T0320174

Strengthening Social Protection in East Asia

This book focuses on relatively unexplored areas in pension and health care arrangements, including financing, in East Asia. The book aims to fill the literature gap on social protection in East Asia by covering issues such as pension and health care arrangements in the depopulating high income countries of Japan and Korea; the challenges of the pay-out phase in Defined Contribution (DC) arrangements in Australia, New Zealand, and Singapore; and the extension of coverage of social protection schemes in China, India, and Indonesia. It also reviews social protection from a much wider perspective and extends coverage of social protection in terms of both the proportion of the population with access to the social protection scheme and the types of risks faced by the households and by society as a whole. The book also gives attention to reforms of civil service pensions.

Mukul G. Asher is an Indian national, specializing in social security and public financial management issues in Asia. He has published widely in national and international journals and has authored or edited more than 10 books. He is on the editorial advisory boards of several journals, including the *International Social Security Review*. He has been a consultant to multilateral organizations and has led executive training programs for officials of several countries, including Indonesia, India, Sri Lanka, Kazakhstan, Brunei, and Tanzania. His interactions with media have been extensive.

Fukunari Kimura has been Chief Economist of the Economic Research Institute for ASEAN and East Asia (ERIA) since 2008 and Professor at the Faculty of Economics, Keio University, since 2000. He obtained his PhD (in Economics) from the University of Wisconsin–Madison in 1991.

"This collection of essays by the leading authorities in the field is a superb addition to the literature and provides a most reliable guideline to the public policy makers in East Asia and Oceania Region."

—Yukinobu Kitamura, Professor,
Research Centre for Information and Statistics of Social Science,
Hitotsubashi University, Japan

Routledge-ERIA Studies in Development Economics

Strengthening Social Protection in East Asia

Edited by Mukul G. Asher
and Fukunari Kimura

LONDON AND NEW YORK

First published 2015
by Routledge
2 Park Square, Milton Park, Abingdon, Oxon OX14 4RN

and by Routledge
711 Third Avenue, New York, NY 10017

Routledge is an imprint of the Taylor & Francis Group,
an informa business

British Library Cataloguing in Publication Data

A catalogue record for this book is available from the British Library

Library of Congress Cataloging-in-Publication Data
Strengthening social protection in East Asia / edited by Mukul Asher,
    Fukunari Kimura. — 1 Edition.
        pages cm. — (Routledge-ERIA studies in development economics)
    Includes bibliographical references and index.
    1. East Asia—Social policy.   2. Social security—East Asia.   I. Asher,
Mukul G., editor.   II. Kimura, Fukunari, editor.
    HN720.5.A8S77 2015
    306.095—dc23
    2014038303

ISBN: 978-1-138-81714-2 (hbk)
ISBN: 978-1-315-71766-1 (ebk)

Typeset in Galliard
by Apex CoVantage, LLC

Contents

Figures

Tables

Contributors

Mukul G. Asher is a Professorial Fellow at the Lee Kuan Yew School of Public Policy, National University of Singapore, Singapore, and Councilor at the Takshashila Institution. He specializes in social security issues in Asia and in public financial management.

Hazel Bateman is a Professor of Economics and Head of the School of Risk and Actuarial Studies at the University of New South Wales, Sydney, Australia. She has research interests in the areas of public and private provision for retirement with particular focus on member decisions, financial competence, and information disclosure.

Ngee-Choon Chia is an Associate Professor with the Department of Economics, National University of Singapore, Singapore. Her published work is in the areas of public finance and pension economics. She has served as a consultant to the World Bank and the Asian Development Bank. She has also provided consultancy service to the Civil Service College, the Central Provident Fund Board, and the Ministry of Manpower. She is the co-editor of the *Singapore Economic Review*.

Santanu Gupta is an Associate Professor with Xavier Labour Research Institute, Xavier School of Management, Jamshedpur, India. His published work is in the areas of public economics and political economy. He has an active interest in public policy issues in the South Asian context.

Yuwei Hu is currently Banco Bilbao Vizcaya Argentaria's China Representative (Pensions and Insurance). He has published various articles in refereed journals and has provided technical assistance on Chinese pensions to international organizations, including the European Commission, International Monetary Fund, and World Bank.

Fukunari Kimura has been Chief Economist of the Economic Research Institute for ASEAN and East Asia (ERIA) since 2008 and Professor at the Faculty of Economics, Keio University, since 2000. He obtained his PhD (in Economics) from the University of Wisconsin–Madison in 1991.

Budi Kuncoro graduated from Harvard University's Kennedy School and the National University of Singapore's Lee Kuan Yew Public Policy School in Public Management. He had been an advisor to the Canadian International Development Agency and is currently the Green Prosperity Director of Millennium Challenge Account – Indonesia.

Hyungpo Moon was a Chief Economist at and Vice President of the Korea Development Institute. He has been extensively involved in the pension policy of South Korea. He now serves as the Minister of Health and Welfare in the Republic of South Korea.

Friska Parulian was a researcher at the Economic Research Institute for ASEAN and East Asia (2009–May 2011). She is a macroeconomist who graduated from Hitotsubashi University, Tokyo, with specialization in public finance and taxation.

Noriyuki Takayama is Professor Emeritus at Hitotsubashi University, Tokyo, and Distinguished Scholar at the Research Institute for Policies on Pension and Aging, Tokyo, Japan. He holds a PhD from the University of Tokyo, Japan. He is known as a distinguished key player on the topic of Japanese pensions.

Albert K. Tsui is an Associate Professor in the Department of Economics at the National University of Singapore. His research interests are in the fields of financial economics, pension economics, and time series analysis. He has published in various economics and statistics journals. He has also served as a consultant to the Ministry of Foreign Affairs, Central Provident Fund Board, and Ministry of Manpower in Singapore.

Acknowledgments

This edited volume focuses on relatively unexplored areas of pension and health care arrangements in the Asia-Pacific region. The editors would like to express sincere gratitude to the Economic Research Institute for ASEAN and East Asia (ERIA) for organizing and funding this research project, and to the ERIA leadership for their intellectual support. The contributors to this volume have been immensely cooperative as a group in bringing the research project to the final publication stage. They richly deserve our special thanks. The editors and the contributors received strong cooperation and support from the relevant government agencies in the respective countries, and from many researchers at academic institutions and think tanks.

We owe a special debt of gratitude to Shujiro Urata, who was instrumental in facilitating the publication with Routledge. We appreciate the thorough professionalism with which Fauziah Zen, Batari Saraswati, Astrid Dita, and Ma'rifatul Amalia assisted in preparing the typescript. This volume is therefore a collective effort, and we have been privileged to be a part of this effort.

Mukul G. Asher and Fukunari Kimura
September 2014

1 Selected issues in *Strengthening Social Protection in East Asia*

An overview

Mukul G. Asher and Fukunari Kimura

1. Introduction

The importance of addressing the challenges of ageing populations in a coherent, competent, sustainable, and fair manner is increasingly recognized globally, including in Asia. Demographic trends portending rapid ageing, decreases in medium-term growth prospects in the aftermath of the 2008 global crisis, the increasing importance of sound public financial management, and changing labour market dynamics impacting on the generation of jobs, along with relative stagnation in real wages, are some of the major factors which have contributed to this recognition.

It is in the above context that this volume, comprising specially commissioned papers on addressing selected challenges of ageing populations in East Asia, is conceived. The issues covered include pension and healthcare arrangements in the depopulating high-income countries of Japan and Korea; the challenges of the pay-out phase in Defined Contribution (DC) arrangements in Australia, New Zealand, and Singapore; civil service pension arrangements in India, Thailand, and the Philippines; and extension of the coverage of social protection schemes in China, India, and Indonesia, three countries with large populations but low coverage by formal social protection.

This volume represents a second phase of the ERIA (Economic Research Institute for ASEAN [the Association of Southeast Asian Nations] and East Asia) project on social protection. The first phase was completed in March 2010 and was published as an ERIA report entitled "Social Protection in East Asia: Current State and Challenges". The 2010 report comprised 13 country chapters (covering Japan, Korea, Singapore, Brunei, China, Indonesia, India, the Philippines, Thailand, Vietnam, Cambodia, and Laos) and an overview chapter (Asher et al., 2010).

The first ERIA report focused on providing an overview of social protection systems in individual countries. Recent contributions on Asian pension systems (Park, 2011) have also focused on the overall pension systems in individual countries. The limitations of such an approach are that an issue-specific comparative analysis involving similarly situated countries, and a more detailed policy-relevant analysis of how specific issues have been addressed in different Asian countries, cannot be fully developed.

The main distinguishing characteristic of this volume is that it analyses specific issues in social protection which have been relatively neglected, using a comparative context of countries with similar levels of income, demographic status, financial sector development, and other relevant characteristics. Thus, it avoids over-generalizations about social protection systems in Asia and permits a detailed policy-relevant analysis of specific issues designed to meet the challenges of ageing populations. The above characteristics are evident in the selection of specific issues and in the sub-groups of similar countries chosen for the analysis.

The chapters on Japan and Korea, by Noriyuki Takayama and Hyungpyo Moon respectively (Chapters 2 and 3), focus on pension and healthcare management in affluent ageing depopulating countries. The dynamics of the two sectors are different, and the health challenges, particularly the funding of healthcare in an effective and fair manner, may prove to be even more difficult than finding societal resources for pensions. The challenges of the two depopulating countries are qualitatively different than those of the other Asian countries.

The chapters on Japan and Korea highlight the need to consider pension and healthcare costs in an integrated manner, with policy and organizational coherence within the pension and healthcare sectors, as well as between these two sectors.[1] The experience of these two countries would have implications for public policies towards ageing in other East Asian economies, especially Singapore, Australia, and New Zealand. Policymakers in the middle-income countries of Asia – particularly countries with large populations, such as China, India, and Indonesia – may also find the experiences of Japan and Korea useful in coordinating pension and healthcare policies.

As relatively greater emphasis is placed on the DC method for pensions, the phase of paying out the balances accumulated during the working years becomes of greater significance. The chapter by Hazel Bateman on Australia and New Zealand (Chapter 4), and that by Ngee-Choon Chia and Albert K. Tsui on Singapore (Chapter 5) focus on the challenges in the pay-out phase of pension systems using DC methods. All three countries are comparable as a sub-group. The chapters have implications for other East Asian countries, such as Malaysia and India, in whose pension systems DC method plays a significant role.

In many countries, there have been separate pension arrangements for civil servants. In Chapter 6, Mukul G. Asher and Friska Parulian analyse recent civil service reforms in India, the Philippines, and Thailand. India's shift from the Defined Benefit (DB) to the DC method of providing pensions to civil servants, and setting up of a pension regulator for a modern pension architecture, may have policy implications for other countries planning civil service pension reform. As demands for fairness in pension arrangements become more pressing, and as fiscal constraints become more acute, the re-examination of civil service pension arrangements will acquire greater urgency.

2. Selected issues: chapter summaries

The following two chapters in the volume focus on the management of pension and healthcare costs in the rapidly ageing depopulating countries of Japan (Chapter 2) and South Korea (Chapter 3) respectively. Just as Japan led the Asian countries in rapid industrialization and progress towards high-income-country status during the second half of the 20th century, it has been leading the rest of Asia in the rapid ageing of its population. Similarly, South Korea has followed Japan in the rapid ageing process. As a result, both countries are expected to exhibit a decline in population.[2] The decline in absolute population, in conjunction with uncertain longevity trends, has significant implications for both pensions and healthcare costs. How these two countries manage these costs could offer significant lessons for other Asian countries that are also experiencing ageing of the population.

2.1. Pensions and healthcare in depopulating countries

The main findings of the chapter on Japan, by Noriyuki Takayama, may be summarized as follows. In the past, families and occupational schemes were the major old-age safety net in Japan. The principal social security pension program was introduced during World War II. It had developed gradually, during the period of rapid economic growth, and the growth of pension and healthcare programs appeared as a dividend of economic growth. An enormous shift of the population from farmers to salaried employees took place during the rapid growth period, along with increases in life expectancy. The household size became smaller on average. The rise and fall of private enterprises was very common in this period. These factors forced a major source of old-age income to shift from families and occupational schemes to social security pension programs. The future demographic and economic situations of Japan will, however, make the current generous social security pensions hard to sustain.

One of the major objectives of the 2004 pension reforms was to eventually eliminate the huge excess liabilities of JPY 500 trillion on the balance sheet of the Kosei-Nenekin-Hoken. The plan is to generate a surplus equal to this amount by (1) hiking contributions, (2) increasing payments from the national treasury, and (3) reducing benefits. But the combination of higher contributions and lower benefits will mean the future participants will end up getting back less than they pay into the system. It is estimated that their benefits will amount to only about 80 percent of their contributions. This is hardly likely to encourage people to participate. Higher contributions will further alienate younger workers from the pension system and deepen their distrust of politics.

The decision to keep the model income replacement ratio at 50 percent at the point when pension benefit payments commence represents, in effect, the adoption of a DB formula. Maintaining both fixed contributions on the one hand and defined benefit levels on the other is not an easy task, for there is no room to deal flexibly with unforeseen developments. If the government is to keep its promise regarding an upper limit for contributions and a lower limit for benefits, the only policy option it will have in the event of a financial shortfall will be to raise the age at which people begin receiving benefits. The 2004 reform package makes no mention of such a possibility; the drafters of the bills no doubt chose to simply put off this task until a future date.

There are several unique features in the current Japanese healthcare system. First, the coverage is virtually 100 percent, with four major programs for different sectors of the population. Second, at retirement, employees are usually obliged to move to a municipal-based scheme. Third, a revenue-sharing scheme has been established for those aged 75 and over. The "old-old" pay a lower share of medical costs (co-payments and 10 percent of remaining costs), the major part of which are financed by transfers from social insurance contributions to the remaining programs and from the general revenue of both central and local governments.

Fourth, the social security coverage of medical care services and its reimbursement to providers are the same for all the programs. The social insurance coverage of medical care services (including co-payments) is still very high (around 90 percent in terms of the aggregate cost). Reimbursement to healthcare providers is principally based on a fee-for-service schedule that is uniform across different regions. Each patient in Japan enjoys free access to any medical service providers at any time, purchasing most available medical treatments at a publicly determined price through social insurance programs for healthcare. Fifth, in contrast to the benefit side, each program for healthcare adopts a different financing method.

Older people are heavy users of medical care services, and the medical cost per person per annum for those aged 75 and over was about 8.2 times the cost for those between 15 and 44 years old. Consequently, in 2008, 55 percent of aggregate medical expenses were incurred by people aged 65 and above, while their share of the total population was 22 percent. Social security programs for healthcare are becoming very similar to those for pensions, in that the basic feature of the program is income redistribution from younger and middle-aged people to older people.

The annual healthcare expenditure in 2007 in Japan was 7.3 percent of the gross domestic product (GDP), which was relatively low among Organisation for Economic Co-operation and Development (OECD) countries. Owing to the rapidly ageing population, this will increase very sharply.

In reforming the healthcare payment schedule, a prospective payment system would be advisable. Insurers can evaluate the quality of providers, giving them strong incentives through rewards based on outcome, not on input. There should also be more competition among providers and among insurers. Many people propose that the programs should be divided up on a prefectural basis. In addition, many people advocate introduction of gatekeepers, which would place some restrictions on free access to service providers.

Socio-economic conditions will change very rapidly. The changes that take place will often be beyond previous expectations. Never-ending reforms of social security are therefore inevitable in Japan as it copes with the trends of depopulation. The need for greater coordination and coherence in the pension and in healthcare systems, and in both systems taken together, also emerges from the chapter on Japan.

Hyungpo Moon in Chapter 3 analyses the policies being adopted by Korea to manage depopulating trends. He notes that the drastic decrease in the birth rate as well as the lengthened life expectancy will bring enormous demographic changes in Korea. The population aged 65 years or older is expected to reach 16.2 million in 2050, 3.7 times larger than the 4.4 million in 2005, while the working-age population aged from 15 to 64 will drop a record 35 percent during the same period.

Although the rapid demographic change affects various sectors of an economy, the most direct and significant impact will fall on age-related public programs, including public pension and healthcare systems. The biggest challenge facing social insurance systems in Korea is to contain growing public expenditures driven by population ageing and to secure adequate financial resources to maintain a sustainable social protection system for the elderly.

At the same time as a rapidly ageing population will make social protection of the elderly more important, Korea needs to strengthen its public pension and healthcare systems, which are still immature in terms of both their coverage and their benefit provisions, without sacrificing its financial stability.

It is in the above context that Moon examines the impact of population age-ing on public pension and healthcare systems in Korea and discusses the policy issues for providing more sustainable and adequate risk protection for the elderly (as in the case of Japan, a need for greater coordination and coherence in the pension and healthcare systems, taken individually and jointly, is also evident in Korea).

Expanding coverage of the National Pension

Despite the nominal framework of a universal pension system that covers the whole nation, more than a third of the target individuals of the National Pension currently fail to pay contributions, including those who are exempted from contributions and delinquents. Considering that the majority of non-participants are the poor or those with low incomes, such low participation in the National Pension is likely to increase the potential risk of pulling them into old-age poverty. The empirical analysis in the chapter shows that participation behaviour is highly sensitive to variables such income, age, and gender and that the participation probability of non-regular workers is less than half that of regular workers or the self-employed. It was also shown that participation rates are lower particularly for workplaces with 10 or fewer employees in the construction and wholesale and retail trade industries.

These empirical results clearly imply that the primary target group for cover-age expansion should be non-regular workers in small businesses. To prevent the spread of old-age poverty in advance by promptly enhancing the participation rate, it is necessary to devise active measures that aim to improve the participa-tion of non-regular workers, such as provision of matching-contribution subsidies to non-regular workers or the poor self-employed, as well as to strengthen the administrative capability to manage the insured.

Enhancing the long-term financial sustainability of the National Pension

The National Pension scheme in Korea has had a serious structural problem, specifically, the imbalance between generous benefits and low contribution rates, since its introduction in 1988. This internal structural imbalance, combined with the external factor of a rapidly ageing population, seriously threatens its long-term financial sustainability. To respond to this situation, the Korean government made a parametric reform in 2008 containing measures to decrease the benefit level by one-third by 2028. Despite a huge decrease in benefit expenditures in the long term, however, it is estimated that the financial stabilization measures do not seem to be sufficient for achieving the actuarial balance of the pension fund.

Moon discusses policy directions for enhancing financial sustainability that should be pursued in the future, as follows: first, with the extremely low fertility and rapidly increasing longevity, the prefunding method needs to be strengthened for financial stability and intergenerational equity; second, a considerable increase in the contribution rate will be inevitable if the partially funded system is to be maintained; and, third, increasing the profitability of the National Pension Fund will not only improve the pension finance but also lower the contribution burden of future generations.

Containing the growth of healthcare expenditure

The biggest challenge facing Korea's healthcare system is the rapid increase in health expenditure, mainly driven by population ageing and by increasing medical costs per elderly person. Unless measures are taken to contain the expenditure hike effectively, contribution rates are projected to more than double within the next two decades to maintain the financial balance of the healthcare insurance system in Korea. At the same time, the current healthcare system still relies heavily on private financing, and the government's role in risk protection needs to be strengthened so as to reduce the burden of excessive out-of-pocket payments for patients.

The extended insurance benefits will eventually put additional pressure on healthcare financing. Hence, the current healthcare system in Korea faces challenges including the sustainability of financing, the strengthening of health protection, and the enhancing of administrative efficiency. Some of the reform measures for increasing the efficiency of Korea's healthcare system that need immediate attention are as follows: first, the payment mechanism for providers needs to be redesigned to give better incentives for more efficient use of medical resources; second, policy measures on drug pricing are urgently needed to contain growing pharmaceutical expenditures; and, third, cost containment of long-term care insurance through demand control will be an imperative issue as population ageing puts growing pressure on its financing.

2.2. Managing the pay-out phase in the DC method

Australia, New Zealand, and Singapore are also high-income countries, with the first two being members of the OECD along with Japan and Korea. However, unlike Japan and Korea, the other three countries primarily rely on mandatory DC arrangements for financing retirement. A major characteristic of a DC arrangement is that while contributions are specified, the benefits received, and therefore retirement adequacies, are left undefined. Unlike in the DC method, social insurance arrangements promise a lifetime annuity, thus addressing longevity risk (the risk that a person may run out of resources in retirement if he or she lives longer than anticipated), and often inflation-indexing features address inflation risk. In social insurance arrangements, there is also provision for family benefits, thus addressing the survivors' risk. In contrast, in the DC arrangement, longevity, inflation, and survivors' risk have to be explicitly incorporated into the design. In Chapter 4 Hazel Bateman analyse the structuring of the pay-out phase in Australia and New Zealand, while in Chapter 5 Ngee-Choon Chia and Albert K. Tsui undertake a similar analysis for Singapore.

Retirement income provision in both Australia and New Zealand differs from the prototypical OECD structure. In both countries, current retirees rely on a universal public age pension funded from general revenue, paid according to age and residency. The Australian version (the Age Pension) pays 27.7 percent of the average earnings for a single retiree and is means tested but not taxed. The New Zealand version (called the New Zealand Superannuation) pays 43 percent of the average earnings for a single retiree and is taxed at standard personal marginal tax rates. Neither country adopted contributory earnings-related pay-as-you-go public pensions, common in other OECD countries.

Until recently private retirement savings played a secondary role. However, this is changing, particularly in Australia, with the introduction of mandatory private retirement saving, known as the superannuation guarantee, in 1992. Currently the superannuation guarantee mandates a 9 percent employer contribution; however, this is gradually being increased to 12 percent over the next decade. Australia has a long history of encouraging voluntary superannuation through tax concessions, and the superannuation guarantee increased coverage from just below 50 percent to over 95 percent of workers. Future Australian retirees can expect their retirement incomes to consist of contributions from the public pension, the superannuation guarantee, and voluntary superannuation.

Policies for private retirement savings are less developed in New Zealand. Retirement income policy has long emphasized a central role for the public age pension with a very minor role for private savings. This changed in 2007 with the introduction of Kiwisaver, a voluntary government-subsidized but tax-preferred "automatic enrolment" retirement saving structure. The default employee contribution rate is 2 percent (with options to contribute 4 or 8 percent) and is matched by a 2 percent employer contribution. However, with an allowance to withdraw the accumulated balance for the purchase of a first home, many years before system maturation, and no culture of retirement income streams, it is questionable whether Kiwisaver will reduce reliance on public provision.

Common to retirement provision policies in both Australia and New Zealand is freedom of choice of retirement benefits, a long-term practice of taking lump sums, and an undeveloped market for longevity products. Almost all retirement accumulations in New Zealand are taken as lump sums. In Australia there is a growing trend to take account-based pensions (a form of phased-withdrawal product). Under current trends around 50 percent of retirement benefits are taken as a lump sum and 50 percent as account-based pensions. Owing to system immaturity, the size of a typical lump sum is quite small, and lump sums are largely used for debt consolidation and investment in non-annuitized investment products. In both Australia and New Zealand the life annuity market has virtually disappeared, and amounts to around 50 life annuities per year in the aggregate (Bateman and Piggott, 2011; Bateman and Kingston, 2010; Mercer, 2009).

Neither Australia nor New Zealand has escaped demographic transition. In both countries the old-age dependency ratio is expected to double over the next 40 years from around 20 percent currently. Consequently, the cost of financing Australia's Age Pension is projected to increase from 2.7 percent to 3.9 percent of GDP (Australian Treasury, 2010), and the New Zealand Superannuation from 4.3 percent to 8 percent of GDP (New Zealand Government, 2009). With healthcare and old-age care competing for public funds, this also raises questions about the long-term sustainability of a retirement income system centred on public provision.

When DC pay-out structures in both Australia and New Zealand are assessed, against the economic and financial risks faced by individuals in retirement, it is clear that some gaps remain. In particular, because of the gaps in the retirement benefits market, future retirees in both countries are vulnerable to investment risk, longevity risk, and inflation risk.

Feasible reform measures in both Australia and New Zealand are quite complex and involve a more sophisticated approach than just mandating life annuities at retirement or providing incentives for purchasing annuities. In both countries, co-operation between the private and public sectors is required to rejuvenate the market for longevity products. Policies to address these issues must address weak consumer demand, behavioural biases, risk management for product providers (specifically longevity risk, inflation risk, and investment risk), ineffective product distribution channels, and poor public policy coordination. Overall, there is greater cause for optimism in Australia than in New Zealand.

The main points emphasized by Chia and Tsui in Chapter 5 may be summarized as follows. Singapore relies almost exclusively on a DC social security system under the Central Provident Fund (CPF) system. Countries with DC systems enjoy fiscal advantages because the benefit pay-outs are directly correlated to contributions, but the trade-off is that retirement provision may be inadequate and have limited fairness. The DC system exposes individuals to risks – longevity, interest rate, and inflation risks. Whether a DC system can successfully provide an adequate retirement income and help protect against longevity and inflation risks depends both on the design of the accumulation and pay-out phases and on other components of the pension system such as budget-financed non-contributory pensions, sometimes called social pensions.

As retirement wealth depends on how much workers save, there are concerns about whether the accumulated savings are adequate. The adequacy of retirement income depends on contribution rates, contribution periods (higher retirement ages), inflation rates, and returns to savings. Thus, macroeconomic variables influencing salary growth, unemployment episodes, and rates of return will influence the accumulation of retirement savings during the accumulation phase.

One unique feature of the Singapore's CPF system is that retirement savings can be withdrawn to help finance housing consumption. Public housing provided by the Housing Development Board is the most important non-financial asset for most Singaporeans. In examining the pay-out phase in such an asset-based social security system, there is a need to look at monetization of housing assets. Although annuities are the classical answer to retirement financing during the pay-out phase, they are not the only one. As part of the de-accumulation process, the Singapore government has put in place several mechanisms to help asset-rich, cash-poor Singaporeans to monetize housing. These instruments include reverse mortgages, subletting, downsizing, and lease buyback scheme. Flat owners can choose an option that best balances their preference for retirement adequacy, ageing in place, and leaving a bequest. Reverse mortgages are the least preferred option, and subletting is most preferred as it allows the elderly to age in place and to leave a bequest. The lease buyback scheme has a low take-up rate as Housing Development Board owners have strong bequest motives.

The challenge for adequate old-age provision during the pay-out phase lies in the existence of annuity markets to provide financial instruments that yield a steady monthly stream of income until death. One early criticism of the adequacy of the CPF system was its lack of mandatory annuitization. Before the introduction of a national annuity scheme, the CPF Board had attempted to enhance the retirement savings in the retirement account (RA) by improving its rate of returns. However, the issue of longevity risk remained, and it became necessary to introduce an insurance scheme to address the uncertainty. In 2009 the CPF Board introduced mandatory annuitization to convert accumulated savings into a stream of retirement incomes under the CPF Lifelong Income Scheme (CPF LIFE).

The implementation of CPF LIFE can be regarded as one of the main structural reforms in Singapore's social security system, as most earlier CPF changes were mainly parametric in nature. CPF LIFE pools longevity risk among all annuitants – those who die younger will share the interest accumulated on their annuity premium with those who survive longer, but on the basis of commercial insurance principles rather than social insurance principles. CPF LIFE thus does not increase the resources available for retirement. It enables individuals to use accumulated balances differently as compared to a lump sum withdrawal for the minimum sum specified. CPF LIFE thus insures retirees against longevity risk, so that they will not outlive their accumulated savings. The product is an outcome of public consultation. It has been refined using some perspectives from behavioural economics.

The design of CPF LIFE complements the existing minimum sum scheme and is thus integrated into that scheme. It is designed to balance the CPF members' preference for meeting retirement needs and fulfilling bequest motives. When a CPF member joins CPF LIFE, a portion of his/her cash savings in the RA is used to pay for the premium for a deferred life annuity at a stipulated drawdown age.

The remaining RA is allocated to a spend-down account, with phased withdrawal starting at the age of 65 and continuing to the drawdown age of the annuity. The withdrawal amount is managed in a way to ensure that the payment will last until the deferred annuity date. This amount withdrawn from the managed spend-down account, together with the life annuity, provides monthly pay-outs until the member dies. The design and structure of CPF LIFE thus complement the DC system to enhance retirement adequacy.

2.3. Extending coverage of pension systems

There are three chapters focused on the issue of extending the coverage of pension and healthcare systems in three Asian countries with large populations, namely China (Chapter 7), India (Chapter 8), and Indonesia (Chapter 9). This is an important issue in all these countries, as the coverage of formal social protection schemes is relatively low. However, their rapid economic growth and the rising expectations of their populations, along with rapid ageing, are generating pressures to extend pension and healthcare benefits to larger and larger proportions of the population, particularly in the rural areas.

Yuwei Hu analyses the experience of China in extending the coverage of social protection schemes in Chapter 7. He notes that since initiating the economic reform and open-door policy in the late 1970s, China has witnessed a tremendous transformation. A once centrally planned and impoverished country has gradually been transformed into a market-oriented economy and had become the second largest economy after the United States of America by 2010. Against this background of impressive growth, the Chinese economy is still associated with a number of key problems which remain to be solved. Among others, demographic trends portending rapid ageing and the consequent un-sustainability of the existing pension system are a major challenge for the Chinese government. Failure to tackle any of these problems may well have a devastating impact on the Chinese economy.

China's current pension system may be divided between urban and rural areas. The current urban pension system consists of three pillars with four components, described as follows:

A. **Pillar 1A:** This pillar is run on a 'pay-as-you-go' basis and serves as a social pooling mechanism. Contributions are made solely by employers, while the contribution rate is 20 percent of payroll. The expected replacement rate is approximately 35 percent of the average local wages with 35 years of contribution.

B. **Pillar 1B:** This pillar is a mandatory individual account, designed to be fully funded. The contribution is 8 percent of employees' salary, contributed solely by employees. The expected replacement rate is about 24.2 percent. To receive benefits from pillars 1A and 1B certain vesting requirements need to be met, notably a minimum 15 years of contribution, a retirement age of 60 (for men) or 55 (for women), etc.

C. **Pillar 2:** It is often referred to the enterprise annuity scheme in China, which is the equivalent of occupational pension schemes in Western countries. Participation in this pillar is voluntary.

D. **Pillar 3:** It refers to the voluntary individual saving/pension schemes and is designed to meet the needs of the population who want to receive a higher income after retirement.

Despite the large rural population in China (over 50 percent of the national population lives in the countryside), a formal pension system had been practically non-existent until recently. In June 2009 the central government announced the introduction of a new voluntary rural pension scheme after various local experiments. A flat-rate pension of RMB 55 per month was to be paid. Meanwhile, an individual account would be created to which contributors could choose to pay between RMB 100 and 500 annually, in increments of RMB 100. The local government must pay at least RMB 30 per year to the account. The central government would pay the entire cost of the flat-rate pension in central and western provinces, whereas in the east the provincial governments would pay half. Local governments are free to add to the basic pension and make payments to the individual accounts.

Despite significant efforts and achievements in the past, China's pension system still suffers from insufficient coverage in rural areas, uneven coverage in urban areas, fragmentation of the system, unsatisfactory investment return, and poor coordination between ministerial agencies.

Given the above limitations, Hu proposes a new, modified urban pension system so as to improve pension coverage and increase the financial sustainability of the system.

A. **Pillar 0:** A universal old-age social assistance system. All urban citizens – regardless of whether or not they have contributed to the system over their career life – are entitled to this benefit. This pillar is fully financed from the general budget.

B. **Pillar 1:** A mandatory urban pension system. The basic structure is the same as the existing one, i.e. consisting of two components, and participation is mandatory. However, pillar 1B would be transformed into a notional DC scheme, while pillar 1A would still be run on a pay-as-you-go basis. The contribution should be 10 percent and 5 percent, respectively for the two components.

C. **Pillar 2:** Enterprise annuity. This pillar will carry the current enterprise annuity, i.e. voluntary, fully funded, trust based, and professionally managed. The expected contribution rate is 10 percent.

D. **Pillar 3:** Commercial life insurance products, again in keeping with the current system. This pillar is mainly relevant for the high-income population group; i.e. high income throughout one's career life leads to higher expectations regarding the standard of living post-retirement.

Hu argues that the proposed model has several features designed to improve the sustainability and efficiency of the current pension system in China. It remains consistent with the current pension structure, helps to move towards establishing a national integrated system, mitigates against reform resistance, improves the fairness of the system, offers incentives for participation and for less evasion of contributions, and helps to develop private pensions.

The chapter on India, by Santanu Gupta (Chapter 8), focuses on the extension of coverage of social protection among informal workers in India. He defines employees as being in informal employment if their employment is not subject to national legislation, income taxation, or social protection, or does not entitle them to benefits such as paid leave or sick leave, amongst others. He notes that India's labour force for 2009–2010 was 520 million; assuming that even 10 percent of the labour force is in the formal sector would imply that the size of informal sector employment is around 468 million. This underlines the importance of extending the social protection coverage to informal workers.

The Annual Report of the Ministry of Labour, Government of India, 2009–2010[3] mentions that the unorganized sector suffers from cycles of seasonality of employment, lack of a formal employer-employee relationship, and absence of social protection. Given that labour in the informal sector is quite heterogeneous, providing social security to all types of workers will require a number of schemes. Keeping in mind that people below the poverty line will be the most hurt by fluctuations in the informal sector, the government has initiated some employment-oriented schemes, old-age pension schemes, and health insurance schemes. The Indira Gandhi National Old Age Pension Scheme is sponsored by the central government's budget; however, state governments were urged to contribute towards the total pension benefit for poor households. The coverage of such schemes that target the elderly destitute (65+ in this case) has risen steadily over the years from 34.51 percent in 2002–2003 to 67.66 percent in 2008–2009.

Rashtriya Swasthya Bima Yojana (RSBY) provides health insurance coverage for people below the poverty line (BPL). A key feature of the RSBY is that every BPL family is issued a biometric-enabled smart card containing the fingerprints and photographs of family members. All hospitals under RSBY are information technology enabled and connected to the server at the district level. Issuance of smart cards has ensured that the grants under RSBY are not misused; patients have the option of using the card at any of the hospitals empanelled by RSBY. The card can be split for migrant workers who carry a share of their coverage with them separately. Beneficiaries of RSBY get cashless benefits after providing verification through their fingerprint. Health providers need not send any paper documents to the insurer, as payment is electronic. As for the coverage, until March 2011, enrolment has been completed in about 225 districts, which is 33 percent more districts than those covered by RSBY. About 43.9 million BPL families have been identified in the selected states, and 23.2 million BPL families have been enrolled.

Social security for the formal organized sector is provided by the Employee State Insurance Corporation and Employees' Provident Fund Organization. The former provides for health and unemployment benefits, while the latter looks into provision of social security in old age. The coverage for both of these schemes has been low to date, and the New Pension System (NPS), operational since May 1, 2009, is expected to improve coverage to a large extent. Although mandatory for people employed in the public sector, it is voluntary for others and based on the DC pension system, therefore sustainable in the long run. It is open to all citizens of India, and it also gives citizens the flexibility to choose an investment plan and a fund manager. It is simple to open such an account at any one of the Points of Presence and to get a Permanent Retirement Account Number. It is portable, as it is operational even if an individual changes cities or jobs. The NPS is regulated by the Pension Funds Regulation and Development Authority and therefore has transparent investment norms, regular monitoring, and performance reviews of fund managers by the NPS Trust.

At present, to meet their social security needs in old age, many individuals prefer to purchase the schemes of India Post, which offer either a monthly or a quarterly income at guaranteed rates of return of 8 percent or above. Though there is a ceiling on the amount of investment in these schemes, the ceiling is large enough to generate an adequate income on a monthly or quarterly basis. About a million individuals have subscribed to the Senior Citizens Savings Scheme, and about 24.9 million people have subscribed to the monthly income scheme. There are private companies selling pension products, but their premiums are generally high, and the target population has generally been the high-income classes. Recent efforts by the government to open a no-frills bank account for individuals and to assign every individual a unique identification number are not just expected to increase coverage but would also go a long way to directing public resources to their most efficient use.

2.4. Civil service pension arrangements

In Chapter 6 Mukul G. Asher and Friska Parulian analyse civil service pension arrangements in three middle-income Asian countries: India, the Philippines, and the Thailand. As anxiety about the credibility and sustainability of pension promises increases owing to rapid ageing and fiscal stringency in the aftermath of the global crisis, civil service pension arrangements, which account for a substantial proportion of those covered by relatively generous DB pensions, and for a disproportionate share of the resources devoted to pensions in relation to these workers' share in the labour force, have become a major public policy issue.

The premise of the chapter is that parametric and systemic reforms of civil service pensions could help allocate the total national resources devoted to the elderly more equitably and efficiently. Both inter-generational and intra-generational equity issues are therefore relevant.

For analysing civil service pensions, it is the dynamics of the demographic profile of the civil servants which is relevant. But as the relevant databases are weak in these countries, data for the population as a whole are used as a proxy.

The three countries are projected to experience more rapid ageing than the global average, whether considered as a proportion of persons over 60 years of age or as the number of elderly. A brief examination of the public debt levels and overall fiscal deficits in the three countries suggests relatively limited fiscal space for higher levels of government expenditure. This lends additional urgency to reforming civil service pensions in these three Asian countries.

India

An analysis of the civil service pension arrangements in a federal state of India suggests that the non-contributory DB pension systems, with generous commutation benefits (i.e. lump sum provision of a certain proportion of the monthly pension benefits), price and wage indexing, and survivors' benefits, have increased fiscal costs which need to be financed. Sustaining the projected fiscal costs has become particularly challenging for fiscally weak states. It is estimated that civil servants in India constitute 4.4 percent of labour force, but their pension costs are approaching about 2.0 percent of GDP.

Recognizing the fiscal costs and the challenges in financing them, the central government introduced a DC method for civil servants employed since January 1, 2004. The NPS has since been implemented by all but three of the states in the country. More than a million civil servants have become mandatory members, with the pace expected to quicken during the decade of 2010–2020. The phase-in period for the NPS will therefore be over next three to four decades.

The NPS architecture is designed to minimize administrative and investment management costs, and it is scalable. It can also be adapted to voluntary participation in the NPS by any citizen of the country, potentially providing contestability.

The pay-out phase of the NPS currently permits 60 percent to be withdrawn as a lump sum, but 40 percent must be annuitized. This phase requires reconsideration as annuity markets, unless organized by the state, raising its contingent liabilities, are unlikely to develop sufficiently. This is also the international experience.

As the NPS matures, the current practice of mandating only domestic investment of the funds may also need to be reconsidered. The analysis also has scope for parametric reforms in the traditional civil service schemes.

The Philippines

Unlike in India and Thailand, pension arrangements for civil servants and for private sector workers in the Philippines are based on the same social insurance principles. The Government Service Insurance System (GSIS), the agency administering the DB pensions for the civil servants, was set up in 1936. It has a membership of 1.4 million (3.63 percent of the labour force). The government as an employer contributes 12 percent; employees contribute 9 percent, for a total of 21 percent. There is no wage ceiling. The GSIS is an unusual social security organization as it provides life insurance and has a mutual fund program.

The actuarial life of the GSIS reserve fund in 2007 was projected to be till 2055. So there is little immediate pressure on the GSIS to reform. Nevertheless, it faces several challenges. First, the GSIS governance structures need to be strengthened, with a view to enhancing its transparency, accountability, and competence. Second, the operating costs as a percentage of contributions, at 14 percent in 2007, are much higher than for its private sector counterpart, the Social Security System (SSS). The SSS costs are themselves already high, at between 6 and 10 percent of the contributions. Third, the equity issue between the GSIS and SSS members needs to be addressed. In 2008 the average pension for a GSIS pensioner was Peso 7,800, 2.5 times the corresponding amount for the SSS member.

Thailand

The civil servants have traditionally received DB pensions, without any contribution from them being required. In 1997, before the Asian financial crisis, the pension formulation was revised to make it less generous. In return, a DC scheme to which the employee and the government as an employer contribute 3 percent each, administered by a separate statutory organization called the Government Pension Fund, was set up.

Civil servants in Thailand thus receive a major part of their pension under a traditional DB scheme, supplemented by the DC scheme, which provides a lump sum at retirement. There are financial incentives for those who convert it into an annuity instead of taking a lump sum.

In 2008 the Government Pension Fund assets were equivalent to 4.3 percent of GDP. They were invested domestically as well as globally, using both in-house expertise and specialized investment mandates. The real annual return credited to members averaged 3.97 percent during the 1997 to 2009 period. This compares favourably with the corresponding annual return of 0.54 percent for the bank deposits.

The evidence presented in this chapter lends strong support to the premise that reform of the civil service pension arrangements in the three countries should be an essential element in the pension reform agenda of the three countries.

The final chapter of this volume, Chapter 9 by Budi Kuncoro, Friska Parulian, and Mukul G. Asher analyses the issue of extending social protection to informal sector workers in Indonesia. They regard it as one of the greatest challenges faced by Indonesia.

In practice, the most basic protections, such as a minimum wage, are not ensured, as the majority of workers engaged in the informal sector usually have low incomes, such that it would be very difficult to make contributions to any social security scheme. In addition, the Act No. 3 of 1992 on the Worker's Social Security limits the mandatory coverage to firms with more than 10 employees with a monthly payroll of more than one million Rupiah. This in effect excludes the informal sector workers from the mandatory social security scheme administered by Jamsostek.

A milestone in the development of the social security system in Indonesia is the enactment of the Act No. 40 of 2004 on the National Security System Law (Sistem Jaminan Sosial Nasional), which came into effect in October 2004. The law stipulates that every citizen has the right to social security and that the state has the role of providing universal social security coverage. The law also mandates the enforcement of universal coverage (in a staged manner), whereas its implementation (to extend the coverage) for workers in the informal sector, which constitutes two-thirds of employment in Indonesia, should become a major public policy issue.

Consistent with the spirit of implementing the act and achieving a universal coverage of social security in Indonesia, this chapter explores the possibility of extending the coverage to informal sector workers. It provides an overview of the current initiatives for the informal sector workers, examines the challenges, and explores possible options for extending the social protection coverage to informal sector workers in Indonesia.

The current social protection arrangements in Indonesia face three major challenges. The first concerns the fragmentation of the programs. Currently, there are three public pension institutions with three programs, and three public health institutions with five programs. PT Jamsostek manages the pension scheme, work-related insurance, and health benefits intended for private sector workers in the formal sector. PT Taspen manages a pension scheme for current and retired civil servants and their families; Asabri manages the pension program and health benefits for armed forces members; and Askes provides health insurance for civil servants and government employees. In addition, there is no coordination between the above-mentioned three institutions.

The second challenge is low coverage. It is estimated that in Indonesia currently only about 20 million workers (18 percent of the labour force) out of a total of 110 million people in the labour force are covered by the Taspen, Asabri, and Jamsostek schemes. In terms of health protection, with 116.8 million people (50 percent of the population) currently covered, this still leaves another 114 million people without health protection. The coverage needs to be expanded for healthcare protection as well. If the National Security System Law is effectively implemented, it has the potential to expand the coverage of social protection schemes.

The third issue is the protection for the informal sector. Roughly 70 percent of the labour force is in the informal sector; most of them are unskilled workers. A large portion of this group (approximately 45 percent) works in the rural agricultural sector, while the rest are distributed within the service production sectors. Therefore, a failure to protect informal sector workers is actually a failure to protect the largest section of Indonesian workers from loss of income resulting from death or accidents at work.

The above suggests that the social protection system in Indonesia is highly fragmented in the formal sector, while informal workers and the poor do not have any protection against social risks.

As the Indonesian constitution mandates that every citizen has the right of social security the government launched a National Social Security System in October 2004; social security is also imperative for workers outside formal working relationships, who form the bulk of the labour force in Indonesia. Such workers have special characteristics so that the provision of a social security scheme for these workers needs to be organized separately. An improvement in the coverage of health insurance by the Jamkesnas program is considered a good start. However, the existing state health insurance carriers, PT Askes and PT Jamsostek, may need to discuss their new roles within a social health insurance system, including new business models and management systems. In addition, further efforts in extending the existing legal social security schemes (Jamsostek) to include informal sector workers, creating a special scheme for the informal sector workers, and encouraging the development of micro-insurance schemes merit the urgent attention of the policymakers.

3. Concluding remarks

Managing social protection systems, and making promises regarding pensions and healthcare in East Asia credible, will represent a major continuing challenge. This volume extends the empirical evidence–based analysis of social protection systems in East Asia in several ways. First, specific issues are addressed, such as the challenges of ageing depopulating countries, the pay-out phase arrangement under DC methods, civil service pension reforms, and the extension of the coverage of social protection in highly populated Asian countries.

Second, each specific issue is analysed for a small sub-sample of countries with similar income, demographics, and other relevant characteristics, thereby avoiding over-generalization for Asia as a whole. Nevertheless, possible implications of the analysis of specific issues for other Asian countries which may in the future experience similar challenges are recognized.

Third, a strong need for greater policy and organizational coordination and coherence within the pension and health sectors, and between the two sectors, is evident from the analysis of Japan and Korea, two affluent depopulating countries. This need is likely to arise in other Asian countries as well, especially Singapore, Australia, and New Zealand, and to result from rapid ageing and robust growth in incomes in China.

While there has been a strong empirical evidence–based and data-intensive research tradition in such East Asian countries as Japan, Korea, Australia, and New Zealand, in others such a research tradition is in an early phase. Such research on social protection issues thus needs to be encouraged and pursued vigorously. This requires developing social security and ageing studies as a specialization in Asian universities and think tanks, with a view to producing competent professionals in these areas. The studies in this volume suggest a need for a regular forum where policymakers, academics, and researchers from Asian countries can exchange ideas on managing the challenges of ageing populations.

Notes

1 For a preliminary exploration of the issue of coordination between pension and healthcare sectors, see Bali and Asher (2012).
2 According to United Nations projections (2008 revision), the population of Japan is expected to decline from 127.9 million in 2007 to 102.5 million in 2050, while

the corresponding numbers for South Korea will be 48.2 million and 42.3 million respectively.
3 http://labour.nic.in/upload/uploadfiles/files/Reports/Annual%20Report%20 2009-10%20English.pdf

References

Asher, M. G., Oum, S., and Parulian F. (Eds.). (2010). *Social Protection in East Asia – Current State and Challenges*. ERIA Research Project Report 2009–9, March. Jakarta: Economic Research Institute for ASEAN and East Asia. www.eria.org/ publications/research_project_reports/images/pdf/y2009/no9/SP_Compiling_ corrected_2010-09-15_FINAL.pdf

Australian Treasury. (2010). *Australia to 2050: Future challenges*. Canberra: Australian Government.

Bali, A. S., and Asher, M. G. (2012). *Coordinating Healthcare and Pension Policies: An Exploratory Study*. ABDI Working Paper Series (No. 374). www.adbi.org/files/ 2012.08.16.wp374.coordinating.healthcare.pension.policies.pdf

Bateman, H., and Piggott, J. 2011. "Too Much Risk to Insure? The Australian (non-) Market for Annuities." *Centre for Pensions and Superannuation Discussion Paper*, no. 01/10. www.researchgate.net/publication/228292473_Too_Much_Risk_to_ Insure_The_Australian_(Non-)_Market_for_Annuities/file/504635205a35 38355e.pdf.

Bateman, H., and Kingston, G. (2010a). The Henry Review and Super and Saving. *Australian Economic Review*, 43(4): 437–448.

Mercer. (2009). *Time to act: Risks, challenges and opportunities with New Zealand's retirement income system*. Auckland, New Zealand: Author. www.workplacesavings. org.nz/assets/KiwiSaver/SecuringretirementincomesAug09.pdf

New Zealand Government. (2009). *Challenges and choices: New Zealand's long term fiscal statement*. October. Wellington, New Zealand: Author.

Park, D. (2011). *Pension Systems and Old-Age Income Support in East and Southeast Asia: Overview and Reform Directions*. Oxford, UK: Taylor & Francis.

2 Managing pension and healthcare costs in rapidly aging depopulating countries

The case of Japan

Noriyuki Takayama

1. Introduction[1]

In the past, families and occupational schemes were the major old-age safety nets in Japan. The principal social security pension program was introduced during World War II. It had developed gradually during the period of high-speed economic growth. Its development appeared to be a dividend of economic growth. An enormous shift of the population from farmers to salaried employees took place during the period of rapid growth, along with increases in life expectancy. The household size has become smaller and smaller on average. The rise and fall of private enterprises was very common in this period. These factors forced a major source of old-age income to shift from families and occupational schemes to social security pension programs.

The future demographic and economic situations of Japan will make the current generous social security pensions hard to maintain, however. It is still an open question whether or not Japan will manage to contain the increasing social security pension cost, while assuring its people stable lives over the whole life cycle. Social security healthcare programs in Japan are becoming very similar to those for pensions, since their basic feature is income transfers from younger and middle-aged people to older people.

This chapter first explains changes in Japan's social security pension programs. Second, it discusses future pension policy options in Japan. Third, it addresses healthcare issues. The final section concludes this chapter.

2. Changes in Japan's social security pension programs

Japan had six social security pension programs covering different sectors of the population. The earliest plan was established in 1890, the most recent in 1961. The earliest plan was for military servants and required no individual contributions. It was totally financed by general revenue. The scheme was then expanded to civil servants. The old-age benefit for military and civil servants was based on their final salary, and its benefit level was generous from the outset.

The principal program that is mandatory for private sector employees is the Kosei-Nenekin-Hoken (KNH), which was introduced during wartime in 1942.

The old-age pensions of the KNH had to be suspended immediately after the end of the war, and the KNH contribution rate was reduced from 11 percent to 3 percent. The KNH was rebuilt in 1954, shifting from an earnings-related pension to a two-tier benefits system with flat-rate basic benefits.

2.1. The high-speed growth period

The social security pension system was, and is, to be reformed at least every five years. In the early stages, the KNH benefit level was not enticing, and for old-age retirees at that time, a lump-sum retirement benefit provided on a private basis by their employers was often of much more significance. In contrast, pension benefits for civil servants were considerably higher. This difference induced "gap-decreasing" adjustments in benefit levels between private and public sector employees. Drastic improvements in the KNH old-age benefits occurred in 1965 and 1973; the replacement ratio in terms of gross wages was increased to 40 percent and then to 60 percent. In 1973 the updating of past salary history together with benefit indexing enabled retired people to manage on the generous KNH benefits in their old age. In the meantime, there happened to be a sharp decline in the real significance of the lump-sum retirement benefits provided privately by employers.

Under the KNH, equal percentage contributions are required of employees and their employers. The 3 percent contribution rate was gradually increased, and the total percentage went up to 7.8 percent in 1973.

At the outset, the KNH was established as a defined-benefit plan on a fully funded basis. It was initially regarded as a compulsory saving program to prevent inflation. Its financing gradually shifted from fully funded to pay-as-you-go. The KNH had a reserve fund of about JPY 118 trillion in March 2013. KNH contributions used to be accumulated in a reserve fund, to be invested in social overhead capital for the construction of highways, railways, bridges, airports, and other public projects.

Before 1961 the self-employed; people engaged in agriculture, forestry, and fishery; the unemployed; persons with no occupation; and employees working in small firms were still excluded from the social security pension system. The Kokumin-Nenkin (KN) Law went into effect in April 1961, embracing all previously uncovered people under social security. Participation in the KN has been compulsory for everyone between 20 and 59 years old (even for the unemployed).

The basic structure of the KN is a flat-rate basic benefit and a flat-rate contribution on an individual basis. One-third of the KN benefits were financed by subsidies through general revenue. The full old-age benefit of the KN was payable initially after 25 years of contributions from age 65, although an actuarially reduced or increased benefit could be claimed at any age between 60 and 70. The transitional KN old-age benefit with a special 10-year contribution requirement began to be paid in 1971. A majority of the elderly came to enjoy receiving this special benefit, which contributed to making the public aware of the significant role of social security pensions in old-age income security. The benefit formula of the KN was revised to be more and more generous. Meanwhile, automatic indexation of the KN benefits began in 1973.

2.2. The period of diminished expectations

The KN started with a very small contribution, and it was politically difficult to increase it. The KN soon faced severe difficulties in financing benefits. An enormous shift of the population from farmers to salaried employees during the rapid growth period necessitated some revenue-sharing scheme between employees' and non-employees' pensions. The scheme was established in 1986, and since then the first-tier basic flat-rate benefits of all the pension systems have been financially integrated. Currently the flat-rate pension benefit is financed on a full pay-as-you-go basis. The 1986 reform changed some requirements of the KN; the full old-age pension is payable after 40 years of contributions, provided the contribution were made before 60 years of age. Also introduced were special transitional provisions for those born after 1926 with at least 25 years of coverage. They can receive the maximum pension even with fewer contribution years, provided they have been contributing since 1961.

It should be noted that those covered by the KNH (and the other employee pension systems) are not required to make individual contributions to the KN, while employers and employees are responsible for the financial participation in the integrated first-tier, flat-rate basic pensions.

Since the 1986 reform, if the husband has his contribution deducted from his salary and placed in the KNH, his dependent wife would automatically be entitled in her own name to the flat-rate basic benefits, and she is not required to make any individual payments to the public pension system. Through this, women's right to a pension was comprehensively established.

The 1986 reform included another advance in the flat-rate disability pensions. A dependent child less than 20 years of age would be entitled to the flat-rate basic benefits in case of disability. Though the medical check was (and is) very strict, handicapped children largely came to be supported by the social security pension system, and not by the special welfare program.

Through the 1986 pension reform, the accrual rate for the earnings-related component of the KNH old-age benefits was to be reduced gradually from 1.0 percent per year to 0.75 percent, cohort by cohort. The reductions corresponded to the longer average contribution years of the younger cohorts. On average, each cohort was expected to receive 30 percent of their career average monthly real earnings as the earnings-related component.

The future demographic situation of Japan was getting darker and darker; the total fertility rate (TFR) showed an unexpected sharp decline from 1975, and the level in 2013 was 1.43. There is still little sign that the TFR will return to a higher level. Japan's total population began to fall beginning in 2005 and is projected to reach less than 40 percent of its current level by 2100. On the other hand, life expectancy has steadily increased. Consequently, the proportion of the elderly (65 years and above) in Japan was 25.9 percent in 2014, the highest proportion in the world. It is expected to reach 30 percent by 2025 and more than 40 percent by around 2060. In the 1990s the Japanese economy changed dramatically, too, when the asset bubble finally burst. The colorful dreams that Japanese youth had had for their economy were likely to be destroyed.

Both demographic and economic factors in the future will probably impose greater stresses on social security pension programs that are based on pay-as-you-go defined-benefit financing. The biggest political issue in the Japanese pension system has been when to start benefit payments. The pension age was 60 years for workers in the 1990s. The government twice, in 1979 and 1989, proposed raising the eligibility age for all workers to 65. The proposal was turned down by the parliament both times, since trade unions and opposition parties were strongly against the bill.

In the summer of 1993, the political situation changed dramatically. The Liberal Democratic Party (LDP), which had been ruling Japan ever since the end of World War II, fell from power. It was replaced by a coalition of opposition parties (excluding the Japanese Communist Party). It was this coalition that prepared the 1994 legislation.

The approved legislation guaranteed that the second-tier earnings-related benefits for retired employees between 60 and 64 would be paid without any reduction. The first-tier basic benefits for this age group were to be phased out in stages (between 2001 and 2013 for men), and eventually no one under 65 will receive full basic benefits (the phasing out of basic benefits for female employees was delayed by five years, starting only in 2006). Until October 1994, benefits were adjusted in line with hikes in gross wages, but since 1994 they have been aligned with net wages.

In December 1998, the government decided to increase existing pension benefits in fiscal year 1999, to reflect changes only in the consumer price index over the previous calendar year, though fiscal year 1999 was previously anticipated as seeing net-wage indexing of existing pension benefits after a five-year interval.

In July 1999, the government submitted the 1999 pension reform bill to the parliament, and the bill was passed in March 2000. Its main points are as follows:

a)   Earnings-related benefits are to be reduced by 5 percent; specifically, the current annual accrual rate of 0.75 percent is to be decreased to 0.7125 percent from fiscal year 2000.

b)   Both the flat-rate basic benefits and the earnings-related pension benefits once paid are to be adjusted based on the consumer price index after age 65 from fiscal year 2000.

c)   The normal pensionable age for earnings-related old-age benefits is to be increased step by step from age 60 to 65 for men, from fiscal year 2013 to 2025. The phasing out of earnings-related old-age benefits for female employees in their early 60s will be delayed by five years, starting only in 2018. In exchange, those between 60 and 64 will become eligible for newly provided advance payments, at a reduced rate, out of the earnings-related benefits. The rate of reduction will be 0.5 percent per month (6 percent per year).

If a person begins to receive an advance payment from age 60, his/her benefit level will be 70 percent of the normal amount.

d) An earnings test for those aged 65 to 69 was to be introduced from fiscal year 2002.

e) Employers are to be exempted from paying their share of social security pension contributions for their employees on child-care leave from fiscal year 2000.

f) The monthly standard earnings base for social security pensions is upgraded to the JPY 98,000 to JPY 620,000 range from October 2000.

g) The benefit/contribution base is to be shifted from monthly standard earnings to annual earnings, including semi-annual bonuses from fiscal year 2003. The shift is to be adjusted to induce no changes in aggregate income from contributions in 2003.

h) The rebates on contributions for contracted-out schemes are to be frozen from fiscal year 1999.

i) A 50 percent reduced flat-rate contribution for non-employees is to be newly introduced from fiscal year 2002. This is mainly for low-income groups. Their basic benefits will be two-thirds of the full amount. Students aged 20 and over are to be able to postpone paying their flat-rate contributions for 10 years at most. They are, however, eligible for the full basic disability benefit during the years of non-payment.

By these measures, aggregate pension benefits will be reduced by 20 percent by 2025. As a result, the contribution rate for the KNH will peak at 25.4 percent by 2025, instead of the 34.5 percent anticipated without any reforms (the rate estimated on the basis of monthly standard earnings). The flat-rate monthly contributions for non-employees will peak by 2021 at JPY 18,500 (instead of JPY 26,400), at 1999 prices.

2.3. The 2004 pension reform

The administration of Prime Minister Koizumi Junichiro submitted a set of pension reform bills to the National Diet on February 10, 2004, and they were enacted on June 5, 2004. This section will describe the gist of the approved reforms and explore issues that remain to be addressed.

Salaried workers are, as a rule, enrolled in the KNH, which is part of the public pension system. Contributions under this plan had, since October 1996, been set at 13.58 percent of annual income, with half paid by the worker and half by the employer, but the newly enacted reforms raised this rate by 0.354 percentage points every year starting in October 2004. The rate has risen every September thereafter and will do so until 2017, after which it will remain fixed at 18.30 percent. The portion paid by workers will accordingly rise to 9.15 percent of annual income.

For an average male company employee earning JPY 360,000 a month plus annual bonuses equivalent to 3.6 months' pay, contributions will increase by nearly JPY 20,000 a year, starting from October 2004. By the time they stop rising in September 2017, contributions will have reached just under JPY 1.03 million a year, and the share paid by the worker would be just over JPY 514,000. This is 35 percent more than the 2013 level of contributions.

Those who are not enrolled in the KNH or another public pension scheme are required to participate in the KN, which provides just the so-called basic pension. (The basic pension also forms the first tier of benefits under the KNH and other public pension systems.) Contributions under this plan will rise by JPY 280 each April, from the existing JPY 13,300 per month, until they plateau at JPY 16,900 (at 2004 prices) in April 2017. The actual rise in KN contributions is adjusted according to increases in general wage levels.

In addition, the government increased its subsidies for the basic pension. One-third of the cost of basic pension benefits is paid from the national treasury; this share was to be raised in stages until it reached one-half in 2009.

2.4. Lower benefits despite higher contributions

Benefits under the KNH consist of two tiers: the flat-rate basic pension, which is paid to all public pension plan participants, and a separate earnings-related component. The latter is calculated on the basis of the worker's average preretirement income, converted to current values. The index used to convert past income to current values was the rate of increase in take-home pay. Under the 2004 reform, though, this index was subject to a negative adjustment over the course of an "exceptional period" based on changes in two demographic factors, namely, the decline in the number of participants and the increase in life expectancy. This period of adjustment was expected to last through 2023.

The application of the first demographic factor means that benefit levels will be cut to reflect the fact that fewer people are supporting the pension system. The actual number of people enrolled in all public pension schemes was ascertained each year, and the rate of decline would be calculated based on this figure. The average annual decline was projected to be around 0.6 percentage points.

Introducing the second demographic factor, meanwhile, will adjust for the fact that people are living longer and thus collecting their pensions for more years; the aim is to slow the pace of increase in the total amount of benefits paid as a result of increased longevity. This factor will not be calculated by tracking future movements in life expectancy; instead, it has been set at an annual rate of about 0.3 percentage points on the basis of current demographic projections for the period through 2025. Together, the two demographic factors were thus expected to mean a negative adjustment of about 0.9 points a year on average during the period in question.

How will these changes affect people's benefits in concrete terms? Let us consider the case of a pair of model KNH beneficiaries as defined by the Ministry of Health, Labour, and Welfare: a 65-year-old man who earned the average wage throughout his 40-year career and his 65-year-old wife who was a full-time homemaker for 40 years from her 20th birthday. In fiscal year 2004 (April 2004 to March 2005), this model couple would receive JPY 233,000 a month.

How does this amount compare to what employees are currently taking home? The average monthly income of a salaried worker in 2004 was projected to be around JPY 360,000, before taxes and social insurance deductions. Assuming that this was supplemented by bonuses totaling an equivalent of 3.6 months' pay, the average annual income was roughly JPY 5.6 million. Deducting 16 percent of this figure for taxes and social insurance contributions left an annual take-home pay of about JPY 4.7 million, or JPY 393,000 a month.

The JPY 233,000 provided to the model pensioners was 59.3 percent of JPY 393,000. But this percentage, which pension specialists call the "income replacement ratio," will gradually decline to an estimated figure of 50.2 percent as of fiscal year 2023 (assuming that consumer prices and nominal wages will rise according to government projections by 1 percent and 2.1 percent a year, respectively). Over the next two decades, then, benefit levels will decline by roughly 15 percent in comparison with wage levels.

The revised pension legislation stipulates that the income replacement ratio is not to fall below 50 percent for the model case described above, and so the exceptional period of negative adjustment will end once the ratio declines to 50 percent. This provision was included to alleviate fears that benefits would continue to shrink without limit.

How would the reforms affect those who are already receiving their pensions? Previously, benefits for those 65 years of age and over were adjusted for fluctuations in the consumer price index. This ensured that pensioners' real purchasing power remained unchanged and helped ease postretirement worries. But this cost-of-living link would effectively be severed during the exceptional period, since the application of the demographic factors would pull down real benefits by around 0.9 points a year. In principle, however, the negative adjustment of nominal benefits is suspended during deflation. Once the exceptional period is over, the link to the consumer price index is to be restored.

2.5. Provisions for working seniors and divorcees

People aged 60–64 who were receiving pensions and wage income had had their benefits reduced by a flat 20 percent, regardless of how much or little they earned. This rule was abolished so as not to discourage older people from working. But these people are still subject to the existing rule that if the sum of wages and pension benefits exceeds JPY 280,000 a month (after factoring in annual bonuses), the pension benefits are to be cut by 50 percent of the amount in excess of this level.

Workers aged 70 and over, meanwhile, have been exempt from paying into the KNH, even if they are still on a company's payroll, and they did not have their benefits reduced no matter how much they earned. Beginning in April 2007, though, their benefits have been reduced if they are high-income earners. Those receiving more than the equivalent of JPY 480,000 a month in wages and pension benefits will have their benefits cut by 50 percent of the amount in excess of this level. This is a rule that currently applies to those aged 65 to 69, and it will be maintained for this age group. The over-70 group will still be entitled to the full amount of the basic pension, and they will continue to be exempt from paying contributions.

Divorced wives were not legally entitled to any portion of their former husbands' earnings-related pension benefits, but this was changed under the revised legislation. Couples who divorce after April 2007 are able to split the rights to the earnings-related portion of the husband's pension that accrued during their marriage. The wife is able to receive up to 50 percent of these rights, although her actual share is determined by agreement between the two. For rights accruing after April 2008, moreover, a full-time homemaker is able to automatically receive half of her husband's benefits in case of divorce, by filing a claim at a social insurance office. Underlying this rule is the assumption that even though the contributions are paid in the husband's name, the wife has provided half of the couple's livelihood through her work as a homemaker. (Note that the provisions for working husbands and dependent homemaker wives apply conversely in cases where a homemaker husband is dependent on the wife.)

Widowed spouses younger than 30, and without children under the age of 18, had been entitled to lifelong benefits under the survivor's pension scheme (based on the earnings of the deceased spouse). After April 2007, however, they receive benefits for no longer than five years.

Workers taking child-care leave are exempt from making pension contributions, and to prevent a decrease in their future benefits resulting from this period of nonpayment, they are treated as having continued their full payments, even when they have no income. This special exemption was initially for up to one year after childbirth, but in April 2005 the period was extended until the child reaches the age of three.

Also from April 2005, parents who change their working arrangements to put in shorter hours so as to care for children under age three and who take a corresponding cut in pay are treated as having worked full time and earned a full salary. Actual contributions during this three-year period are based on the lower earnings, however.

2.6. Additional adjustments

As a rule, a person cannot simultaneously receive more than one public pension benefit. But the recent reforms have created an exception. People with disabilities who had gainful employment and paid pension contributions from April 2006 were entitled to not only their basic disability pension but also the earnings-related component of the old-age pension or survivor's pension. This measure is designed to encourage employment among people with handicaps.

Participants in the KN who have low incomes currently pay either half of the regular contributions or none at all. There was a fine-tuning of payment exemptions starting in July 2006, when low-income earners became exempt from paying one-quarter or three-quarters of the regular contributions.

The reform covered private pension plans as well. The upper limit of the amount that could be put aside each month under company-funded defined-contribution pension plans was raised from JPY 36,000 to JPY 51,000 in cases where there was no other corporate pension plan and from JPY 18,000 to JPY 25,500, in cases where there was another plan in effect. The ceiling on monthly installments under individually funded defined-contribution plans for salaried workers was raised from JPY 15,000 to JPY 23,000 where there was no corporate pension coverage, while the cap for the self-employed remained unchanged at JPY 68,000. The higher ceilings for private plans were designed to make up for the anticipated smaller benefits of public old-age schemes.

3. Some discussions on the 2004 pension reform

Social insurance contributions in Japan already exceed the amount collected in national taxes, and contributions to the pension system are by far the biggest social insurance item. If this already huge sum is increased by more than JPY 1 trillion a year, as the government plans, both individuals and companies are bound to change their behavior. Government projections of revenues and expenditures, though, completely ignore the prospect of such changes.

Companies will likely revamp their hiring plans and wage scales to sidestep the higher social insurance burden. They will cut back on recruitment of new graduates and become more selective about midcareer hiring as well. Many young people will be stripped of employment opportunities and driven out of the labor market, instead of being enlisted to support the pension system with a percentage of their income. Most of the employment options for middle-aged women who wish to re-enter the work force will be low-paying ones. Only a few older workers will be able to continue commanding high wages, causing a likely dramatic rise in the number of aging workers who will be forced to choose between remaining on the payroll with a pay cut and settling for retirement. Many more companies will either choose or be forced to leave the KNH, causing the number of subscribers to fall far below the government's projections and pushing the system closer to bankruptcy.

The jobless rate on the whole will rise. The government plans to increase pension contributions annually up to 2017 would exert ongoing deflationary pressure on the Japanese economy. For the worker, a rise in contribution levels means less take-home pay; as a result, consumer spending is likely to fall, and this will surely hinder prospects for a self-sustaining recovery and return to steady growth.

Another problem with increasing pension contributions is that they are regressive, since there is a ceiling for the earnings on which payment calculations are based, and unearned income is not included in the calculations at all.

One major objective of the reforms is to eventually eliminate the huge excess liabilities of JPY 500 trillion on the balance sheet of the KNH. The plan is to generate a surplus equal to this amount by (1) hiking contributions, (2) increasing payments from the national treasury, and (3) reducing benefits. But the combination of higher contributions and lower benefits will mean the future participants will end up getting back less than they pay into the system. It is estimated that their benefits will amount to only about 80 percent of their contributions. This is hardly likely to encourage people to participate. Higher contributions will further alienate younger workers from the pension system and deepen their distrust of politics.

As noted above, those who are already receiving their pensions would see their benefits decline in real terms by an average 0.9 percent per year. The government scenario sees consumer prices eventually rising 1 percent a year, and take-home pay 2.1 percent a year. This means that the model beneficiary who began receiving JPY 233,000 a month at age 65 in 2004 would get roughly JPY 240,000 at age 84 in 2023; nominal benefits, in other words, will remain virtually unchanged for two decades, despite the fact that the average take-home pay of the working population would have risen by over 40 percent. The income replacement ratio, which stood at nearly 60 percent at age 65, would dwindle to 43 percent by the time the model recipient turns 84. The promise of benefits in excess of 50 percent of take-home pay does not apply, therefore, to those who are already on old-age pensions.

The so-called demographic factors are likely to continue changing for the foreseeable future. The government itself foresees the number of participants in public pension plans declining over the coming century. The estimated figure of 69.4 million participants as of 2005 is expected to fall to 61.0 million in 2025, 45.3 million in 2050, and 29.2 million in 2100. This corresponds to an average annual decline of 0.6 percent through 2025, 1.2 percent during the quarter century from 2025, and 0.9 percent for the half century from 2050 on. In other words, the decline in the number of workers who are financially supporting the public pension system is not likely to stop after just two decades.

The 2004 reform, though, adjusts benefit levels in keeping with the decline in the contribution-paying population for the next 20 years only; the government's "standard case" does not foresee any further downward revisions, even if the number of participants continues to fall. If the government really anticipates an ongoing decline, there is no good reason to abruptly stop adjusting benefit levels after a certain period of time. Sweden and Germany, for instance, have adopted permanent mechanisms whereby benefit levels are automatically adjusted for fluctuations in demographic factors.

The decision to keep the model income replacement ratio at 50 percent at the point when pension benefit payments commence represents, in effect, the adoption of a defined-benefit formula. Maintaining both fixed contributions on the one hand and defined-benefit levels on the other is not an easy task, for there is no room to deal flexibly with unforeseen developments. The government will be confronted with a fiscal emergency should its projections for growth in contributions and a reversal in the falling birthrate veer widely from the mark.

The government based its population figures on the January 2002 projections of the National Institute of Population and Social Security Research.[2] Under these projections, the medium variant for the TFR (the average number of childbirths per woman) falls to 1.31 in 2007, after which it begins climbing, reaching 1.39 in 2050 and 1.73 in 2100. Actual figures since the projections were released have been slightly lower than this variant, and there are no signs whatsoever that the fertility rate will stop declining.

If the government is to keep its promise on an upper limit for contributions and a lower limit for benefits, the only policy option it will have in the event of a financial shortfall will be to raise the age at which people begin receiving benefits. The 2004 reform package makes no mention of such a possibility; the drafters of the bills no doubt chose to simply put this task off to a future date.

In fiscal year 2009, the share of the basic pension benefits funded by the national treasury was raised from one-third to one-half. This means that more taxes will be used to cover the cost of benefits. Taxes are by nature different from contributions paid by participants in specific pension plans, and there is a need to reconsider the benefits that are to be funded by tax revenues.

The leaders of Japanese industry tend to be quite advanced in years. For the most part, they are over the age of 65, which means they are qualified to receive the flat-rate basic pension. Even though they are among the wealthiest people in the economy, they are entitled to the same basic pension as older people hovering around the poverty line. Using tax revenues to finance a bigger share of the basic pension essentially means asking taxpayers to foot a bigger bill for the benefits of wealthy households as well. For an elderly couple, the tax-financed portion of the basic pension will rise from JPY 530,000 a year to JPY 800,000. If a need arises to raise taxes at a future date, who will then actually agree to pay more? Few people will be willing to tolerate such wasteful uses of tax money.

4. Brief outline of the 2012 pension reform

On August 30, 2009, there was a dramatic change in the political arena of Japan. The LDP fell from power and was replaced by the Democratic Party. On August 10, 2012, Japan's parliament passed a package of social security and tax reform bills after the ruling Democratic Party succeeded in reaching an agreement with the two major opposition parties, the LDP and New Komeito. The core of the bills is that the consumption tax rate is to be raised from 5 percent to 8 percent in April 2014 and further to 10 percent in October 2015. Moreover, consumption tax revenue is to be earmarked exclusively for financing social security expenditures, i.e., for pensions, healthcare for the elderly, long-term care, and childcare.

This section provides a brief outline of the reforms of the pension system that form part of the package of social security and tax reform bills, and it also highlights some remaining challenges in Japan's pension system.

4.1. Transfers from general revenue

In the past, one-third of the flat-rate basic pension used to be financed through general government revenues. In 2009 this share was raised to one-half, but no specific source for the required funds was designated. With the passage of the reforms, it was finally decided that from April 2014 the additional funds would come solely from the increase in consumption tax revenues.[3]

4.2. Inclusion of civil servants in the general pension scheme

So far, civil servants have been covered by a special pension system of their own, which is independent of the general pension system for private sector employees (KNH). From October 2015, civil servants in the central and local governments are to be included in the general pension program. Further, when the two pension systems are integrated, the third-tier pension for civil servants, which has been a component of their social security provisions, will be abolished. Their earned third-tier pension entitlements, however, are assured, as they are paid from a separate part of the existing reserve fund. The remaining part of the reserve fund will be absorbed into the general pension scheme. The first- and second-tier (earnings-related) pensions for current public sector retirees are to be paid from the general system.

The current government also established a new defined contribution–type occupational pension program for civil servants to supplement their social security. To finance this new program, the government has decided to reduce the lump-sum retirement payment for civil servants.

4.3. Reduction of the required years of coverage for old-age pensions

From October 2015 on, the years of coverage required to entitle a person to an old-age pension will be reduced from the current 25 years to only 10 years. This change will lead to an increase in the number of retirees with smaller old-age pensions owing to their shorter contribution periods.

A danger of this change is that many of the self-employed and atypical workers may decide to stop paying contributions after completing the minimum of 10 years, turning this originally mandatory pension scheme into a virtually optional (voluntary) one. This kind of situation might arise if implementation is weak and might be exacerbated by the introduction of a supplementary benefit for low-income pensions (see below).

4.4. Introduction of a supplementary benefit for low-income pensioners

From October 2015 on, low-income pensioners with annual pension benefits of less than JPY 780,000 will be entitled to a supplementary monthly benefit of up to JPY 5,000. The scheme is to be established as a welfare program outside the pension system and will be financed from the increase in consumption tax revenues. The detailed contents of the supplementary benefit were set down in another bill, which was passed by the parliament in November 2012.

4.5. Extension of the coverage of the KNH to employees with shorter working hours

The KNH currently covers employees with 30 working hours or more per week. From October 2016 on, coverage will be extended to employees working between

20 and 30 hours a week. Although there are estimated to be about 4 million employees in Japan who work between 20 and 30 hours a week, the expected increase in covered employees is only around 250,000, since the following four conditions will also be put in place. Only employees (1) with a monthly salary of JPY 88,000 or more, (2) with an employment contract for at least one year, and (3) working for a company with more than 500 employees (i.e., a large company) will qualify. Further, (4) students are excluded. These conditions were incorporated to placate strong opposition from employers.

4.6. Survivor benefits for single fathers

Currently, only mothers whose husband is deceased or children whose parents are deceased are entitled to survivor benefits. From April 2014, fathers whose wife is deceased will also be entitled to survivor benefits, unless the wife was a full-time housewife.

4.7. Contribution exemption during maternity leave

From April 2014 on, the system is changed to exempt the employer and the employee herself from pension contributions when an employee takes maternity leave. The employee continues to accrue pension entitlements as though both she and her employer had continued contributing. The pension entitlements accruing during this period are financed through contributions by other employees and their employers.

4.8. Major challenges ahead

The changes introduced in the social security and tax reform bills went some way toward putting the pension system on a sounder financial footing and creating a more equitable pension system overall. Nevertheless, challenges remain. Four of the major challenges ahead are the following.

First, in 2004 Japan introduced an "automatic balancing mechanism (negative adjustment)," according to which pension benefits were to be adjusted upward below the rate of inflation. However, Japan has been suffering from deflation for more than a decade, so that the automatic balancing mechanism has not taken effect. This means that the mechanism needs to be redesigned to apply also in times of deflation (with benefits falling faster than the price level).

Second, the proportion of atypical employees has been increasing, reaching 40 percent in 2010. A growing number of young employees are forced to enter the job market as irregulars and are given few opportunities thereafter to obtain a position as a regular-status employee with a higher and more stable salary. Japan is seriously affected by the "Bad Start, Bad Finish" problem identified by Takayama and Shiraishi (2012).[4]

Third, the normal pensionable age in Japan is still 65. Its automatic indexation to longevity is essential to the long-term adequacy of the pension benefit.

Fourth, under the current system, full-time housewives married to regular employees are automatically entitled to the flat-rate basic pension without making any contributions of their own. This system is being viewed as grossly unfair by dual-income couples and single women. A solution to this problem would be to introduce an equal income split between an income-earning husband and his dependent wife in determining their pension entitlements (while keeping the husband's pension contributions unchanged).

5. Healthcare issues in Japan

5.1. Brief outline of the program

The Japanese system of social security healthcare is universal. Currently, it is broadly composed of four programs covering different sectors of the population.[5] The first is the scheme for the "old-old" (those age 75 and over). For those age 74 or younger, the major program is the healthcare system for employees in large firms (Kumiai) and for civil servants (Kyosai). It is financed on an individual employer basis. The third is the scheme for all other employees not covered by the second. Employees in small and medium-sized firms are usually covered by the third scheme, which is managed by the central government (Kyokai, formerly Seikan). The fourth scheme is for independent workers, self-employed people, and retired workers. It is operated on a municipal basis (Kokuho). Dependents are covered by one of the three schemes for those age 74 or younger.[6]

There are several unique features in the current Japanese healthcare system. First, at retirement, employees are usually obliged to move from the second or third scheme to the fourth one. Second, a revenue-sharing scheme has been established for those aged 75 and over. The old-old pay a lower share of medical costs (co-payments and 10 percent of remaining costs), the major part of which are financed by transfers from social insurance contributions to the three remaining programs mentioned above and from the general revenue of both central and local governments.[7]

Third, the social security coverage of medical care service and its reimbursement to providers are the same for all of the programs. The social insurance coverage of medical care service (including co-payments) is still very broad (around 90 percent in terms of the aggregate cost). Reimbursement to healthcare providers is principally based on a fee-for-service schedule that is uniform across different regions. The schedule is revised every two years by the central government. Each patient in Japan enjoys free access to any medical service provider at any time, purchasing most available medical treatments at a publicly determined price through social insurance programs for healthcare.

Fourth, in contrast to the benefit side, each program for healthcare adopts a different financing method. Generally speaking, the principal source of income is the contribution from enrollees (and their employers in the second and third programs). Transfers from the general revenue of the central and/or local governments are given to the first, third, and fourth programs to compensate for the relatively low income of these groups.

5.2. Financing the healthcare costs of the elderly population

Average medical costs vary among different age groups. In 2011 the annual cost per person was JPY 149,000 for those less than 15 years old, JPY 110,000 for those between 15 and 44, JPY 276,000 for those between 45 and 64, JPY 721,000 for those 65 and above, and JPY 892,000 for those 75 and over (USD 1 = JPY 107, approximately). Older people are heavy users of medical care services, and their medical costs per person per annum for those aged 75 and over are currently about 8.1 times the cost for those between 15 and 44 years old. Consequently, in 2011, 56 percent of aggregate medical expenses were incurred by people aged 65 and above, while their share of the total population was 23 percent. Social security programs for healthcare are becoming very similar to those for pensions, in that the basic feature of the program is income redistribution from younger and middle-aged people to older people.

Annual healthcare expenditure in 2011 in Japan was 8.2 percent of the gross domestic product, which was relatively low among countries in the Organisation for Economic Co-operation and Development. Owing to the rapidly aging population, it will, however, increase very sharply. There is a broad consensus among Japanese economists that it will grow by around 40 percent in 15 years in real terms.[8]

The problems of financing social security healthcare were getting more and more serious in Japan, especially with respect to the medical costs of the elderly population. There was growing dissatisfaction within the second and third groups (*Kumiai*, *Kyosai* and *Kyokai*) about transferring their money to the scheme for the old-old.

Before the scheme for the old-old (*Roken*) was set up in 1983, the medical costs of the elderly population were mainly financed by the *Kokuho*, the lowest income group, with substantial transfers from general revenue. The *Roken* changed the main financial source for the elderly's healthcare, from transfers from general revenue to transfers (contributions) from the respective healthcare programs. The medical costs of the elderly population had been supported by all of the above programs.

Substantially increased transfers, especially from the *Kumiai* and *Kyosai*, forced their current account to repeatedly run a deficit, causing steady increases in their contribution rate for healthcare. Their complaints about subsidizing the *Roken* were becoming extreme.

5.3. The 2008 reform

After heated debates among stakeholders, the latest healthcare reform was went into effect April 2008. The main contents of the reform are as follows:

- The eligible age for the scheme for the old-old was raised from 70 to 75.
- A 10 percent co-payment is applied to those age 75 and above. A 30 percent co-payment is exceptionally applied to those who have a high income.

- 50 percent of medical expenses for the scheme for the old-old are to be covered by transfers from the general revenue of central and local governments.
- The co-payment for employees in the second and third programs (*Kumiai, Kyosai* and *Kyokai*) is increased from 20 to 30 percent, while the rate for infants less than three years old is reduced from 30 to 20 percent.
- The ceiling on co-payments is increased from JPY 63,600 to JPY 80,100 a month for the employees' group, while it is lifted to JPY 12,000 for elderly outpatients and JPY 44,400 for elderly inpatients.
- The contribution base for the second and third programs was expanded to include semi-annual bonuses, whereas the rate for the *Kyokai* was increased from 7.5 to 9.34 percent.

5.4. Future options

Social security healthcare in Japan is by and large on a command-and-control model operated by the central government. There is a growing demand for Japan to introduce a contracting model. An agency relationship, formed whenever a principal delegates decision-making authority to another party (the agent), should be built up between patients and service providers, and between insurers and insured persons. Each player would be equal in making contacts. Contracts should include incentive schemes for efficient supply of good-quality medical services. In this sense, an insurer should play a more active role than in the traditional indemnity policy. The insurer should be permitted not only to do the *ex post* review of medical practice but also to contract directly with medical service providers, applying a different payment schedule from that determined by the central government.

In reforming the healthcare payment schedule, a prospective payment system (PPS) would be advisable. Insurers can evaluate the quality of providers, giving them strong incentives through rewards based on outcomes, not on inputs. The PPS was first introduced into the inpatient fee for older patients in 1990. It was not mandatory, but it induced lower service inputs. The area of medical treatments that the PPS covers is expected to be widened.

There should be more competition among providers and among insurers. Many people propose that the programs should be divided up on a prefectural basis.[9] In addition, many people advocate the introduction of gatekeepers, which would place some restrictions on free access to any service provider.

6. Conclusion

In January 2012, the National Institute of Population and Social Security Research released future population projections that made the problem of social security financing look more serious. The majority of the population has recognized the gravity of the problem. They will be sure to drastically change all the existing programs of social security.

Many younger people in Japan are currently atypical workers, and their working status is quite unstable. They are not assured to enjoy adequate and stable income during their working age, and consequently their pension benefits will be less than adequate. Higher employability with a stable income is missing for them.

Socio-economic conditions will change very rapidly. The changes that take place will often be beyond our previous expectations. Never-ending reforms of social security are inevitable in Japan, where only fine-tuning of programs in the face of changing circumstances is acceptable in the political arena.

Notes

1 This chapter is a revised and extended version of Takayama (2002) and Takayama (2010a).
2 See www.ipss.go.jp/pp-newest/e/ppfj02/top.html
3 The burden of the consumption tax levied at a uniform rate would be largely proportional if the denominator is lifetime income (see Caspersen and Metcalf, 1994). A partial shift from payroll tax to consumption tax for financing pension benefits will temporarily induce an income transfer from pensioners to actively working generations (see Takayama, 2010b).
4 The problem was first highlighted by Italian pension experts (see Galasso and Boeri, 2012).
5 Yoshikawa et al. (1996) give a detailed explanation of social security healthcare in Japan.
6 Those with very low incomes are exempt from participating in any social insurance programs for healthcare, and their medical costs are wholly covered by public assistance.
7 Since 1984 another revenue-sharing scheme has been set up for retirees under 70. From 2008 the age ceiling has been lifted to 75.
8 See the Ministry of Health, Labour and Welfare (2012).
9 See Tanaka (2000) and Ogata (2001) for more details.

References

Caspersen, E. and Metcalf, G. (1994). Is a value added tax regressive? Annual versus lifetime incidence measures. *National Tax Journal*, 47(4), 731–746.

Galasso, V. and Boeri, T. (2012). Is social security secure with NDC? In Holzmann, R., Palmer, E. and Robalino, D. (Eds.), *NDC pension schemes in a changing pension world: volume 2*. Washington, DC: World Bank.

Ministry of Health, Labour and Welfare. (2012). *Benefit and cost of social security: projections updated*. Tokyo: Ministry of Health, Labour and Welfare.

National Institute of Population and Social Security Research. (2012). *Population projections for Japan: 2011–2060*. Tokyo: National Institute of Population and Social Security Research.

Ogata, H. (2001). *Health care reform and the role of insurers: in the international perspective*. Mimeo. Department of Health Care Administration and Management, Graduate School of Medical Sciences, Kyushu University, Fukuoka, Japan.

Takayama, N. (2002). Japan's never-ending social security reforms. *International Social Security Review*, 55(4), 11–22.

Takayama, N. (2010a). *Development of pension arrangements and future pension policy issues in Japan (report)*. Tokyo: Pacific Economic Cooperation Council (PECC) .

Takayama, N. (2010b). *Pensions and child allowance*. Tokyo: Iwanami Shoten (in Japanese).

Takayama, N. and Shiraishi, K. (2012). *Does a bad start lead to a bad finish in Japan?* Project on Intergenerational Equity / Center for Intergenerational Studies, Tokyo DP-547, http://takayama-online.net/pie/stage3/Japanese/d_p/dp2011/dp547/text.pdf.

Tanaka, K. (2000). Financing increased medical expenditure and allocation of specific risks in health insurance. In Von Maydell, B. et al. (Eds.), *Entwicklungen der Systeme sozialer Sicherheit in Japan und Europa*. Berlin: Duncker & Humblot.

Yoshikawa, A., Bhattacharya, J. and Vogt, W.B. (Eds.). (1996). *Health economics of Japan*. Tokyo: University of Tokyo Press.

3 Managing pension and healthcare costs in rapidly aging depopulating countries

The case of Korea

Hyungpo Moon

1. Introduction

The rapidly growing phenomenon of population aging and low birth rates is expected to bring enormous demographic changes in Korean society. According to the future population prospects released by the National Statistics Office (2006), the average life expectancy of Koreans is projected to rise from 78.6 years in 2005 to 86.0 years in 2050. As a result, the population aged 65 years or older is expected to reach 16.2 million in 2050, 3.7 times larger than the 4.4 million in 2005. The drastic decrease in the birth rate as well as the increased life expectancy will affect the demographic structure of Korean society to a serious degree. In particular, the working-age population (ages 15–64) is expected to drop by a record 35 percent, from 34.5 million in 2005 to 22.4 million in 2050. Among them, the prime working-age population (ages 25–49) is also projected to fall by half during the same time frame. Such a large increase in the elderly population and decrease in the working-age population will place a huge burden on Korean society in supporting the elderly. The aging population structure will cause a comprehensive impact on the overall national conditions including the labor market, the financial market, and the national fiscal plan. Such an impact will become more apparent a decade from now, and expected impacts include a relative reduction in the working-age population as the number of elderly increases, combined with a decrease in the accumulation of productive capital as a result of a low savings rate. Therefore, if other conditions remain the same, the aging population will adversely affect the growth potential of the Korean economy.

The aging of the population is expected to affect the overall economy by reducing the savings rate, putting more burdens on the pension system and health insurance, and creating additional demands for welfare, which will lead to an aggravated fiscal condition. Since the economic implications of population aging accompany issues related to social and economic institutions, institutional reform forms a major part of the policy to counter the aging of society. However, it is not easy to reform institutions entangled with conflicting interests among the different social levels. Moreover, since matters related to population aging cannot be changed easily, it can be said that the current situation faced by the Korean economy is quite serious. Under such conditions, it is important to promptly determine the policy direction to prepare for the aging of society, formulate a comprehensive national consensus on the direction, and carry out the relevant policy consistently in accordance with the direction.

Although the rapid demographic change will affect various sectors of the economy, the most direct and significant impacts will be on age-related public programs, including public pension and healthcare systems. Population aging puts increasing pressure on the spending of public pension and healthcare programs, while a decrease in the working population shrinks the revenue basis, thus threatening the financial sustainability of the system. Hence, the biggest challenge facing the social insurance system in Korea is to contain growing public expenditures driven by population aging and to secure adequate financial resources to maintain a sustainable social protection system for the elderly. At the same time, a rapidly aging population will make social protection of the elderly more important. However, because of their short history, the Korean public pension and healthcare systems are still immature in terms of both their coverage and their benefit provisions. As strengthening income and health protection through extended coverage or additional insurance benefits requires more funding, it will not be an easy task to expand social protection without sacrificing financial stability. In this regard, this chapter examines the impacts of population aging on public pension and healthcare systems in Korea and discusses the policy issues for providing more sustainable and adequate risk protection for the elderly.

2. Population aging and the public pension system in Korea

2.1. The narrow coverage of the National Pension

Inclusion of the urban self-employed among the targets of the National Pension Scheme in 1999 has created, at least nominally, the framework of a universal pension system that covers the whole nation. However, it is true that there exists a wide loophole: the insured who are exempted from making contributions, and those who have deferred their payments because of business closure, unemployment, or temporary leave. The official statistics show that as of 2009 the insured who were exempted from contribution payments numbered above 5 million, which accounts for 27.1 percent of the total number of insured and 58.2 percent of the individually insured, as shown in Table 3.1.

Table 3.1 Number of insured persons in the National Pension, 2009 (% in parentheses)

Total	Workplace-based insured	Individually insured	Income reporter	Exempt from contribution
18,623,845	9,866,681	8,679,861	3,627,597	5,052,264
(100.0)	(53.0)	(47.0)	(19.9)	(27.1)

Source: National Pension Service, 2009.

Table 3.2 Number of those exempt from contribution payments, 2009 (% in parentheses)

Total	Jobless	Business closure	Students	Temporary leave	Livelihood difficulties	Other*
5,052,264	3,817,904	433,544	278,259	92,695	7,229	422,633
(100.0)	(75.6)	(8.6)	(5.5)	(1.8)	(0.1)	(8.4)

Source: National Pension Service, 2009.

*Includes military personnel, inmates, missing persons, hospital patients, etc.

It is also assumed that a considerable number of insured individuals report their incomes but are unable to pay contributions. As of 2009, the contribution collection rate of the total income reporters including workplace-based insured persons was 92.0 percent in terms of the amount collected but 62.1 percent in terms of individually insured persons. In particular, approximately half of those who have failed to pay the contribution are long-term delinquents who have extended their deferral period to more than two years (National Pension Service, 2009).

The existence of a wide range of insured people who are exempted from contribution of payments is likely to increase the risk of pulling them into the elderly poor. Such risk is clearly found in the cases for the exemption of contribution payments. As shown in Table 3.2, the insured who are exempted from contribution because of subsistence difficulties account for almost 90 percent of the total number of cases, and a third of them turn out to be unemployed. Moreover, the majority of non-regular workers, such as temporary and day laborers and self-employed small business owners, have a greater incentive to evade income reporting or to under-report their incomes as a result of subsistence difficulties. However, it is difficult to know exactly the actual size of their incomes given the poor administrative capability of the National Pension Corporation. As a result, many non-regular workers and self-employed small business owners who are actually engaged in economic activities are considered as insured who are exempted from contribution of payments and therefore excluded from participating in the system. This section closely examines the behavioral characteristics shown in participation in the National Pension and the factors why people decide not to join the scheme.

2.1.1. Participation behaviors of the individually insured

This study uses research data from the Korea Welfare Panel Study, currently the largest panel in Korea, which has accumulated data on over 7,000 households since 2006 and also includes farming and fishing households, which makes it more suitable for this study. This analysis extracts 4,115 samples from the 2008 data for people between the ages of 18 and 59, the target age of the National Pension initiatives.

As shown in Table 3.3, among the total number of people subject to individual insurance, only 34.4 percent contributed payments in 2007, meaning that there is a wide range of uninsured people, including the insured who are exempt from

Table 3.3 Number of the insured in the National Pension by occupational status (% in parentheses)

Category		Total	Self-employed			Wage workers				Other*
			Subtotal	Employer	Self-employed	Subtotal	Regular	Temporary	Day laborer	
Workplace-based (2,156)	Contributing	2,152 (99.79)	62 (99.0)	57 (98.9)	5 (100)	2,081 (99.8)	1,888 (99.8)	171 (100)	22 (100)	9 (100)
	Non-contributing	5 (0.21)	1 (1.0)	1 (1.1)	0 (0.0)	4 (0.2)	4 (0.2)	0 (0.0)	0 (0.0)	0 (0.0)
Individually insured (1,959)	Contributing	674 (34.4)	406 (58.5)	129 (67.0)	277 (55.2)	182 (27.8)	92 (36.4)	29 (17.4)	62 (25.9)	85 (14.0)
	Non-contributing	1,285 (65.6)	288 (41.5)	64 (33.0)	225 (44.8)	474 (72.2)	161 (63.6)	136 (82.7)	176 (74.1)	523 (86.0)
	Contribution exemption	1,111 (86.8)	195 (67.8)	46 (71.9)	149 (66.6)	412 (87.3)	146 (90.8)	115 (85.1)	151 (85.9)	504 (96.7)
	Contribution deferral	169 (13.2)	92 (32.2)	18 (28.1)	75 (33.4)	60 (12.7)	15 (9.2)	20 (14.9)	25 (14.1)	17 (3.3)

Source: Calculated from Korea Institute for Health and Social Affairs, 2008.

*Includes unpaid family workers, the unemployed, and the economically non-active population.

payments or who deferred their contributions. In particular, more than half of the respondents who are classified as the insured who are exempted from contribution turn out to be economically active, implying that the "loophole" problems caused by poor administrative capability in gathering accurate information on people's income status are quite serious. It is also noted that among individually insured persons, 33.4 percent turn out to be wage workers, and the majority of them are legally entitled to the status of workplace-based insured; they have remained as individually insured because their status was not reported properly. This also implies that it would be a huge error to consider the individually insured as consisting of employers and the self-employed without employees.

The actual pension participation rate of people subject to individual insurance demonstrates considerable differences by their type of occupational status. The non-participation rate of wage workers was 72.2 percent on average, meaning that over seven out of ten workers have failed to pay the contribution on time. This is 1.7 times higher than the non-participation rate of self-employed persons, which was 41.5 percent. The non-participation rate of wage workers was 63.6 percent for regular workers, 74.1 percent for day laborers, and 82.7 percent for temporary workers, suggesting that the higher the instability of the occupational status, the lower the pension participation rate. This means that the loophole problem for participation in the National Pension is probably the most threatening among non-regular workers, indicating that they should be considered as the primary target in efforts to formulate policy measures to tighten the loophole.

Table 3.4 shows the result of comparing the individual characteristics of persons subject to individual insurance depending on their participation or non-participation in the National Pension. The one that stands out the most is that the average disposable income of uninsured people is over 20 percent lower than that of insured people. Also, as the household income declines, their non-participation rate increases quickly, meaning that economic reasons are a significant determinant of participation in the pension system. At the same time, it is worth noting that for persons with an average educational background, the participation rate turned out to be lower than the non-participation rate. By age group, the younger the person, the lower the participation rate, and in particular the non-participation rate of those in their 30s and younger turned out to be as high as 95 percent. Also, the participation rate of females turned out to be approximately 20 percent lower than that of males, meaning a bigger loophole among women.

In an attempt to closely examine the impacts of individual characteristics on participation behaviors, the study conducts an estimation using the Probit model, and its results are presented in Table 3.5, which is the estimation of the participation probability of 1,993 individually insured persons among the sample. As expected, the probability of participation in the National Pension for individually insured persons turned out to be highly sensitive to variables such as gender, age, and income. It is estimated that the participation probability will increase significantly according to higher income, older age, and male gender. However, contrary to expectations, the estimated coefficients showed negative signs and low statistical significance in the category of educational background, meaning little impact on the participation probability.

Table 3.4 Major characteristics of individually insured persons

Category		Total		Participants		Non-participants	
		Number	%	Number	%	Number	%
Total		1,959	100.0	674	34.4	1,285	65.6
Age	18–30	205	10.5	11	5.2 (1.6)	194	94.8 (15.1)
	31–40	684	34.9	166	24.2 (24.6)	519	75.8 (40.4)
	41–50	650	33.2	264	40.7 (39.2)	385	59.3 (30.0)
	51–59	420	21.5	233	55.4 (34.6)	187	44.6 (14.6)
	Average (years)	42.4		46.5		40.3	
Educational background	Middle school or lower	329	16.8	156	47.3 (23.1)	173	52.7 (13.5)
	High school	957	48.8	319	33.4 (47.4)	637	66.6 (49.6)
	College or higher	673	34.4	199	29.5 (29.5)	475	70.5 (36.9)
	Average years of schooling	12.35		11.98		12.54	
Gender	Male	1,235	63.0	511	41.4 (75.8)	724	58.6 (56.4)
	Female	724	37.0	163	22.5 (24.2)	561	77.5 (43.6)
Spouse	Yes	1,509	77.1	575	38.1 (85.3)	935	61.9 (72.7)
	No	450	22.9	99	22.0 (14.7)	351	78.0 (27.3)
No. of family members	Average	3.51		3.61		3.46	

Householder	Yes	1,205	61.5	518	43.0 (76.8)	687	57.0 (53.5)
	No	754	38.5	156	20.7 (23.2)	598	79.3 (46.5)
Economic status	Regular worker	253	12.9	92	36.4 (13.7)	161	63.6 (12.5)
	Temporary worker	165	8.4	29	17.4 (4.2)	136	82.6 (10.6)
	Day laborer	238	12.2	62	25.9 (9.2)	176	74.1 (13.7)
	Self-employed	695	35.5	406	58.5 (60.3)	288	41.5 (22.4)
	Other	608	31.1	85	14.0 (12.7)	523	86.0 (40.7)
Disposable income* (10,000 won)	1,000 or lower	291	14.8	73	25.1 (10.8)	218	74.9 (16.9)
	1,000–2,000	823	42.0	248	30.2 (36.8)	575	69.8 (44.7)
	2,000–3,000	526	26.8	185	35.3 (27.5)	340	64.7 (26.5)
	3,000–4,000	173	8.8	77	44.9 (11.5)	95	55.1 (7.4)
	4,000 or higher	148	7.5	90	60.8 (13.3)	58	39.2 (4.5)
	Average	2,178.7			2,547.9		1,985.2

Source: Calculated from Korea Institute for Health and Social Affairs, 2008.

*Adjusted for family size using $\sqrt{n}$.

Please note that both vertical and horizontal comparisons appear in this table.

Table 3.5 Estimation results for individually insured persons (Probit)

Dependent variables		Model 1		Model 2	
		dy/dx	SE	dy/dx	SE
Male		0.0758***	0.028	0.0736***	0.028
Age		0.0375**	0.016	0.0355**	0.016
Age^2		−0.0002	0.000	−0.0002	0.000
Economic status (basis: temporary worker)	Regular worker	0.1835***	0.063	0.1822***	0.063
	Day laborer	0.0023	0.058	0.0048	0.058
	Self-employed	0.3129***	0.052	0.3150***	0.052
	Other*	−0.0513	0.052	−0.0492	0.052
Educational background (basis: middle school or lower)	High school	−0.0475	0.037		
	College or higher	−0.0399	0.042		
Years of schooling				−0.0146	0.021
ln (disposable income)^a		0.1144***	0.023	0.1140***	0.023
Observations		1,933		1,933	

Source: Calculated from Korea Institute for Health and Social Affairs, 2008.

^{a}Adjusted for family size using $\sqrt{n}$.

*** $p < 0.01$, ** $p < 0.05$, * $p < 0.1$.

It is worth noting that the probability of participation in the National Pension var-ies significantly depending on the occupational status of individually insured persons. With temporary workers as the standard dummy, the study finds that the participa-tion probability of day laborers has no statistically significant difference, whereas that of regular and self-employed workers is estimated to be 18.4 percentage points and 31.3 percentage points higher, respectively. Given that the National Pension participation rate of temporary workers was 17.4 percent, if all other conditions are equal, the participation probability of regular workers is two times higher than that of temporary workers, while that of the self-employed is 2.8 times higher than for temporary workers. In other words, even when individual characteristics are con-trolled for, the participation probability of wage workers and of the self-employed with employees, among types of individually insured persons, shows a considerable difference. It is estimated that the participation probability of those facing job inse-curity, such as temporary and day laborers, will turn out particularly low.

2.1.2. Participation behaviors of wage workers

Table 3.6 is the result of a close comparison between individually insured wage workers and workplace-based insured workers, which apparently is the most seri-ous loophole for pension participation. The table shows a clear difference in the

Table 3.3 Major characteristics of wage workers

		Individually insured						Workplace-based insured	
		Subtotal		Insured		Non-insured			
		Number	%	Number	%	Number	%	Number	%
Total		663	100.0	184	27.8	479	72.2	2,085	99.82
Age	18~30	69	10.5	4	6.0 <2.3>	65	94.0 <13.6>	466	99.7 <22.3>
	31~40	233	35.2	47	20.3 <25.7>	186	79.7 <38.9>	838	99.8 <40.2>
	41~50	233	35.2	76	32.8 <41.5>	157	67.2 <32.8>	560	99.8 <26.9>
	51~59	127	19.1	56	44.4 <30.5>	71	55.6 <14.7>	222	100 <10.7>
	Average (years)	42.3		45.8		40.9		38.15	
Educational background	Middle school or lower	116	17.5	49	42.3 <26.6>	67	57.7 <14.0>	171	100 <8.2>
	High school	373	56.2	88	23.7 <47.9>	284	76.3 <59.4>	729	99.6 <35.0>
	College or higher	175	26.3	47	27.0 <25.5>	127	73.0 <26.6>	1,185	99.9 <56.9>
	Average years of schooling	12.1		11.6		12.2		13.57	
Gender	Male	451	68.0	137	30.3 <74.1>	314	69.7 <65.7>	1,390	99.7 <66.6>
	Female	212	32.0	48	22.5 <25.9>	164	77.5 <34.3>	696	100 <33.4>
Economic status	Regular worker	255	38.6	93	36.4 <50.5>	162	63.6 <34.0>	1,892	99.8 <90.7>
	Temporary worker	166	25.1	29	17.4 <15.7>	138	82.6 <28.7>	171	100 <8.2>
	Day laborer	241	36.3	62	25.9 <33.8>	178	74.1 <37.3>	22	100 <1.1>
Workplace size (no. of persons)	1~4	229	35.2	53	23.3 <29.6>	176	76.7 <37.4>	132	99.1 <6.4>
	5~9	157	24.2	34	21.9 <19.1>	123	78.1 <26.2>	216	98.8 <10.5>
	10~99	185	28.5	61	33.1 <34.0>	124	67.0 <26.4>	728	100 <35.4>
	100~299	26	4.0	10	38.0 <5.5>	16	62.0 <3.4>	296	100 <14.4>
	300 or higher	52	8.1	21	41.1 <11.9>	31	59.0 <6.6>	686	100 <33.3>

(*Continued*)

Table 3.6 (Continued)

Total		Individually insured						Workplace-based insured	
		Subtotal		Insured		Non-insured			
		Number	%	Number	%	Number	%	Number	%
Business type	Agriculture, forestry, and fishery	6	1.0	1	17.1 <0.6>	5	83.0 <1.1>	7	100 <0.4>
	Manufacturing	68	10.2	20	29.3 <10.7>	48	70.7 <10.0>	763	100 <36.7>
	Construction	171	25.8	46	26.9 <25.0>	125	73.1 <26.2>	147	98.4 <7.1>
	Wholesale and retail trade and accommodation	148	22.5	20	13.6 <11.0>	129	86.4 <26.9>	223	100 <10.7>
	Transportation and telecommunications	51	7.6	20	39.2 <10.7>	31	60.8 <6.4>	171	99.1 <8.2>
	Other services	169	25.5	61	35.9 <32.9>	108	64.1 <22.6>	508	100 <24.4>
	Public administration, defense, and education	49	7.4	17	33.9 <9.0>	33	66.1 <6.8>	262	100 <12.6>
	Average	2,066.6		2,241.7		1,999.2		2,673.6	
Disposable income[a] (10,000 won)	1,000 or lower	77	11.6	17	21.5 <9.0>	61	78.5 <12.7>	62	100 <3.0>
	1,000–2,000	331	49.9	78	23.6 <42.4>	253	76.4 <52.9>	658	99.8 <31.6>
	2,000–3,000	178	26.8	56	31.4 <30.3>	122	68.6 <25.5>	716	99.6 <34.3>
	3,000–4,000	44	6.7	19	41.8 <10.1>	26	58.2 <5.4>	389	100 <18.6>
	4,000 or higher	33	4.9	15	46.8 <8.3>	17	53.3 <3.6>	261	100 <12.5>
	Average	2,066.6		2,241.7		1,999.2		2,673.6	

Source: Calculated from Korea Institute for Health and Social Affairs, 2008.

[a] Adjusted for family size using $\sqrt{n}$.

Please note that both vertical and horizontal comparisons appear in this table.

individual characteristics of workplace-insured workers and individually insured workers. First, the average income level of individually insured workers amounted to only 77.3 percent of that of the workplace-based insured workers, meaning that low-income workers are more often left out from the workplace-based insured status. Also, among persons subject to individual insurance, there is an average income gap of over 10 percent between the insured workers who pay the contribution to the National Pension and those who do not. The participation behavior varies significantly according to the occupational status of workers. For regular workers, 88.1 percent of the total sample (2,147) are workplace-based insured, whereas for temporary and daily laborers, only 32.2 percent are workplace-based insured. Also, the ratio of uninsured workers to the total was 7.6 percent for regular workers, 41 percent for temporary workers, and 37.7 percent for day laborers, reconfirming that the higher the instability of the occupational status, the lower the pension participation rate.

Significant differences are observed in the individual characteristics, such as age, educational background, and gender. The average age of workplace-based insured workers is younger than for individually insured workers, while among persons subject to individual insurance, those who are insured are approximately five years older than those who are uninsured, meaning that the loophole problems experienced by younger workers are relatively more serious than for other age groups. Moreover, the percentage of individually insured male workers (24.5 percent) is slightly higher than that of female workers (23.1 percent), while the percentage of uninsured female workers (18.6 percent) is slightly higher than that of male workers (17.1 percent). With regard to educational background, workplace-based insured workers have approximately 10 percent more years of schooling on average than individually insured workers do, while among individually insured persons the uninsured workers have more years of schooling, which is an interesting result.

It should be noted that the ratio of workers who are left out from the workplace-based insured status and participation in the National Pension varies significantly according to the workplace size and business type. As shown in Figure 3.1, the poorer and smaller the workplace that individuals belong to, the more unlikely they are to report incomes and participate in the National Pension. In particular, workplace-based insurance covered only 36.6 percent of total workers. By business type, the ratio of workplace-based insured workers was 91.8 percent in the manufacturing industry but only 46.2 percent in the construction industry, in which the majority of employees are day laborers. In the service industries, the proportion of workplace-based insured workers was approximately 60 percent in the wholesale and retail trade and accommodation sector, which includes a large number of small and poor businesses.

Table 3.7 shows the estimates of the participation behaviors of the total number of 2,746 wage workers, including workplace-based and individually insured persons. According to the estimation that uses the Probit model, for wage workers, variables such as income, educational background, and age affect the decision to participate in the National Pension. Also, the occupational status turns out to be correlated with the participation rate in the National Pension. To be specific, the

A. By Workplace Size

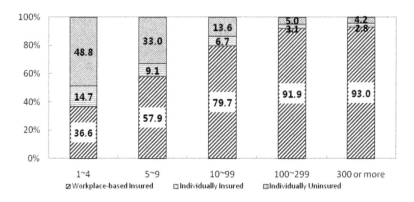

B. By Business Type

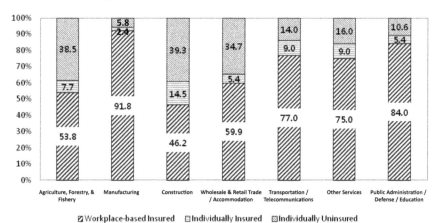

Figure 3.1 Participation behaviors of wage workers by workplace size and business type
Source: Korea Institute for Health and Social Affairs, 2008.

participation rate of regular workers is higher by 23.0 percentage points than that of temporary workers, which is a large gap, but the participation rate of day laborers is estimated to be lower than that of temporary workers, by 8.4 percentage points, which suggests that the higher the instability of the occupational status, the lower the pension participation rate.

The participation rate of workers turns out to be influenced by the business type or workplace size where they work, even when the individual characteristics are statistically controlled for. In other words, workers in poorer and smaller workplaces tend to show lower participation rates. In particular, the participation rate of workers in workplaces with fewer than 10 employees is lower by 8–11

Table 3.7 Estimation results for wage workers

Dependent variables		Participation or non-participation	
		dy/dx	SE
Male		0.0109	(0.013)
Age		−0.0138***	(0.005)
Age^2		0.0002**	(0.000)
Educational background (basis: middle school or lower)	High school	−0.0823***	(0.027)
	College or higher	−0.0223	(0.026)
Economic status (basis: temporary worker)	Regular worker	0.2301***	(0.027)
	Day laborer	−0.0840**	(0.034)
Workplace size (basis: fewer than 5 employees)	5–9	0.0235*	(0.014)
	10–99	0.0885***	(0.012)
	100–299	0.0864***	(0.009)
	Over 300	0.1138***	(0.012)
Business type (basis: manufacturing)	Agriculture, forestry, and fishery	−0.1820*	(0.111)
	Construction	−0.1080***	(0.033)
	Wholesale and retail trade and accommodation	−0.1547***	(0.033)
	Transportation and telecommunications	−0.1140***	(0.039)
	Other services	−0.0919***	(0.023)
	Public administration, defense, and education	−0.0430	(0.029)
ln (disposable income)[a]		0.0280**	(0.012)
Observations		2,746	

Source: Korea Institute for Health and Social Affairs, 2008.

[a] Adjusted for family size using $\sqrt{n}$.

*** $p < 0.01$, ** $p < 0.05$, * $p < 0.1$.

percentage points than that of workers in workplaces with 10 or more employees. With regard to business type, in comparison to the manufacturing industry, the participation rate in the National Pension in other industries is estimated to be considerably lower. In particular, the participation rate of workers in agriculture, forestry, and fishery and in wholesale and retail trade and accommodation is significantly lower, by over 15 percentage points, than for those in the manufacturing industry, suggesting that they are experiencing the most serious loophole problems. Also, the participation rate of employees in other services and the construction industry turns out to be around 10 percentage points lower than for those in the manufacturing industry. Such estimates imply that the loophole problem of the National Pension is far more serious among non-regular workers in the low-income class, particularly in the small and poor conventional sector as well as the wholesale and retail trade and accommodation sectors.

2.2. The financial sustainability of the National Pension[1]

The National Pension Scheme, which serves as the backbone of Korea's public pension system, was first implemented in 1988. The scheme started to be extensively applied in 1999 to include self-employed people in urban areas, establishing a framework for the full-scale National Pension Scheme. Despite this external growth, however, the National Pension Scheme had a serious structural problem, specifically, the imbalance between generous benefits and low contribution rates since its introduction. To resolve this "low contribution–high benefit" discrepancy, the first amendment to the National Pension Act was done in 1998. At that time the average income replacement rate for insured people with 40 years of coverage was adjusted to 60 percent from 70 percent, the age at which a person is entitled to receive the first pension benefits was increased to 65 years, and the actuarial valuation was adopted (conducted every five years starting in 2003), while maintaining the basic framework of the previous unified pension scheme.

Despite the reform according to the actuarial valuation conducted in 2003, a pension deficit would still occur by 2036, and the pension fund would be completely exhausted by 2047 (National Pension Development Committee, 2003). Accordingly, the long-term financial instability of the National Pension Scheme became a serious issue again, damaging pensioners' confidence in the government's pension plan. To respond to the situation, the government conducted a second reform of the National Pension Scheme in 2008, which contained measures to strengthen the financial stability of the fund and to ensure the sustainability of various systems. The second reform of the National Pension Scheme consisted of "parametric" reform measures to alleviate the financial imbalance through an adjustment of benefit and contribution levels, while maintaining the structural framework of the existing scheme, much as in the first reform. More specifically, the financial stabilization measures of the second amendment included a decrease in the income replacement ratio, based on average income earners with 40 years of contributions, from 60 percent to 50 percent by 2008, and then further progressive decreases by 0.5 percentage points per year, down to 40 percent in 2028, while maintaining the same 9 percent contribution rate. In addition, the Deferred Pension System was drawn up to encourage the elderly to engage in income-earning activities. The other amendments included (i) an increase in the scale of the benefit cuts to prevent early retirement; (ii) an improvement of the Concurrent Benefits Adjustment System;[2] (iii) the prohibition of the seizure of paid pensions; (iv) continuous payment of the Divided Pension, which is originally paid to a divorced spouse, even after a beneficiary remarries; and (v) the expansion of the scope of beneficiaries for the Dependents' Pension. Table 3.8 summarizes the major contents of the amendment to the National Pension Act.

Table 3.8 Major contents of the amendment to the National Pension Act

		Before amendment	After amendment
Long-term financial stabilization measures	Contribution rate	9 percent of average monthly income	Same
	Income replacement rate	Average income replacement rate for insured people with 40 years of coverage:* 1988–1997: 70 percent 1998–2007: 60 percent	2008: 50 percent 2009–2028: Decrease by 0.5 percentage points per year After 2028: 40 percent
Measures to rationalize and complement the National Pension Scheme	Abatement Old-Age Pension	Additional 2.5 percent abatement rate applied to pensioners with fewer than 10–20 years coverage:	Abolishment of additional reduction rate
	Early Old-Age Pension	• Applicable five years before the normal benefit payment age, which is currently 55 • Decrease of 5 percent in the benefit amount per year for the period of early payment	Upward adjustment of the abatement rate per year for the duration of early payment (5–6 percentage points)
	Incentives for inducing early old-age pensioners to engage in income-earning activities	• Suspension of benefit payment if beneficiaries engage in income-generating activities • Application of Early Old Age Pension to people over 60	• Suspension of benefit payment if pensioners generate income • Application of the Active Old-Age Pension to workers aged 60 and above • Increase in benefit payment rate for the period of re-subscription (6 percent per year for the re-subscription period)

(*Continued*)

Table 3.8 (Continued)

		Before amendment	After amendment
	Deferred Pension System	None	• Payment of an increased benefit when beneficiaries who reach the pension age defer the receipt of the pension • Additional rate: 0.5 percentage points per month (6 percentage points per year)
	Military Service Credit System	None	When a person has successfully finished his/her military service, an additional insured period (6 months) is granted to the person
	Childbirth Credit System	None	When a person gives birth to more than two children, an additional insured period (up to 50 months) is granted to one of the children's parents
Measures to expand the pension coverage	Introduction of Basic Old-Age Pension System	None	• Expansion of the scope of beneficiaries: from 60 percent to 70 percent of the elderly population aged 65 and over • Increase in the benefit rate: from 5 percent to 10 percent of the average earnings of all national pensioners by 2028

Source: Moon.

*Based on the amount of the monthly benefit in the first year of pension payments compared to the recalculated average lifelong earnings of middle-income earners.

Together with these reform measures, the non-contributory Basic Old-Age Pension Act was introduced to expand the pension coverage among elderly people with low incomes. Under this act, a benefit payment amounting to about 5 percent of the average monthly income (Value A) is provided for people over 65 with an income lower than the basic income determined by the Presidential Decree issued in January 2008. The benefit level, however, will be adjusted gradually from 5 percent of Value A to 10 percent by 2028, while the scope of its beneficiaries expanded from the current 60 percent of people older than 65 (as of 1 July 2008 at its first benefit payment) to 70 percent by January 2009.

The purpose of the amendment to the National Pension Act is to obtain long-term financial stability for the National Pension Scheme in preparation for an aging society. Thus, it seems reasonable to prioritize the evaluation of how much the National Pension Act's amendment can contribute to the enhancement of the sustainability of the scheme. Table 3.9 shows the results of comparing the financial prospects for the pension fund before and after the amendment of the National Pension Act.[3] As shown in Table 3.9, the instability of the pension finance is expected to be alleviated considerably in the long term owing to the second set of financial stabilization measures introduced in 2008. More specifically, with the stabilization measures implemented, the financial deficit of the pension fund is likely to occur in 2035, 10 years later than previously expected. Also, under the assumption that there will be no additional institutional changes, the point in time when the fund runs out of money will be postponed by 15 years, from 2045 to 2060. Moreover, the ratio of the fund reserve amount to the gross domestic product (GDP) is likely to reach 46.2 percent by 2035, while the speed of decreases in the fund size is expected to slow down after the amendment.

Therefore, it is estimated that the amendment to the National Pension Act has considerably improved the sustainability of the pension finance through the decrease in benefit levels and has significantly alleviated the structural imbalance between pension benefits and contributions at the same time. In particular, not only is this gradual decrease by 20 percentage points in the average income replacement rate based on insured people with 40 years of coverage (from 60 percent to 40 percent) substantial, but it is also meaningful that this adjustment has been applied at the *initial* stage of the system implementation. Nevertheless, the financial stabilization measures do not seem to be sufficient to fundamentally change the "high benefit–low contribution" structure of the National Pension Scheme and achieve the actuarial balance of the pension fund. As shown in the projection results, the gap between pension benefits and contributions remains despite a huge decrease in benefit expenditures in the long term (a decrease of 2.5 percentage points compared to the projected GDP value in 2070).

As a result, it seems inevitable that the pension fund will be exhausted by 2060 if the current contribution rate stays at the same level. After that, the financial system will have to be replaced by a pay-as-you-go (PAYG) system. In this case, however, the contribution burden on the workers of future generations will

Table 3.9 Comparison of financial prospects before and after the amendment, in trillions of won (% of GDP in parentheses)

	Total revenue		Total expenditures		Account balance		Reserve		Necessary contribution rate (%)	
	Before	After	Before	After	Before	After	Before	After	Before	After
2005	30.2 (3.5)	30.2 (3.5)	3.2 (0.4)	3.2 (0.4)	27.0 (3.1)	27.0 (3.1)	173.0 (20.1)	173.0 (20.1)	9.0	9.0
2010	50.7 (4.0)	50.7 (4.0)	8.1 (0.6)	7.6 (0.6)	42.6 (3.3)	43.1 (3.4)	353.7 (27.7)	357.3 (27.9)	9.0	9.0
2015	79.9 (4.3)	80.4 (4.3)	17.6 (1.0)	15.5 (0.8)	62.3 (3.4)	64.9 (3.5)	625.3 (33.8)	638.4 (34.5)	9.0	9.0
2020	117.1 (4.5)	119.1 (4.6)	39.3 (1.5)	30.5 (1.2)	77.8 (3.0)	88.6 (3.4)	988.8 (37.8)	1,031.9 (39.4)	9.0	9.0
2025	160.6 (4.5)	167.8 (4.7)	78.7 (2.2)	57.9 (1.6)	82.0 (2.3)	109.9 (3.1)	1,397.6 (39.2)	1,535.0 (43.1)	9.0	9.0
2030	206.2 (4.4)	225.5 (4.8)	143.2 (3.1)	101.3 (2.2)	63.0 (1.3)	124.2 (2.7)	1,761.8 (37.7)	2,124.1 (45.5)	9.0	9.0
2035	242.1 (4.1)	285.7 (4.8)	236.4 (4.0)	163.5 (2.7)	5.7 (0.1)	122.2 (2.1)	1,924.1 (32.3)	2,748.8 (46.2)	9.0	9.0
2040	259.9 (3.5)	348.3 (4.7)	376.9 (5.0)	258.1 (3.5)	-116.9 (-1.6)	90.2 (1.2)	1,619.6 (21.7)	3,298.9 (44.1)	9.0	9.0
2045	237.3 (2.6)	403.0 (4.3)	553.8 (6.0)	377.3 (4.1)	-316.5 (-3.4)	25.6 (0.3)	478.4 (5.1)	3,613.3 (38.9)	9.0	9.0
2050	234.4 (2.0)	443.6 (3.8)	772.8 (6.7)	524.9 (4.5)	-538.4 (-4.7)	-81.2 (-0.7)	—	3,488.9 (30.2)	29.7	9.0

2055	284.4 (2.0)	454.1 (3.2)	992.2 (6.9)	672.5 (4.7)	-707.8 (-4.9)	-218.4 (-1.5)	—	2,781.5 (19.4)	31.4	9.0
2060	346.4 (1.9)	424.5 (2.4)	1,295.8 (7.3)	876.6 (4.9)	-949.5 (-5.3)	-452.1 (-2.5)	—	1,131.2 (6.3)	33.7	9.0
2065	425.5 (1.9)	425.5 (1.9)	1,671.4 (7.5)	1,128.5 (5.1)	-1,246.0 (-5.6)	-703.0 (-3.2)	—	—	35.4	23.9
2070	525.1 (1.9)	525.1 (1.9)	2,101.1 (7.6)	1,415.3 (5.1)	-1,576.0 (-5.7)	-890.2 (-3.2)	—	—	36.0	24.3

Source: Moon.

become much heavier. It is estimated that the per capita contribution rate of economically active people after the conversion to the PAYG system will surge from the current 9 percent to 23.9 percent by 2065, and to 24.3 percent by 2070 (Moon, 2009). That is, compared to the situation where the National Pension Scheme continues to have the current partially funded system, not only will the future workers have to bear the burden of over 1.5 times higher contribution payments (refer to Section 4 for more information), but they will also receive benefits far less valuable than the present value of what they have paid, which will inevitably cause an excessive income transfer from the next generations to generations in the future.

To analyze the role of the National Pension Act's second amendment in alleviating the fundamental imbalance of the pension scheme and its limitations, it seems more reasonable to conduct the actuarial valuation of the National Pension Scheme using a "closed measure." Table 3.10 present the calculation results of the changes in the scale of total pension liability and total reserve for losses, using the "projected benefit obligation" method. In Table 3.10 the "unfunded actuarial liability" (UAL) means the difference between the total pension liability and the actual fund reserve, while the funding ratio is the ratio of the fund reserve to the total pension liability. Therefore, in the case of a fully funded pension scheme, the UAL value becomes zero (the funding rate will be 1.0), while in the case of using a PAYG system, the UAL value will be equal to the total reserve for loss.

As observed in Table 3.10, with the amendment to the National Pension Scheme, the size of the UAL is expected to be reduced considerably, from 278 trillion won in 2005 (pre-amendment period) to 150 trillion won (post-amendment period). The reason this UAL value decreases with the reform is because the projected benefit obligation method considers the future subscription period of current pensioners in calculating the amount of total pension liability. That is, if the benefit rate for the future subscription period decreases with the amendment, the average payment rate over the total subscription period will also decrease, which in turn will have an impact on the size of the past service liability. As a result, the funding rate is estimated to have increased from 38 percent before the amendment to 53.5 percent after the amendment, which will considerably improve the actuarial imbalance.

Despite this improvement, however, the ratio of the UAL to GDP is likely to increase continuously after 2030 and to reach 100 percent around 2070. The funding ratio will also plunge after it reaches its peak rate, over 70 percent, by 2035. This implies that the actuarial imbalance of the National Pension Scheme remains and will actually be aggravated as the pension system enters a mature stage and population aging accelerates. Therefore, to strike a more fundamental financial balance for the National Pension Scheme, it seems necessary to make an upward adjustment of the current contribution level, or an additional decrease in pension benefits within a short time frame.

Table 3.10 Actuarial assessment before and after the amendment to the National Pension Act, in trillions of won (% of GDP)

	Pension reserve (A)		Total pension liability (B)		Unfunded actuarial liability (UAL) (B − A)		Funding ratio (%)	
	Before	After	Before	After	Before	After	Before	After
2005	173 (20.1)	173.0 (20.1)	451 (52.2)	323.2 (37.5)	278 (32.2)	150.1 (17.4)	38.4	53.5
2010	354 (27.7)	357.3 (27.9)	801 (62.7)	569.7 (44.6)	448 (35.0)	212.4 (16.6)	44.1	62.7
2015	625 (33.8)	638.4 (34.5)	1,320 (71.2)	928.6 (50.1)	694 (37.5)	290.1 (15.7)	47.4	68.8
2020	989 (37.8)	1,031.9 (39.4)	2,071 (79.1)	1,430.4 (54.6)	1,082 (41.3)	398.5 (15.2)	47.7	72.1
2025	1,398 (39.2)	1,535.0 (43.1)	3,110 (87.3)	2,138.9 (60.0)	1,712 (48.1)	604.0 (17.0)	44.9	71.8
2030	1,762 (37.7)	2,124.1 (45.5)	4,221 (90.4)	2,891.7 (61.9)	2,459 (52.7)	767.6 (16.4)	41.7	73.5
2035	1,924 (32.3)	2,748.8 (46.2)	5,782 (97.2)	3,940.0 (66.2)	3,858 (64.8)	1,191.2 (20.0)	33.3	69.8
2040	1,620 (21.7)	3,298.9 (44.1)	7,846 (104.9)	5,342.5 (71.5)	6,226 (83.3)	2,043.7 (27.3)	20.6	61.7
2045	478 (5.1)	3,613.3 (38.9)	10,853 (116.7)	7,386.4 (79.4)	10,374 (111.6)	3,773.1 (40.6)	4.4	48.9
2050	—	3,488.9 (30.2)	14,504 (125.5)	9,865.3 (85.4)	14,504 (125.5)	6,376.4 (55.2)	—	35.4

(Continued)

Table 3.10 (Continued)

	Pension reserve (A)		Total pension liability (B)		Unfunded actuarial liability (UAL) (B − A)		Funding ratio (%)	
	Before	After	Before	After	Before	After	Before	After
2055	—	2,781.5 (19.4)	18,351 (127.8)	12,473.9 (86.8)	18,351 (127.8)	9,692.4 (67.5)	—	22.3
2060	—	1,131.2 (6.3)	23,645 (132.5)	16,050.8 (89.9)	23,645 (132.5)	14,919.6 (83.6)	—	7.2
2065	—	—	30,765 (138.7)	20,845.3 (94.0)	30,765 (138.7)	20,845.3 (94.0)	—	—
2070	—	—	39,550 (143.5)	26,754.1 (97.1)	39,550 (143.5)	26,754.1 (97.1)	—	—

Source: Moon (2009).

3. Population aging and the healthcare system in Korea

The healthcare system of Korea has three components: the National Health Insurance (NHI) program, the Medical Aid program, and Long-Term Care Insurance (LTCI) program. The NHI program covers the whole population as a compulsory social insurance benefit scheme, financed mainly by contributions from the insured and government subsidies. The Medical Aid program is a public assistance scheme to secure the minimum livelihood of low-income households by providing medical services for free or at a reduced price. In 2008, 1.84 million people, or 3.7 percent of the total insured, were covered by the Medical Aid program (National Health Insurance Corporation [NHIC], 2009). In addition, the Korean government recently introduced the separate LTCI program to meet the needs of elderly with difficulties resulting from geriatric disease; this section briefly examines the financial state and policy issues related to population aging and the healthcare system in Korea.

3.1. National health insurance system

The Korean government first implemented the mandatory NHI program for workplaces with 500 employees or more in 1977. The coverage of the NHI program was gradually expanded to smaller workplaces and to self-employed people in rural and urban areas, until the program achieved universal coverage by 1989. The rapid coverage expansion of the NHI has contributed greatly to improving the health conditions of the public by ensuring low-cost access to healthcare. Compared to several decades ago, the health outcomes have improved markedly in terms of life expectancy and infant mortality; life expectancy at birth of the total population increased to 79.9 years in 2008, which surpasses the Organisation for Co-operation and Development (OECD) average, from 61.9 years in 1970. The infant mortality rate was reduced drastically, from 81.5 per 1,000 in 1970 to 4.4 in 2010 (Organisation for Economic Co-operation and Development, 2010).

The Ministry of Health and Welfare currently manages and supervises the operation of the NHI program, while the NHIC, a non-profit public institution, is a single insurer that provides health insurance to all Korean citizens.[4] The NHIC is in charge of administering the program, including the management of enrollment of the insured and their dependents, collection of contributions, and the setting of medical fee schedules through negotiation with providers, as well as the provision of health insurance benefits. The Health Insurance Review and Assessment Service is responsible for evaluating medical fees, the quality of healthcare institutions, and the adequacy of medical service. The operational structure of the NHI is depicted in Figure 3.2.

Despite the universal coverage of the NHI and the remarkable improvement in health conditions, Korea has been able to keep health expenditures at a relatively low level, and Korea's total health expenditures accounted for 6.3 percent of the GDP in 2007, the fourth lowest in OECD countries (Figure 3.3). This is partly due to Korea's relatively young population structure. The elderly population aged

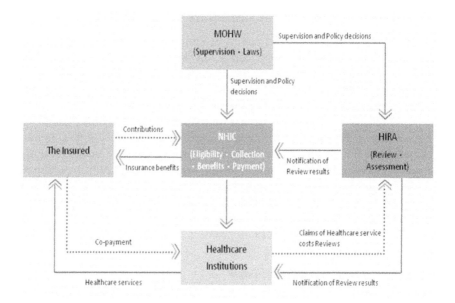

Figure 3.2 National Health Insurance Operational System

Source: National Health Insurance Corporation (2009).

Note: HIRA = Health Insurance Review and Assessment Service; MOHW = Ministry of Health and Welfare.

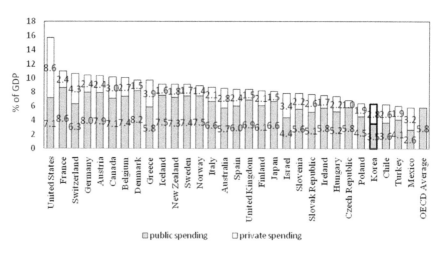

☐ public spending   ☐ private spending

Figure 3.3 Total Expenditure on Health in OECD Countries, 2007

Source: OECD (2010) Health Statistics (database).

Note: OECD = Organisation for Economic Co-operation and Development.

65 and over in Korea, for instance, accounted for 11.0 percent of the total population in 2010, which is less than half that in Japan (22.1 percent) in 2008. However, a more direct reason for low total health expenditure is the insufficient role of the public sector. As shown in Figure 3.2, public spending on health accounted for 3.5 percent of the GDP in 2007, the second-lowest level in OECD member countries. The Korean government has traditionally kept public health expenditure under control by limiting the range of benefits covered by the NHI and by fixing medical prices at low levels. The containment of public spending played a critical role in rapidly achieving universal coverage (Jones, 2010). However, as a result, the level of risk protection fell short of being adequate; public expenditure on health accounted for only 55.3 percent of total expenditure, much lower than the OECD average.

The NHI benefits are payable to the insured and their dependents in cases of prevention and treatment of sickness and injury, childbirth, health promotion, and rehabilitation. Benefits are granted both in cash and in kind. The financial resources of the NHI program come mainly from the contributions from the insured and government subsidies. The current contribution rate for the workplace-insured is 5.64 percent of the monthly average wage, including the LTCI premiums, and the contribution is shared equally by employer and employee. The contribution rate has been adjusted upward continuously, from 3.63 percent in 2002 to 5.64 percent in 2011, to finance the ever-increasing medical costs. The contribution for the self-employed is calculated separately based on their income, using a formula in which the insured persons' properties, income, motor vehicles, age, and gender are taken into consideration.[5] In 2009 contributions from the insured constituted 83.2 percent of total revenue. The government subsidized 15.3 percent of the total revenue in the same year; 12.1 percent comes from the General Account financed by general tax revenue, and 3.3 percent from the Health Promotion Fund financed by a surcharge on tobacco.

Private financing consists of co-payments on covered services and out-of-pocket payments for non-covered services. The co-payment rate is currently set at 20 percent of the total treatment cost for inpatient service. The co-payment rates range from 30 percent to 60 percent for outpatient service depending on the level and type of care institutions.[6] The share of out-of-pocket payments made by patients for non-covered services is declining as a result of the government's continuous effort to provide the people with adequate health protection. However, it still accounts for more than 20 percent of the total health expenditure. The high co-payment rate together with existence of many non-covered healthcare services makes the Korean healthcare system still rely heavily on private financing and limits the government's role in terms of health-related risk protection of the public.

Recently, the benefit payments of NHI are increasing at a very rapid pace. The size of NHI's total expenditure more than doubled during the last decade, showing an average increase rate of 12.7 percent per annum (Table 3.11). The recent skyrocketing health cost is driven both by automatic increases resulting from demographic changes and by discretionary increases resulting from the government's

Table 3.11 Financial indicators of the National Health Insurance Corporation (2009), 2000–2009, in trillions of won (% increase in parentheses)

Year	Revenue				Expenditure				Balance	Accumulated balance
	Total		Contributions	Government subsidies	Others	Total		Benefits	Administrative costs	Others		
2000	9,828	(10.5)	7,229	1,553	1,046	10,744	(11.8)	9,286	696	763	-916	-916
2001	11,928	(21.4)	8,856	2,625	447	14,106	(31.3)	13,196	629	281	-2,177	-3,094
2002	14,305	(19.9)	10,928	3,014	364	14,798	(4.9)	13,824	598	377	-493	-3,587
2003	17,467	(22.1)	13,741	3,424	302	15,972	(7.9)	14,893	634	445	1,494	-2,093
2004	19,408	(11.1)	15,579	3,483	347	17,330	(8.5)	16,265	693	372	2,079	-14
2005	21,091	(8.7)	16,928	3,695	469	19,980	(15.3)	18,394	759	827	1,111	1,097
2006	23,263	(10.3)	18,811	3,836	616	22,818	(14.2)	21,588	779	451	445	1,542
2007	26,050	(12.0)	21,729	3,672	649	25,889	(13.5)	24,560	720	609	161	1,704
2008	29,787	(14.3)	24,973	4,026	788	28,273	(9.2)	26,654	672	947	1,514	3,217
2009	31,500	(5.8)	26,166	4,683	651	31,189	(10.3)	30,041	660	489	311	3,529

Source: National Health Insurance Corporation (2009), by year (2000–2009).

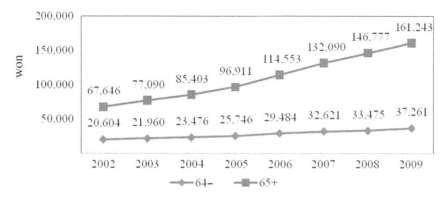

Figure 3.4 Monthly benefits per capita
Source: National Health Insurance Corporation (2010).

effort to secure better protection. On the automatic side, population aging is the major driver for the cost hike; the number of elderly aged 65 and over in Korea has increased by 160 percent during the last decade, from 3.4 million in 2000 to 5.4 million in 2009. It is inevitable that health spending should increase with the rising share of the elderly, as the medical costs per capita are usually higher for the elderly. What's more serious is the fact that health spending per older person is rising much faster than for younger generations. As depicted in Figure 3.4, benefit payments per capita for the elderly were 3.2 times higher than the payments for those under 65 in 2002. However, the gap has widened to 4.3 times in 2009.

On the discretionary side, there have been continuous efforts to enhance the government's role in health protection in response to people's growing expectations for better and cheaper health services. During the last decade, the Korean government tried to alleviate the financial burden resulting from patients' heavy out-of-pocket payments by expanding the range of services covered by the NHI and by introducing ceilings on co-payments. As a result, the public share in total health spending rose from 50.4 percent in 2003 to 55.3 percent in 2009 (OECD 2010). The enhanced government involvement put additional pressure on the increase in the NHI's benefit payments. To finance the growing outlays of the NHI, the government increased contribution rates almost every year during the last decade, and, consequently, the contribution rate for the workplace-insured rose by more than 2 percentage points during the period from 2002 to 2011 (Figure 3.5).

Despite the continuous increases in contribution rates, the current rates are still far too low to finance the rapidly rising health spending of the NHI in the years to come. According to the most recent financial projection results by the NHIC (2010), the deficit of the NHI is expected to increase exponentially in the near future, even if we assume that medical fees are kept constant in real terms (Figure 3.6). Considering that medical fees, which were set too low initially, are likely to increase faster than the inflation rate owing to technological progress and that

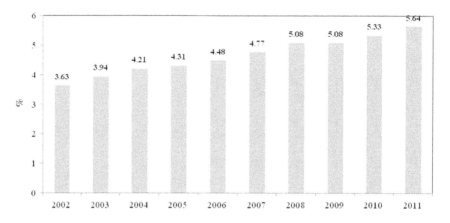

Figure 3.5 National Health Insurance program contribution rates for the workplace-insured

Source: National Health Insurance Corporation (2009), by year (2000–2009).

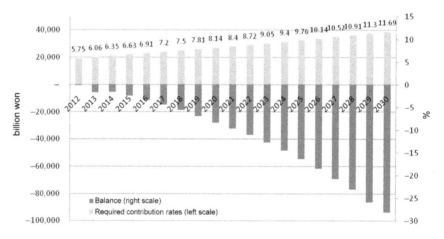

Figure 3.6 Financial projection results of the National Health Insurance Corporation

Source: Park and Lee (2010).

* Medical fees in nominal terms are assumed to increase 2.5 percent per annum, in line with the consumer price index.

the range of the services covered by the NHI will continue to be extended, the NHI's future financial situation is expected to be more pessimistic than indicated in the projections of the NHIC. The NHIC also predicts that a substantial increase in the contribution rate will be inevitable to balance the system financially; the contribution rate for the workplace-insured should be more than doubled over the next two decades, from 5.64 percent in 2011 to 11.69 percent in 2030.

3.2. The LTCI system

With rapid population aging, growing female participation in the labor market, and longer life expectancies, the demand for long-term care has increased continuously. In particular, the demand for formal involvement of the government in long-term care is growing, as the informal family network, which was traditionally responsible for providing healthcare support to the elderly, is weakening with the increase in the number of elderly who have difficulties performing daily living activities due to old age or geriatric disease that needs long-term treatment and continuous aid. To alleviate these burdens, Korea introduced the LTCI system in July 2008. It aims to promote the stability of senior citizens' health and life as well as increasing the quality of people's lives by mitigating the physical, mental, and financial burden of care on family members. The LTCI has various forms of benefits to support the insured including giving baths, providing meals, cooking, doing laundry, cleaning, nursing, providing medical treatment aid, or offering consultation on care.

The LTCI provides coverage for all those over the age of 65, as well as for younger people with geriatric disease like Alzheimer's disease, stroke, etc. As the LTCI is targeted to cover only age-related care needs, individuals need to obtain prior approval for services. There are three levels of functional status/limitations, each with different benefits. The LTCI system largely provides service benefits: in-home services and institutional services. In-home services include home-visit care, home-visit bathing, home-visit nursing, day and night care, short-term respite care, and welfare equipment services. The type of payment varies: pay per hour for home care, pay per visit for home nursing and baths, and pay per day for institutional care and day and night care. Cash benefits are also provided in exceptional cases as a form of family care cash benefits, exceptional care cash benefits, and nursing expenses in long-term care hospitals (NHIC, 2009).

In July 2008, at the time of its inception, LTCI covered only 2.9 percent of the total elderly, around 140,000 persons, but the coverage has rapidly expanded to 4.3 percent of the elderly at the end of 2008, 5.4 percent in 2009, and 5.6 percent in April 2010 (Table 3.12). Among LTCI beneficiaries so far, the very old, aged 80 and over, make up 45 percent, and more than half of the total beneficiaries are stricken with Alzheimer's disease and stroke. The current coverage of LTCI is very narrow, mainly because LTCI provides basic minimum coverage to the most needy. Despite the tight restrictions on eligibility, the number of elderly who applied, or are qualified, for LTCI benefits is rapidly rising (it more than doubled in two years) as the public's awareness of the availability of LTCI increases.

The central agency, the NHIC, currently manages both the NHI program and the LTCI program to gain economies of scale. Like the NHI program, the LTCI program is financed by premium payments, government subsidies, and co-payments by patients. The LTCI premium payments account for 60–65 percent of the total revenue, while 20 percent of the revenue comes from subsidies of the central and local governments. To prevent moral hazard or the excessive use of LTCI and to encourage home-based care, the co-payment rate was set at a

Table 3.12 The expansion of the Long-Term Care Insurance program

Category	July 2008	December 2008	December 2009	April 2010
No. of elderly who applied for benefits	271,298	376,032	596,235	663,741
% of total elderly	5.4	7.5	11.3	12.3
No. of elderly found eligible for benefits	146,643	214,480	286,907	304,826
% of total elderly	2.9	4.3	5.4	5.6
No. of elderly receiving benefits	70,542	147,801	228,980	236,004
% of total elderly	1.4	3.0	4.3	4.4

Source: National Health Insurance Corporation, 2010.

relatively high level of 20 percent of the cost for institutional care and 15 percent for in-home service. The contribution rate of LTCI is determined as a fixed percentage of the NHI contribution, with the two contributions collected together. The contribution rate of LTCI was initially set at the level of 4.05 percent of the NHI premium in 2008. However, with the soaring demand for LTCI, the government had to increase the rate to 4.78 percent in 2009 and to 6.55 percent in 2010, thereby adding to the financial burden of the insured who are already suffering from the increase in the NHI premium.

Since its inception, the LTCI expenditure has been increasing at a rapid pace. In 2008 the total expenditure for LTCI accounted for merely 0.05 percent of the GDP (Table 3.13). However, it went up to 0.23 percent of the GDP by the first half of 2010 as people became more aware of the LTCI program. In 2010 the expenditure for in-home service recipients represented more than half of the total expenditure. However, the share of institutional service is expected to grow quickly with the expansion of long-term care facilities. As the long-term care cost per LTCI beneficiary is higher for institutional care compared to that for in-home care service, the institutionalization trend is expected to put additional pressure on the growth of expenditures in the near future.

Even though the balance of LTCI is positive now, the future of LTCI's financial situation is expected to be pessimistic. The demand for LTCI, which was expected to be low initially, is likely to increase faster due to demographic factors; the population share of those aged 80 and over, who are the major target group of LTCI, will increase from 2 percent in 2010 to 14 percent in 2010 (National Statistics Office, 2006). As LTCI services should be given to the elderly with long-term disease or with difficulties in their daily life activities, the needs for long-term care services should increase accordingly. The decrease in the number of families with available caretaking females, due to women's extended participation in the labor market, will also contribute to the increase in demand for institutional care. An OECD study (Martins and de la Maisonneuve, 2006) predicted that the public

Table 3.13 Financial status of the Long-Term Care Insurance program, in billions of won

Year	Expenditure			Revenue		
	Total (%of GDP)	In-home	Institution	Total	Contribution	Subsidy
2008	554.9 (0.05)	164.6	262.9	869.0	477.0	386.8
2009	1,908.5 (0.18)	985.0	754.5	2,084.9	1,200.0	864.4
2010 1st half	1,304.6 (0.23)	761.0	543.6	1,610.8	905.7	332.3

Source: National Health Insurance Corporation, 2010.

expenditure on LTCI will increase to as much as 3 to 4 percent of the GDP by 2050, which is higher than the OECD average of 2.4–3.3 percent.

4. Policy implications

4.1. Policy implications for the National Pension

As observed in Section 2.1, despite the extended coverage of the National Pension Scheme in 1999, more than a third of the target individuals have actually failed to pay the contributions, including the insured who are exempted from contribution and delinquents. Furthermore, considering that the majority of these individuals are the poor or those with low incomes who are experiencing employment insecurity, such low participation in the system might mean that working-age poverty leads to old-age poverty. The participation rate in the National Pension might be expected to increase at a gradual pace as the public awareness of the National Pension matures and the government's capability to gather accurate information on the incomes of insured individuals improves. However, in order to prevent the spread of old-age poverty in advance through promptly enhancing the participation rate, it is necessary to devise active measures that aim to improve the participation of non-regular, low-income workers and self-employed small business owners as well as to strengthen the administrative capability to manage the insured.

There are a number of alternatives to consider as ways to tighten the loophole in the participation rate of the National Pension. For instance, some people in academia and politics claim that there is a need to introduce a tax-financed and universal basic pension, which is a radical reform that accompanies a fundamental change in the existing institutional framework. Moreover, since the rapidly aging population would require a huge fiscal expenditure, any such approach should be highly cautious regarding the feasibility and sustainability of the system. On the other hand, the government has actively reviewed another alternative to increase the participation rate in the existing system, which is subsidizing a part of the contributions for the low-income class. It would be more effective to remove possible causes of old-age poverty beforehand than to increase fiscal assistance afterwards. To put it another way, before considering a measure to provide old-age income assistance for those beyond the coverage of the National Pension, it would be appropriate to first draw up a measure that actually encourages the low-income class to participate in the National Pension. To that end, it would be necessary to actively consider allocating a part of the fiscal resources for ex-post old-age income support to non-regular workers or self-employed small business owners to lessen their burden of contribution.

As discussed in Section 2.2, the financial instability and intergenerational inequity problems of the National Pension Scheme were caused by the internal structural imbalance between contributions and benefits, combined with the external factor of a rapidly aging population. In truth, if it were not for such fast demographic changes, the problem of equity among different generations or sustainability caused by differences in pension financing methods such as PAYG or a funded system could be noticeably alleviated. However, with such drastic changes in population structure as are actually occurring in reality, the best alternative to enhance the sustainability of the pension finance and intergenerational equity would be to maintain a financing method based on the funded system for as long as possible (Moon, 2005). The amendment to the National Pension Act implemented in 2008 can be assessed positively in that it sought a preemptive response to the upcoming aged society by considering various measures to stabilize the pension finance, reinforce the vesting rights, and rationalize the relevant institutions. At the same time, there are additional issues that should be resolved and complemented from the economic and welfare perspectives. In particular, the amendment has its limitations when it comes to resolving the structural imbalance of the National Pension Scheme, although it has made a remarkable contribution to the sustainability of the pension finance and the equity of the scheme. Moreover, the huge benefit cuts will inevitably reduce its role as old-age income security. Policy directions for enhancing financial sustainability that should be pursued in the future are as follows.

First, in the discussion of reform measures to stabilize the finances of the National Pension Scheme, top priority must be placed on the clear set-up of the purpose of the reform, which is directly related to the matter of social choice about which financing system should be applied to the National Pension Scheme. If the government decides to keep the partially funded pension scheme, in an effort to respond to a rapidly aging population and to secure the sustainability of the National Pension Fund, the action plan for the reform will have to be prepared in a rational and concrete way to achieve such a goal. In this regard, the contents of the amendment to the National Pension Act in 2008 seem to have limitations in terms of policy goals and future efforts to pursue reforms to stabilize the National Pension Scheme's finances. In-depth discussions about which financing method should be maintained, or what should be the specific goals to achieve financial stabilization, are necessary before any attempts are made to adjust pension benefit or contribution levels.

Second, a leveling off and a decrease in excessive net pension benefits would be a feasible solution to promote the sustainability of the National Pension Scheme and to reduce excessive income transfer from the next generations to the current generations. The level of increase in the contribution rate and the speed of the adjustment should be determined based on the specific goals to achieve the financial stability mentioned above. If the partially funded pension scheme should be maintained in the future, the contribution rate will also have to be adjusted in accordance with the plan, and in that case a considerable increase in the contribution rate will be inevitable. To keep the funding ratio at a stable level from a long-term perspective while maintaining the current benefit system, it is estimated that the contribution rate should increase to 15 percent (Moon, 2009). If the timing and speed of the contribution rate adjustment are delayed and slowed down further, the contribution rate will need to increase more, which will require a bolder decision during future reforms.

Third, unless other complementary old-age income sources are secured in the future, it seems difficult to apply additional cuts in the pension benefit level. However, to restrict the scale of contribution increases to strike a financial balance for the National Pension Scheme, a continuous review will be necessary not only for such a uniform decrease in pension benefits but also for measures to decrease the burden of the benefit payment. In this context, other alternatives could include (i) measures to speed up the scheduled decrease in the future and (ii) introduction of a built-in stabilizer that allows automatic adjustment of the benefit level reflecting a demographic factor, in response to population aging.

Last, not only will the enhancement of the pension fund's rate of return play a pivotal role in promoting the sustainability of the pension finance, but it will also have a huge impact on determining the contribution rate for future generations. Therefore, measures to strengthen the expertise, independence, and accountability of the fund's management are needed to enhance the efficiency of pension fund management. The improvement measures include the establishment of the "National Pension Fund Management Corporation" that is independent from government departments and the political circle, and the imposition of independent roles to determine the investment policy of the newly established "Pension Fund Management Committee," which is composed of experts in the private sector. If fiduciary duties, including the enhancement of the profitability and safety of the national "Pension Fund Management Committee" (Moon et al., 2007), can be reinforced through this effort to advance the fund management system, it will contribute considerably to promoting the financial soundness and alleviating the contribution burden of the current National Pension Scheme.

4.2. Policy implications for the healthcare system

The biggest challenge facing Korea's healthcare system is the rapid increase in health expenditure, mainly driven by population aging and by the increasing medical costs per elderly person. Unless measures are taken to contain the expenditure hike effectively, contribution rates are projected to more than double within the next two decades to maintain the NHI's financial balance. At the same time, the current healthcare system still relies heavily on private financing, and the government's role in risk protection needs to be strengthened so as to reduce the burden of excessive out-of-pocket payments by patients. However, the extended insurance benefits will inevitably put additional pressure on the NHI's finances. Hence, the current healthcare system in Korea is in a dilemma and faces challenges including sustainable financing and the strengthening of health protection and administrative efficiency.

To make the system more sustainable in the long term, the NHI should try to secure more financial resources by increasing insurance contributions at a reasonable level and raising additional funds from other sources like government subsidies. But this alone cannot solve the long-term financial instability unless accompanied by measures to contain the growth of health spending. Some of the reform measures for increasing the efficiency of Korea's healthcare system that need immediate attention are detailed below.

First, the provider's payment mechanism needs to be redesigned to give better incentives for a more efficient use of medical resources. The healthcare costs are currently reimbursed through a fee-for-service system for all medical services and referral levels. However, the fee-for-service payment system often provides incentives for physicians to increase unnecessary healthcare treatments and to substitute uninsured medical services for insured ones. Evidence of supply-induced overtreatments can be found in many cases. For instance, the number of consultations per physician in Korea was three times higher than the OECD average in 2008, the highest in OECD member countries (Jeong, 2010). Also, the average hospital stay in Korea was 10.6 days in 2008, which is much longer than the OECD average of 6.6 days (Jones, 2010). Hence, changing the payment system away from the fee-for-service is essential for more efficient use of medical resources and containment of medical costs. A prospective payment system based on Diagnosis Related Group, which pays a fixed amount depending on the diagnosis, and a capitation payment per enrolled patient should be introduced and expanded in the near future.[7]

Second, policy measures on drug pricing are urgently needed to contain growing pharmaceutical expenditure. In 2009 drug expenditures accounted for 26.6 percent of total NHI spending, which is much higher than in other countries (NHIC, 2010). One of the reasons for high drug costs is that the NHI's reimbursement price for generic drugs is maintained at an artificially high level in order to protect small pharmaceutical companies. The price of generic drugs is currently set at 68 percent of price of the original drug, which is too high by international standards. The high generic drug prices also result in prevalent illegal rebates or rent-seeking behaviors from the drug makers, which negatively affect the NHI's finances. The current reimbursement method using the actual transaction price has also blocked price competition among pharmaceutical companies and thereby undermines the efficiency of the drug market. Hence, it is essential to reform the drug pricing system of the NHI toward facilitating competition in the generic drug market in order to contain pharmaceutical expenditure, and to transform the basis of the reimbursement method into average, rather than actual, transaction prices (Yoon, 2008).

Last but not least, the newly launched LTCI program can help enhance the allocation efficiency of scarce health resources and contain health costs through the relocation of long-term care patients from expensive acute-care hospitals to cheaper chronic beds in long-term care facilities or nursing care in residential homes. However, sufficient long-term care facilities with adequate and affordable care services are not yet available. Hence, in the short run, the policy priority should be given to the supply side, such as the expansion of long-term care facilities and training of necessary care personnel. In doing so, however, an accurate demand forecast is needed, so as not to lead to over-supplied facility capacity and over-institutionalization of the elderly. In the longer term, cost containment of LTCI through demand control will be an imperative issue as population aging puts growing pressure on LTCI finance. The demand for LTCI will increase further since the government has a plan to gradually expand long-term care coverage to the elderly with less serious limitations in their activities of daily living (NHIC, 2009). To combat this situation, de-institutionalization will be essential. As the amount of benefits for institution-based versus home-based care can affect the decision making of the needy elderly, the incentive scheme should be designed to encourage family-based or community-based care, rather than institutional care, and to improve the coordination of medical care and long-term care (Kwon, 2005).

Notes

1 This section is a summarized version of Chapter 2 and Chapter 4 in Moon (2008).
2 When a pensioner has rights to two or more benefits, only one benefit of his/ her choosing is allowed. However, in the case of a survivor's pension, the amendment allowed a fixed amount to be added to the amount of the chosen pension.
3 For more specific information on the actuarial evaluation process of the National Pension Scheme, refer to Moon (2009).
4 At the time of its inception, the NHI program was operated separately by numerous insurance societies. By 1989 the number of insurance societies had reached 367. In July 2000 the Korean government integrated them into a single insurer, the NHIC, in order to resolve inequities among insurance funds and improve managerial efficiency.
5 In 2009 the compliance rates of the workplace-insured and self-employed were 99.6 percent and 96.4 percent, respectively (NHIC, 2010).
6 The Co-payment Ceiling System was introduced in July 2004 to alleviate the financial burden on households resulting from catastrophic or high-cost diseases.
7 In January 2002 a pilot project for the new payment mechanism introduced the Diagnosis Related Group system for seven diagnostic groups to pay medical institutions only for inpatient care services. However, the government failed to extend the Diagnosis Related Group system and make it mandatory because of strong opposition from physicians (Jones, 2010).

References

Jeong, H. S. (2010). Analysis on the budget balance of the national healthcare insurance program. *National Health Insurance, Health Insurance Policy* 9(2) (in Korean).

Jones, R. (2010). *Health-care reform in Korea* (Economics Department Working Paper No. 797). Paris: Organisation for Economic Co-operation and Development.

Korea Institute for Health and Social Affairs. (2008). Korea Welfare Panel Study (In Korean), Seoul: Korea.

Kwon, S. (2005). Population aging and health and long-term care reforms. In Choi, K., et al., (Eds.) *Population aging in Korea: Policy agendas and reform issues.* Seoul: Korea Development Institute (in Korean).

Martins, J. O., and de la Maisonneuve, C. (2006). *The drivers of public expenditure on health and long-term care: An integrated approach* (Organisation for Economic Co-operation and Development Economic Studies No. 43). Paris: Organisation for Economic Co-operation and Development.

Moon, H. (2005). *Sustainability of the National Pension Scheme.* In Moon, H. (Ed.), *Population aging and old age income security,* Seoul: Korean Development Institute.

Moon, H. (2008). Evaluation of the reform in the Government Employee Pension Scheme. *Policy Issues Relating to the old-age income security in Korea II, Collaborative Research Series 25 of the National Research Council for Economics, Humanities and Social Sciences.* Seoul: Korea Development Institute (in Korean).

Moon, H. (2009). *Demographic changes and pension reform in the Republic of Korea* (ADBI Working Paper Series No. 135). Tokyo: Asian Development Bank Institute. www.adbi.org/files/2009.04.07.wp135.korea.pension.changes.reform.pdf

Moon, H., Lee, K.-Y., Han, S.-Y., Park, Y.-S., and Lee, J.-H. (2007). *The plan for the establishment of an advanced national asset management system: Measures to improve the governance of the national pension fund.* Seoul: Korean Development Institute.

National Health Insurance Corporation (NHIC). (2009). *National health insurance statistical yearbook.* Seoul: Author.

National Health Insurance Corporation. (2010). *Long-term care insurance (LTCI) statistical yearbook.* Seoul: Author

National Pension Development Committee. (2003). *Actuarial valuation of the National Pension Scheme and improvement measures.* Seoul: Korean Institute for Health and Social Affairs.

National Pension Service. (2009). *Statistical data.* Seoul: Government of Korea.

National Statistics Office. (2006). *Population projections for Korea: 2005–2050.* Seoul: Government of Korea.

Organisation for Economic Co-operation and Development. (2007). *Pensions at a glance 2007: Public policies across OECD countries.* Paris: OECD. doi: 10.1787/pension_glance-2007-en.

Organisation for Economic Co-operation and Development. (2010). *Health statistics.* OECD database. www.oecd-ilibrary.org/social-issues-migration-health/data/oecd-health-statistics_health-data-en

Park, I., and Donghun, L. (2010). *Medium- and long-term projections of the national health insurance.* Seoul: National Health Insurance Corporation (in Korean).

Yoon, H.-S. (2008). *Issues on drug pricing and reimbursement in Korea.* Seoul: KDI (in Korean).

4 Structuring the payout phase in a defined contribution scheme in high income countries

Experiences of Australia and New Zealand

Hazel Bateman

1. Introduction

Retirement income provision in both Australia and New Zealand differs from the prototypical Organisation for Economic Co-operation and Development (OECD) structure. In both countries current retirees rely on a universal public age pension funded from general revenue, paid subject to age and residency. The Australian version (the Age Pension) is means tested, while the New Zealand version (New Zealand Superannuation) is taxed at standard personal marginal tax rates. Neither country adopted the contributory earnings-related pay-as-you-go public pensions common in other OECD countries.

Till recently, private retirement saving played a secondary role. However, this is changing, particularly in Australia, with the introduction of mandatory private retirement saving, known as the superannuation guarantee, in 1992. Australia has a long history of encouraging voluntary superannuation through tax concessions, and the superannuation guarantee increased coverage from just below 50 percent to over 95 percent of workers. Future Australian retirees can expect their retirement incomes to comprise contributions from the public pension, the superannuation guarantee, and voluntary superannuation.

Policies for private retirement savings are less developed in New Zealand. Retirement incomes policy has long emphasized a central role for the public age pension (known as New Zealand Superannuation) with a very minor role for private saving. This changed in 2007 with the introduction of Kiwisaver, a voluntary government-subsidized but tax-preferred 'automatic enrolment' retirement saving structure. But with an allowance for withdrawals for the purchase of a first home, many years before system maturation, and no culture of retirement income streams, it is questionable whether Kiwisaver will reduce reliance on public provision.

Common to retirement provision policies in both Australia and New Zealand is freedom of choice of retirement benefits, a long term practice of taking lump sums, and an undeveloped market for longevity products. While almost all retirement accumulations in New Zealand are taken as lump sums, there is a growing trend in Australia to take account-based pensions (a form of phased withdrawal product). In both Australia and New Zealand the life annuity market has virtually disappeared (Bateman and Piggott, 2011; Bateman and Kingston, 2010a; Mercer, 2009).

Neither Australia nor New Zealand has escaped demographic transition. In both countries the old age dependency ratio is expected to double over the next 40 years from around 20 percent currently. Consequently, the cost of financing the public age pension is projected to increase from 2.7 percent of the gross domestic product (GDP) to 3.9 percent in Australia (Australian Treasury, 2010) and from 4.3 percent to 8 percent of the GDP in New Zealand (New Zealand Government, 2009). With health and old age care competing for public funds, this also raises questions about the long term sustainability of a retirement income system centered on public provision.

The aim of this chapter is assess the current payout structures for the private defined contributions (DC) retirement savings schemes in Australia and New Zealand and to canvass possible reforms. We commence in the next section with a review of the current arrangements, drawing out similarities, differences, and deficiencies. In Section 3 we assess these policies against standard criteria used to measure the extent to which national retirement income arrangements address the economic and financial risks faced by individuals in retirement. Vulnerability to longevity risk, investment risk, and political risk are highlighted as areas of concern in both Australia and New Zealand. In Section 4 we discuss possible reform measures to revitalize the market for retirement income products. Overall, there is more cause for optimism regarding constructive reform in Australia than in New Zealand. Section 5 concludes the chapter.

2. Current arrangements for the payout phase in Australia and New Zealand

2.1. Australia

2.1.1. Retirement income policies

Retirement income provision in Australia is a multi-pillar arrangement comprising a public pension (the Age Pension), mandatory private retirement saving (the superannuation guarantee), voluntary superannuation, and other long term savings. Voluntary superannuation was first introduced in the 1850s, public pensions in 1909, and the mandatory superannuation guarantee in 1992; yet Australia's retirement income system is still a 'work-in-progress'. Comprehensive reviews of the Age Pension, the taxation of superannuation (including retirement benefits), and the superannuation system were conducted over the period 2008–2010 (Harmer, 2009; Australia's Future Tax System [AFTS], 2010a, 2010b, 2010c; Super System Review, 2010). The main features of Australia's retirement income arrangements are summarized in Table 4.1.[1]

Table 4.1 Retirement income provision in Australia

	Age Pension	Superannuation Guarantee	Voluntary Superannuation
Commenced	1909	1992	1850s
Contributions	Non-contributory	9 percent of earnings (paid by employer), increasing to 12 percent	Average 5.5 percent of earnings
Potential coverage	Available to males aged 65 and over and females aged 64 and over (increasing to age 67 from 2017 for both males and females), subject to residency requirements and income and assets tests	Employees aged 18–70 earning at least AUD 450 per month (around 8 percent of earnings)	Encouraged by overall tax concessions (since 1915), salary sacrifice, government co-contribution for employees and the self-employed on incomes less than AUD 61,920
Funding	General revenue	Individual accounts in privately managed superannuation funds	
Benefits	Full pension: 27.7 percent of average male earnings (single), 41.3 percent of average male earnings (couple). Indexed to the greater of the consumer price index, a pensioner and beneficiary price index, and average male earnings. Additional benefits: Medicare, subsidized pharmaceuticals, access to rent assistance, concessions for public utilities	Preserved to age 55 (increasing to age 60), no early withdrawals, choice of lump sum or income stream. Income streams include phased withdrawal products and life and term annuities.	
Taxation	Taxed but subject to tax offsets	Contributions taxed, superannuation fund earnings taxed, benefits free of tax if aged 60 and over	
Actual coverage:	Around 75 percent of persons of eligible age receive some Age Pension. 60 percent of age pensioners receive the full rate of the Age Pension.	Mandatory and voluntary superannuation – 96 percent of full time employees, 93 percent of all employees	

Source: Derived from Bateman and Piggott (2011); Bateman (2011); Australian Government (2009).

THE AGE PENSION

Retirement provision in Australia relies heavily on the Age Pension, which is financed from general revenue and currently paid at a rate equivalent to 27.7 percent of male full time earnings for a single pensioner and 41.3 percent for a retiree couple. Net replacement rates are higher, as the Age Pension is exempt from income tax, and payments are indexed to the greater of the growth of the consumer price index, a pensioner and beneficiary living cost index, and male average earnings, which ensures that it retains its relativity to wages. Eligibility for the Age Pension brings with it access to other benefits including a pension supplement, a pensioner concession card, and a Health Card and rent assistance. The access age is currently 65, but following a review of public pensions in 2008–2009, this will increase to 67 over the period 2017–2023 (Australian Government, 2009; Harmer, 2009).[2]

The Age Pension is available to all eligible residents regardless of their work history but is means tested. The means tests, applying to both income and assets, have the effect of excluding the best-off quartile of eligible residents from receiving pension benefits. Rather, more than half of the remaining quartiles receives the full pension, with the remainder facing tapers on the means tests that reduce their entitlement to below the full pension level. One way of thinking about the Age Pension is to view it as a poverty alleviation instrument that excludes the rich, rather than as a safety net targeting the poor. The income and assets tested are comprehensively defined, although the value of the retiree's owner-occupied home is excluded from the assets test. Until recently, differential application of these tests provided a mechanism for encouraging different types of retirement benefit products.

MANDATORY PRIVATE RETIREMENT SAVING –
THE SUPERANNUATION GUARANTEE

The superannuation guarantee was introduced in 1992 as a form of mandatory private retirement saving. All employers are required to make superannuation contributions of at least 9 percent of earnings on behalf of their employees to a privately managed superannuation fund.[3] Employees aged 18–70 earning more than AUD 450 per month (around 8 percent of average male earnings) are covered. The self-employed are excluded but have access to tax concessions for voluntary contributions and are eligible to participate in a government co-contribution scheme. Benefits can be accessed at the statutory preservation age – currently age 55, increasing to age 60 by 2024.

The recent review of Australia's tax system recommended against increasing the mandatory rate, extending coverage to the self-employed, or changing the minimum income threshold for mandatory coverage (AFTS, 2010a). However, the government has since announced plans to increase the mandatory contribution rate to 12 percent (Australian Government, 2010b).

VOLUNTARY RETIREMENT SAVING

The Age Pension and superannuation guarantee are supplemented by voluntary superannuation and other forms of long term saving through property, shares, managed investments, and homeownership. Many people have more than 9 percent of their earnings contributed to their accounts, either because employers choose to make more than the minimum contribution or because employees supplement the 9 percent with contributions of their own. Voluntary contributions are encouraged by the overall concessional tax treatment of superannuation savings, the government co-contribution scheme that provides a government contribution of 100 percent of the employee or self-employed contribution for low and middle income earners, and tax rebates for spouse contributions. Some employees also take advantage of 'salary sacrifice' arrangements under which their (employee) contributions are treated as employer contributions for tax purposes and are therefore subject to the 15 percent tax rate applying to employer contributions, as opposed to the contributor's marginal tax rate.

While voluntary contributions on average amount to around 5.5 percent of wages and salaries (in addition to the 9 percent compulsory employer contribution), take-up is concentrated in only part of the income distribution. Survey data from the Australian Bureau of Statistics (ABS) indicate that only around 20 percent of eligible superannuation fund members made 'salary sacrifice' contributions or voluntary contributions under the government co-contribution scheme (ABS, 2009).

Around 93 percent of Australian workers are now covered by mandatory and voluntary superannuation. This represents around 96 percent of full time workers, 80 percent of part time workers, and 73 percent of casual and part time workers. Total superannuation coverage has doubled since the introduction of mandatory arrangements in the late 1980s.

Voluntary retirement saving includes not only superannuation but also other forms of long term saving through property, shares, managed investments, and, especially, homeownership. Homeownership is the most important non-superannuation asset for most Australians. Owner-occupied housing is worth more than half of the nation's private wealth, and more than 80 percent of retirees own their home (most of them with no mortgage).

2.1.2. Payouts from superannuation (DC retirement saving)

Private retirement benefits (from mandatory and voluntary superannuation) can be taken from the legislated 'preservation age'. This is currently age 55, with an increase to age 60 being phased-in by 2024.

When considering current payouts from DC retirement saving (superannuation) in Australia, it is important to remember that mandatory private retirement saving (the superannuation guarantee) was introduced less than 20 years ago. Further, the mandatory contribution rate was phased-in over a ten year period from an initial 3 percent, with the 9 percent pay-in finally reached in 2002. As well, prior to the introduction of the superannuation guarantee, less than 50 percent of Australian workers had access to voluntary superannuation. As a result, current average superannuation balances are quite low, and most Australian retirement savers reach retirement with a modest accumulation.

In 2007 average superannuation balances totaled AUD 87,589 for males and AUD 52,272 for females, with median balances significantly lower, at AUD

31,252 and AUD 18,489 respectively. While mean accumulations are higher for those close to retirement, at AUD 164,679 for persons aged 55–64, this is equivalent to only just over three times average male earnings and is considerably higher than the median accumulation for this age group of just AUD 71,731 (ABS, 2009). Industry estimates indicate that average superannuation accumulations at retirement in 2009 were around AUD 140,000 for men, around AUD 65,000 for women, and around AUD 175,000 for a retiree household (Association of Superannuation Funds of Australia, 2009). Accumulations at retirement will increase over time, as workers reach retirement with progressively more years of mandatory and voluntary superannuation contributions.

CHOICE OF RETIREMENT BENEFITS

Australian retirees can elect to take their superannuation benefits as a lump sum or a retirement income stream, or a combination of both. Retirement income products currently available in the Australian market include account-based pensions (a form of phased withdrawal product) and immediate annuities (including both term and life annuities). Hybrid products have been offered as well from time to time, in response to regulatory incentives.[4]

There have been large changes over the past 15 years in the demand patterns for retirement benefits, from a domination of lump sums to the current 50/50 split between lump sums and retirement income streams of the phased withdrawal variety. All retirement benefits are free of tax for persons aged 60 and above and are equally subjected to the Age Pension income and assets tests. Take-up of both public and private retirement benefits in Australia in 2010 is summarized in Table 4.2.

Table 4.2 Private retirement benefits in Australia, 2010

Benefit Type	Coverage
Lump sum	50 percent of benefits paid
Income stream	50 percent of benefits paid
Private market for income stream products	
Life annuity	Negligible – 13 policies sold in the first nine months of 2010 (29 policies sold in 2008)
Term annuity	2 percent of market for income stream products
Account-based pension	98 percent of market for income stream products
Superannuation pension*	n.a.

Source: Plan for Life Research (2011a, 2011b); Australian Prudential Regulation Authority (2011).

*A superannuation pension is a lifetime pension paid by defined benefit plans. There is no publicly available information on the share of superannuation pensions.

LUMP SUMS

In 2010 around 50 percent of retirement accumulations (by assets) were taken as lump sums. As suggested by the modest size of current retirement accumulations, the average size of lump sum benefits is quite small. A recent survey conducted by the ABS finds that almost 80 percent of total lump sum payments received in the four years to 2007 were less than AUD 60,000, equivalent to average male earnings in a single year (ABS, 2009).

When lump sum payments are taken, the assets are taken out of the superannuation system and no longer receive superannuation tax concessions. However, individuals have the freedom to dissipate a lump sum as they choose. Figure 4.1 illustrates the main use of lump sum payments in the four years to 2007. On average around 23 percent of lump sum payments were used to pay off the family home or to make home improvements; around 10 percent were used to buy or pay off a car or other vehicle (such as a caravan or boat); and around 15 percent were used to pay off outstanding debts. Around 30 percent of lump sum payments are invested either in another superannuation fund or in other financial assets. Overall, data from this national survey suggest that lump sums are dissipated in a way to enable retirees to enter retirement debt free, with a very small proportion of lump sums used for current consumption.

A similar picture emerges in a smaller sample of recently retired industry fund members (more likely to represent workers at the middle and lower end of the income distribution). When asked how they planned to use their retirement savings, 60–70 percent indicated that they would dedicate their retirement

Figure 4.1 Main use of lump sum payments received from 2005 to 2009

Source: ABS (2009, Table 31).

*Estimates for this category are unreliable.

accumulation to debt repayment, short term investments, home renovations, boat or car purchases, and travel (Industry Super Network, 2010).

However, as noted earlier, Australia's mandatory private retirement savings arrangements are immature, and as more workers retire with longer periods of superannuation coverage, it is likely that this pattern of dissipation will change.

INCOME STREAMS

In 2010 around 50 percent of retirement benefits (by assets) were taken as income streams – that is, phased withdrawal products and life and term annuities. Phased withdrawal products have become the most popular form of retirement benefit in Australia in recent years. They are currently marketed as products called 'account-based pensions' and 'transition to retirement pensions'.[5] Both products allow retirees to invest their retirement accumulation in an investment portfolio according to their risk preference and (subject to restrictions, discussed below) to decide how much income they want to receive annually. Retirement benefits paid from an account-based pension are free of tax for a person age 60 and above, and the earnings on the underlying assets are also free of tax where withdrawals satisfy the minimum age-based annual limits as specified in Table 4.3.[6,7]

In theory a comprehensive menu of immediate annuities is available in Australia, including lifetime and fixed term annuities, offered on a nominal basis or indexed, in a single or joint policy, and with the options of a guarantee period, reversion, and/ or a return of capital. However, in practice, only a small menu of annuity types is available. Notably, deferred annuities and variable annuities are absent, due in part to penal tax and Age Pension means test treatment of these particular varieties.

CURRENT RETIREMENT INCOME PRODUCT COVERAGE

It is clear that Australian retirees prefer non-annuitized retirement benefits. As shown in Table 4.2, in 2010 aggregate retirement benefits (by assets) were equally

Table 4.3 Account-based pensions – minimum annual drawdown by age

Age	% of Account Balance
Under age 65	4
65–74	5
75–79	6
80–84	7
85–89	9
90–94	11
95 and over	14

Source: Superannuation Industry (Supervision) Amendment Regulations 2007 (No. 1), Schedule 3.

shared between lump sums and income streams. By far the most popular income streams were phased withdrawal products (account-based pensions and transition to retirement pensions), which accounted for 98 percent of the retirement income stream market. Term annuities accounted for just 2 percent of total income streams purchased (by assets), while the take-up of life annuities was negligible, with only 29 policies sold in 2009 and 13 in the first nine months of 2010.

In the absence of compulsory retirement income streams, the approach of Australian policymakers has been to use tax, Age Pension means tests, and regulatory incentives to encourage the purchase of income streams with particular characteristics. Examples of typical incentives include a tax exemption for the earnings of assets underlying retirement income streams with specific design features, such as longevity or indexation; the exclusion of the return of capital from assessable income for annuity payments; and a 15 percent annuity rebate. Age Pension means test incentives had included full or part exemption from the Age Pension assets test and a concessional treatment of income under the Age Pension income test.

Initially, life annuities received all of these incentives, but in order to encourage the take-up of any form of income stream in place of a traditional lump sum, the incentives were gradually extended to non-annuitized products such as the account-based pensions so popular today. Following reforms in 2006–2007,[8] which abolished taxes on superannuation benefits for persons aged 60 and above and simplified the Age Pension means tests, the government lost the ability to use differential tax-transfer arrangements to encourage particular types of retirement benefits. The elimination of the then minor tax-transfer preference for life annuities has coincided with the effective disappearance of the market (Bateman and Piggott, 2011).

Longer term trends in the take-up of retirement benefits are illustrated in Figures 4.2 (lump sums versus income streams) and 4.3 (retirement income streams by type).

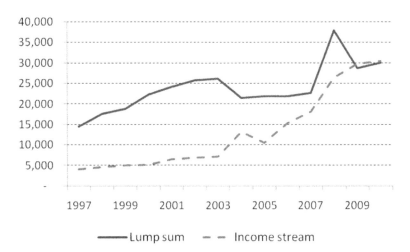

Figure 4.2 Value of retirement benefits – lump sum versus income stream (AUD million)
Source: Australian Prudential Regulation Authority (2007, 2011).

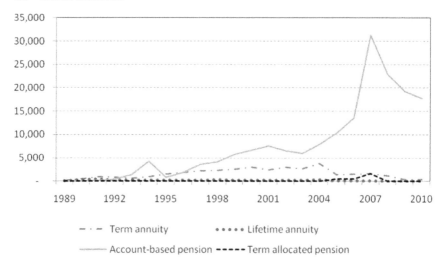

Figure 4.3 Value of private retirement income streams (AUD million)
Source: Plan for Life Research (2011a, 2011b).
Notes: This data includes only products purchased in the private market.

Australian retirees have always preferred non-annuitized products, and their strong predilection for lump sums is clearly illustrated in Figure 4.2, which shows that as recently as 1997, around 80 percent of retirement benefits (by assets) were taken as lump sums. Since then there has been a gradual shift to income streams. These now account for over 50 percent of retirement benefits (Australian Prudential Regulation Authority, 2011), with almost all these account-based pension products (that is, of the non-annuitized variety). By contrast, as indicated in Figure 4.3, the market share of immediate annuities has fallen from a peak of 30 percent of the income stream market in 1999 to around 2 percent currently. Life annuities have always been the least popular type of retirement income stream, and, as illustrated in Table 4.4, demand has fallen severely to almost nothing, from several thousand new policies annually just nine years ago.

Sales of retirement income products offering longevity insurance have been hampered by both demand and supply side constraints. In Australia it is clear that demand for retirement income products has been closely related to policy design. Tax and means test rules, regulations, and prudential requirements have all combined to generate specific conditions to be met by each product, and these have changed significantly over the past 25 years. Many of the trends evident in Figures 4.2 and 4.3 can be explained by these policy changes. For example, the peak in term annuity purchases in September 2004 (see Figure 4.3) preceded a reduction in Age Pension means test preference, applying from late September of that year. Similarly, with the peak in account-based pension purchases in September 2007, the downward trend in term and life annuity purchases over the past decade has

Table 4.4 Sales of life annuities, Australia

	Number	Total Value (AUD million)	Average Value (AUD)
2001	1,927	166.16	86,227
2002	1,750	154.61	88,348
2003	1,477	200.39	135,674
2004	2,801	279.78	99,886
2005	293	27.27	93,072
2006	341	30.16	88,446
2007	403	37.15	92,184
2008	61	11.9	195,082
2009	29	5.91	203,793
2010	13	1.4	127,273

Source: Plan for Life Research (2011a).

coincided with the withdrawal of generous tax and Age Pension means test preference for these products.

Demand is further hampered by product distribution incentive structures, resulting in the tendency of financial advisors to recommend investment-based products that provide the opportunity for ongoing fees, rather than a one-off purchase such as a life annuity. Finally, consistent with the mounting view that behavioral biases lead consumers away from life annuity purchase, it could be argued that Australian consumers turn away from life annuities because of the negative frame in which they are presented (Brown, 2007; Brown et al., 2008; Agnew et al., 2008) by both the government and providers.

On the supply side, product innovation has also been hampered by the ambiguous tax and Age Pension means test provisions mentioned earlier, poor public policy coordination, and, importantly, the lack of products to hedge inflation, interest, and mortality risks (Purcal, 2006; Bateman and Piggott, 2011).

Aside from superannuation, the largest component of household wealth is the family home. Owner-occupied housing is worth more than half of the nation's private wealth, and more than 80 percent of retirees own their homes, largely mortgage free. This has initiated a small but growing market in reverse mortgages as a source of income in retirement. At end 2009, there were just under 39,000 reverse mortgages on issue in Australia, with a total book size of AUD 2.7 million, representing a more than doubling in the market over the past five years. The average age of borrowers is 74, the average loan size is only AUD 70,000 (or around 1.2 times average male earnings), and the most common family structure is an elderly couple (45 percent borrowers, compared with 37 percent single females and 18 percent single males). Both lump sums and income streams are available, although lump sums account for around 95 percent of payments. Typically the lump sum is taken in the form of a 'line of credit', which allows a more flexible withdrawal pattern than a contracted income stream (Deloitte, 2010a).

2.1.3. Main sources of income for elderly Australians

Figures 4.4a and 4.4b consolidate much of the earlier discussion and summarize the main sources of income of current Australian retirees. Government pensions and allowances (typically the Age Pension and associated benefits) dominate. This

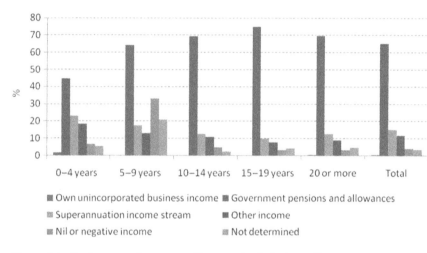

Figure 4.4a Retirees – main source of income (males), Australia
Source: ABS (2009, Table 15).

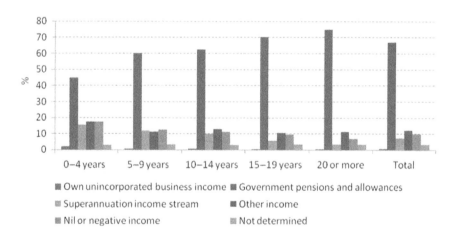

Figure 4.4b Retirees – main source of income (females), Australia
Source: ABS (2009, Table 15).

is not surprising as around 75 percent of Australians of eligible age receive the Age Pension and 60 percent of these (or 45 percent of Australian retirees) are paid at the full rate.

However, the composition of retirement income will change in future years as more Australians retire with a working life of superannuation contributions. Government estimates indicate that over the next 40 years, the proportion of people receiving the full Age Pension will decline from around 45 percent to 28 percent, while those on partial Age Pensions will increase from 30 percent to 45 percent. The proportion of elderly receiving no Age Pension is expected to increase only marginally from 25 percent to 26.5 percent (Department of Families, Housing, Community Services and Indigenous Affairs, 2008; Harmer, 2009). As noted here, and emphasized in recent reviews of the public pension, taxation, and superannuation systems, the aim of the mandatory and voluntary superannuation arrangements is to supplement rather than replace the Age Pension (Harmer, 2009; AFTS, 2010a, 2010b, 2010c).

2.1.4. Retirement income policy under review

The lack of products that retirees can purchase to insure against longevity risk, as well as the very low demand for the currently available products, was highlighted in the Australian tax system review conducted over the period 2008–2010. In its preliminary report the review panel noted that the 'lack of products that retirees can purchase to insure against longevity risk is a structural weakness in the system' (AFTS, 2009, p4). However, the recommendations in the final report fell short of a specific policy prescription. On the demand side, the review panel did not recommend either mandatory annuitization or the re-introduction of tax-transfer incentives. In fact, the final report supports the view that retirees should have the flexibility to 'make decisions in accord with their own retirement needs' (AFTS, 2010b, p121).

However, on the supply side, the review recommends that the 'government should support the development of a longevity insurance market within the private sector' by addressing the interest, inflation, and longevity risks facing existing and potential providers of longevity products (AFTS, 2010b, p121). Possible policy prescriptions included the issuing of more long term securities by the government, government support to develop and maintain a longevity index, the removal of regulatory barriers to product innovation, and possible government participation in the life annuity market.

The focus on longevity continued in the recommendations of the 2009–2010 review of the superannuation system (Super System Review, 2010). Relevant here were recommendations that the duties of superannuation fund trustees be extended to the consideration of longevity risk and that the proposed default superannuation product (called MySuper) be extended from a diversified investment strategy to a lifetime retirement income stream (Super System Review, 2010). While the government deferred a decision on these recommendations, they add to the impetus to address the absence of a private market for longevity products in Australia.

A number of financial service providers are developing retirement income products with longevity features, and several new products have recently entered the market. One of the first, called 'MoneyforLife', was launched by Internationale Nederlanden Groep (ING) in late 2009. 'MoneyforLife' is essentially an account-based pension with guaranteed minimum lifetime payments (or a hybrid account-based pension/variable annuity/life annuity product). It is designed to provide insurance against longevity risk and investment risk, and since it is 'account-based' rather than a life annuity, the full value of the product passes to the estate in the event of the product holder's death (for details, see ING n.d.). It is far too soon to evaluate the success of this product, but there is increased optimism that a market for longevity products in Australia will finally develop.

2.2. New Zealand

2.2.1. Retirement income provision in New Zealand

The key components of retirement income provisions in New Zealand are a public pension called New Zealand Superannuation (NZS), private retirement saving in an automatic enrolment scheme known as Kiwisaver, and personal saving, largely through homeownership. The key focus is the publicly provided NZS, and the overall rationale is to provide a basic guaranteed level of income (from NZS) while encouraging and enabling New Zealanders to take greater responsibility for managing their own finances in a way that best suits their long term interests (Retirement Commission, 2010, p53). Unlike many OECD countries (but like Australia), New Zealand did not introduce a contributory earnings-related public pension, and there has been little support for mandatory private retirement saving arrangements. While government estimates suggest that older people as a group currently have higher living standards relative to the population as a whole (Retirement Commission, 2010), it is not clear that this is sustainable in future.

These features of retirement income provision in New Zealand are summarized in Table 4.5 and are discussed on next page.

NZS

NZS had its beginnings as a public age pension, introduced in 1898. Eligibility was subject to income and assets tests and payable from age 65. By the 1970s this had developed into a combined payment comprising a means tested pension from age 60 and a universal public pension from age 65. In 1977 these payments were replaced by National Superannuation – a flat rate, non means tested but taxable benefit, paid from age 60, indexed to net average wages and financed out of general revenue.

In 1993, following a review of retirement incomes, New Zealand's public age pension was renamed NZS, and the broad parameters decided at that time continue today (St John, Littlewood, and Dale, 2010).[9]

Table 4.5 Retirement income provision in New Zealand

	New Zealand Superannuation	Kiwisaver	Other
Commenced	NZS has existed since 1993. Originated as a means tested pension at age 65 in 1898; combination of means tested from age 60 and universal from age 65 in 1970s, and National Superannuation (universal public pension from age 65) in 1977.	2007	**Homeownership:** 79 percent of elderly own their home mortgage free **Voluntary occupational superannuation:** 14 percent coverage of occupational superannuation schemes **Personal saving:** Modest
Contributions	Non-contributory	Employees: 2, 4, or 8 percent of gross pay Employers: 2 percent matching contributions Government: Up to NZD 1,042.86 per annum Non-covered employees/self-employed: unlimited	
Potential coverage	Available to all New Zealanders aged 65 and above subject to residency requirements. Not income or assets tested (can be paid to those in paid employment) or employment tested.	All New Zealanders starting a new job are automatically enrolled (but can choose to opt-out). Others can opt-in.	
Funding	General revenue (+ New Zealand Superannuation Fund)	Fully funded	

(*Continued*)

Table 4.5 (Continued)

	New Zealand Superannuation	Kiwisaver	Other
Benefits	Paid from age 65 at three rates: • Couple: 66 percent of average wage after tax • Single (sharing accommodation): 60 percent of couple rate • Single (living alone): 65 percent of couple rate Indexed to wages and prices plus supplementary benefits.	Available as a lump sum at the latter of age 65 or being a Kiwisaver for five years. As well, a one-off withdrawal is available after a minimum of three years of saving to help purchase a first home.	
Taxation	Taxed	Fully taxed under the TTE* regime (except 2 percent employer contribution, which is not taxed)	
Actual coverage	94 percent of New Zealanders over age 65. Reasons for lower take-up include migrant inflows in older age groups and high net worth retirees not applying.	1.4 million New Zealanders have joined Kiwisaver, 38 percent of population under 65 One third automatically enrolled, two thirds opted-in	

Source: Retirement Commission (2010), Ministry of Social Development (2010).

Note: Equivalent veterans pension paid to qualified persons.

*Contributions taxed (T), investment income taxed (T), final withdrawal of balances exempted from tax (E).

The aim of NZS is to provide a basic but adequate standard of living in retirement. It is available to all New Zealanders aged 65 and over subject to residency requirements and is paid from general revenue. NZS is taxable, and as it is neither means nor employment tested, it can be paid to those of eligible age in paid employment. It is anticipated that future payments will be partially pre-funded from the NZS Fund (NZSF), set up in 2001 for this purpose. However, government contributions to the NZSF are reliant on strong economic performance, and in the aftermath of the global financial crisis, these have been suspended for at least 10 years (NZSF, 2010).

NZS is paid at three rates – a rate for couples and separate rates for singles living alone and singles in shared accommodation. The standard metric for payment is the 'couple' rate. By legislation this is required to be between 65 percent and 72.5 percent of the average wage after tax. Each individual of a couple receives their own NZS payment of one half the couple rate. The payments are adjusted annually in line with increases in the consumer price index, with further ad hoc increases from time to time to maintain the benchmark net of tax wages. The couple rate is currently 66 percent of the average wage after tax (or 33 percent of the net of tax average wage to each individual), the single living alone rate is 65 percent of the couple rate, and the single shared accommodation rate is 60 percent of the couple rate.

NZS recipients are also eligible for a range of benefits, including an accommodation supplement and a disability allowance. Around 94 percent of New Zealanders over the age of 65 receive NZS. This less than 100 percent coverage is due to increased migrant flows in older age groups (who fail to qualify under the residence test) and a number of retirees with independent means who choose not to apply.

PRIVATE RETIREMENT SAVING

Until the mid-1980s voluntary occupational superannuation schemes were encouraged in New Zealand by virtue of generous tax concessions – effectively EEE (contributions exempted, investment income exempted and final withdrawal exempt) for lump sums and EET for pension payments. A short-lived compulsory DC savings scheme had also existed between 1974 and 1977. Despite these initiatives, less than 25 percent of New Zealand workers belonged to occupational superannuation schemes. Coverage then fell to around 14 percent following the withdrawal of tax preference for all forms of saving in 1990 and the introduction of a TTE regime (contribution taxed, investment income tax and final withdrawal exempt) for private retirement saving, which continues today.

Kiwisaver (a voluntary retirement savings structure) was introduced in 2007 as a means of increasing the level of personal retirement savings. Under Kiwisaver employees aged between 18 and 64 are automatically enrolled in a retirement savings plan when they start a new job but have between the second and eighth week of employment to 'opt-out'. Other employees and the self-employed can 'opt-in'. The default employee contribution rate is 2 percent of gross earnings, and employees can elect to make higher contributions at rates of 4 percent or 8 percent. Employers are must match the minimum 2 percent contribution but are not required to contribute more. Kiwisaver contributions are taxed under a non-concessional TTE regime but are eligible for a government subsidy (effectively tax relief) of NZD 1,000 in the first year of membership and up to NZD 1,042.86 each year (around NZD 20 a week) thereafter.

Kiwisaver contributions are invested in one of a number of Kiwisaver schemes offered by a variety of financial service providers including banks, insurance companies, and investment managers, and most providers offer investment choice. Contributors can choose their own Kiwisaver provider and investment option or can opt for a default provider chosen by their employer and the provider's default investment option.

Kiwisaver accumulations are available at age 65 (contingent upon five years of contributions). All benefits are taken as lump sums. There is no requirement to take the accumulation as an income stream and no incentives to do so. Early withdrawal of some or all of Kiwisaver savings is available after a minimum of three years to help purchase a first home, which the government encourages by offering an additional first home deposit subsidy of NZD 1,000 for each year of Kiwisaver membership, up to a maximum of NZD 5,000.

By March 2010 around 1.4 million New Zealanders (or 38 percent of workers below age 65) had joined Kiwisaver. Of these, around one third were automatically enrolled as new job starters with the remaining two thirds opting-in, often from a fully taxed occupational superannuation scheme (see Table 4.6). As a result, participation in voluntary occupational superannuation schemes has fallen to just 5 percent of New Zealanders of working age.

OTHER SAVING FOR RETIREMENT

The elderly in New Zealand also rely on less formal forms of retirement savings, including personal saving and housing. The policy framework is one of freedom of choice in a tax-neutral saving and investment environment, with this choice supported by financial literacy initiatives and financial market regulation. In fact, financial literacy is considered one of the key components of retirement income policy by the Retirement Commission (2010). However, whether owing to the

Table 4.6 Kiwisaver membership by enrolment method

Enrolment Method	Members	%
Opt-in via provider	706,290	48
Automatically enrolled	541,769	37
Opt-in via employer	211,883	15
Total	**1,459,942**	**100**

Source: Retirement Commission (2010, Table 5.1).

lack of tax incentives or the perceived generosity of the public pension (NZS), private saving for retirement, other than homeownership, is quite modest. As in Australia, homeownership is the largest component of household wealth, and around 80 percent of New Zealanders of retirement age own their own home mortgage free.

2.2.2. Payouts from DC retirement saving in New Zealand

The DC retirement savings schemes operating in New Zealand include Kiwisaver and voluntary occupational superannuation schemes. Benefits are almost always paid as lump sums. Very few annuities are sold in the private markets, although there are a number of retirees still receiving private pensions from discontinued defined benefit plans.

The demand for life annuities has always been small in New Zealand but has shrunk further with the decline of defined benefit schemes (St John, 2009). In 2008 there were only 3,277 annuitants in the country, and over half of these were more than 80 years old. There is currently only one provider of annuities in New Zealand (down from nine in 1993), and only 17 new policies were sold in the first nine months of 2009.

Since the late 1980s New Zealand tax policy has emphasized tax neutrality, and no tax or other concessions are offered to encourage the purchase of retirement income streams. A discussion about retirement income streams is absent from the public debate. There were no recommendations to link the recently introduced Kiwisaver to a retirement income stream. Nor was the lack of a market for retirement income streams in general, or an annuity market in particular, raised in the recent review of retirement income policy by the Retirement Commission (2010).

Financial service providers in the New Zealand market promote investment and home equity products as the means to provide income in retirement, and these options are supported by the government through its financial literacy initiatives.

Home equity release products were first introduced in the New Zealand market in 2005, and by December 2009 there were close to 6,550 loans with a total book value of AUD 447 million. The typical borrower is age 73 and married, with a loan of close to NZD 68,000. Ninety-nine percent of drawdowns were taken as lump sums and primarily used for home improvements (24 percent), followed by debt repayment (Deloitte, 2010b).

2.2.3. Main sources of income for elderly New Zealanders

The main source of income for current retirees in New Zealand is reported in Table 4.7. With the longstanding role of NZS as the central component of retirement income provision it is not surprising that 97 percent of retirees receive government transfers. Nor is it surprising that with an immature Kiwisaver, very low coverage of the fully taxed occupational superannuation schemes, and the prevalence of lump sum retirement benefits, formal private retirement saving arrangements are not listed. Apart from the public pension (NZS), only

Table 4.7 Sources of income in retirement, New Zealand

Income Source	Number Receiving (thousands)	Percentage of All New Zealanders Aged 65+	Average Weekly Amount for Those Receiving (NZD)
Government transfers (mainly NZS)	517.8	96.8	294
Investment income	280.9	52.5	143
Wage or salary income	61.0	11.4	641
Of which:			
Full time employment	31.6	5.9	955
Part time employment	29.0	5.4	299
Other transfers	53.0	9.9	272
Self-employment income	28.4	5.3	448

Source: Retirement Commission (2010, Table 4.1).

Note: NZS = New Zealand Superannuation.

53 percent of retirees receive income from investments, while close to 17 percent receive income from paid employment.

In other words, the majority of the current generation of older New Zealanders is very dependent on NZS and other forms of government support. Estimates from the Ministry of Social Development indicate that 40 percent of those over the age of 65 have virtually no income source other than NZS, with 20 percent depending on NZS and other government transfers for 80 percent of their income and only around 30 percent receiving more than half their income from sources other than NZS (Ministry of Social Development, 2010).

However, despite (and possibly as a result of) NZS, older New Zealanders actually have a higher standard of living than their younger counterparts. According to New Zealand's Economic Living Standards Index, which is scored from 0 (low) to 60 (high), the age 65 and over group scored 47, compared with 40 for the whole population and 36 for children under 18. The distribution of the index scores by age is summarized in Figure 4.5. Living standards of New Zealand retirees also rank high in international comparisons of public pensions (OECD, 2009).

2.2.4. Retirement incomes under review

As in Australia, the retirement income arrangements in New Zealand have been under constant review for the past three to four decades. The most recent is the regular three-year review of New Zealand's retirement income policies carried out by the Retirement Commissioner in 2010. The focus of this review was threefold: to consider the effectiveness of government agencies in delivering retirement income policy, to evaluate the role of the financial services sector in relation to retirement

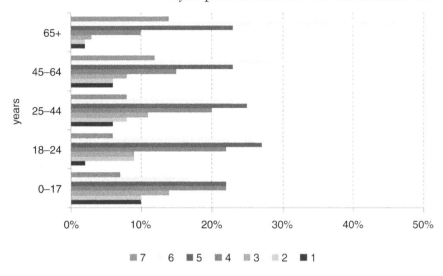

Figure 4.5 Material living standards in 2008, by age group, New Zealand

Source: Retirement Commission (2010, Chart 4.4).

Note: The numbers 7,6, 5, etc. refer to living standards with Level 1 indicating very low living standards, and Level 7 indicating high living standards. The numbers 0–60 are an average for a particular age group but the numbers 1–7 refer to the proportion of population within that age group with a given quality of living standard.

income provision, and to investigate the future wellbeing of retirees. Key recommendations include measures to address the future costs of NZS, specifically by indexing pension payments to the average of wages and prices (rather than benchmarking them to net of tax wages) and increasing the age of eligibility to 67 from 65 (over the period 2020–2030), in conjunction with a means tested payment for those aged 65–67.

Notably absent from the current policy debate in New Zealand is a discussion of the payout phase of private retirement saving schemes. Neither the terms of reference nor the final recommendations of the 2010 review questioned the lack of a private market for longevity products in New Zealand. However, the *2010 Review of Retirement Income Policy* did recommend that the 2013 review include an assessment of the emerging pattern of withdrawals and reinvestments by people aged 65 and over from Kiwisaver (Super System Review, 2010).

2.3. Discussion

There are some similarities, and also important differences, in policy between Australia and New Zealand. In Australia, retirement income provision is a multi-pillar arrangement centered on the mandatory superannuation guarantee, supported by a means tested public pension and tax concessions for voluntary retirement saving. In New Zealand, the focus is a universal public pension, supported by non-concessional personal saving and a recently introduced structure for voluntary retirement saving called Kiwisaver. Homeownership is important in both systems, with the majority of workers reaching retirement mortgage free.

A key difference is the role of private saving. Around 93 percent of Australian workers have superannuation by virtue of the mandatory superannuation guarantee and longstanding tax preference for voluntary superannuation. In New Zealand, private retirement saving is undeveloped: Kiwisaver commenced in 2007, is voluntary, and covers only 38 percent of 15 to 65 year olds, and membership of occupational superannuation schemes has fallen to only 5 percent of workers.

Similarities and differences also emerge at the payout phase. Retirement income policy in both New Zealand and Australia allows freedom of choice in benefits, retirees in both countries have a preference for non-annuitized benefits (lump sums in New Zealand and, increasingly, phased withdrawal products in Australia), and in neither country is there a developed market for longevity products.

However, prospects for change are greater in Australia. Retirement accumulations are larger owing to higher and longer contributions and the availability of a longer menu of retirement benefits (including account-based pensions, which are not available in New Zealand); Australian financial service providers actively developing new 'hybrid' retirement income streams; and the lack of longevity products *is* on the policy agenda in Australia (but not New Zealand).

3. Rationale for reform: Australia and New Zealand

The DC payout structures in Australia and New Zealand can be assessed by the extent to which they address the economic and financial risks faced by individuals in retirement. The main risks are listed in Table 4.8; they include the replacement rate risk (the risk of not adequately replacing pre-retirement income), investment risk (the risk of unevenness in income resulting from the volatility of investment returns), longevity risk (the risk of outliving one's financial resources), inflation risk (the risk of erosion of purchasing power), contingency risk (the risk associated with an unexpected event), and political risk (the risk of government policy changes).

When one is assessing Australia's and New Zealand's public and private retirement provision arrangements against these criteria, a similar pattern emerges. In aggregate, the public and private arrangements appear to address most of the economic and financial risks. However, the reliance on non-annuitized private benefits in both countries leaves retirees particularly susceptible to investment risk, longevity risk, and inflation risk.

The vulnerability of Australian and New Zealand retirees to investment risk was illustrated clearly in the aftermath of the global financial crisis of 2008–2009. As noted earlier, Australians are increasingly taking account-based pensions at retirement. These products allow retirees to choose both the underlying portfolio allocation and the drawdown pattern (subject to the minimum drawdown requirements set out in Table 4.3). In practice, retirees are choosing portfolios with around 65–70 percent allocation to risky assets. The implication of this

Table 4.8 Retirement provision in Australia and New Zealand – retirement risks[a]

Economic and Financial Risks in Retirement	Australia		New Zealand	
	Age Pension	Superannuation Guarantee and Voluntary Superannuation.	New Zealand Superannuation	Other[b]
Replacement risk: the risk of not adequately replacing pre-retirement income	No	Yes	No	Yes
Investment risk: the risk of unevenness in income resulting from the volatility of investment returns	Yes	No	Yes	No
Longevity risk: the risk of outliving one's financial resources	Yes	No	Yes	No
Inflation risk: the risk of erosion of purchasing power	Yes	No	Yes	No
Contingency risk: the risk associated with an uninsurable event, such as unexpected health expenses	No	Yes	No	Yes
Political risk: the risk of government policy changes that eliminate or dissipate benefits	Yes	Moderate	Yes	No

Source: Developed from Bateman, Kingston, and Piggott (2001).

[a] Other risks include annuity risk and regulatory risk.

[b] Includes Kiwisaver, voluntary occupational superannuation, homeownership, and investment income.

reasonably risky asset allocation became clear over 2008–2009, when the Australian stock market fell by close to 40 percent, resulting in large reductions in balances in account-based pensions (Bateman, 2011). Retirees who had self-invested their lump sums were similarly exposed. While these events highlighted the extent to which Australian retirees are exposed to investment risk, they also illustrate the insurance characteristics of Australia's means tested Age Pension, with the fall in privately managed retirement assets and incomes offset by increased public pension eligibility. Between October and December 2008, a period representing the worst of the global financial crisis, the number of new applications for the Age Pension increased by 50 percent (Robertson and Sawyers, 2009).

The impact of the global financial crisis in New Zealand was relatively moderate. Overall, household wealth fell by around 9 percent (Retirement Commission, 2010, p32).

In relation to longevity risk, the extremely low take-up of longevity products increases the likelihood that retirees will outlive their private savings. This may be considered unimportant in New Zealand and Australia, which provide universal public pensions. However, one must remember that the pension paid under NZS is only 66 percent of the after tax average wage for a couple, and 65 percent of the couple rate (around 43 percent of the average wage) for a single retiree. Similarly the full Age Pension provided in Australia is 27.7 percent of gross average male earnings (or around 37 percent after tax). Outliving private retirement savings in Australia and New Zealand will result in a dramatic fall in living standards.

Finally, the combination of aging populations and reliance on public pensions increases the vulnerability of retirees in both Australia and New Zealand to political risk. Australian government estimates suggest that the cost of the Age Pension will rise from 2.7 percent of GDP in 2009 to 3.9 percent of GDP in 2050 (Australian Treasury, 2010). This fiscal burden is quite modest by OECD standards, reflecting the relatively low level of unfunded benefit payable and the gradual encroachment of funded support into the means tested areas of the Age Pension.

New Zealand government estimates of the impact of demographic changes on NZS indicate a doubling of the cost from 4.3 percent to 8.0 percent of GDP over the next 40 years (New Zealand Government, 2009). While the NZSF was established in 2001 to partially pre-fund future payments of NZS, the extent to which it will do this is unclear. Contributions were suspended in the wake of the global financial crisis until at least till 2018/2019 (Retirement Policy Research Centre, 2010).

The increasing proportion of GDP required to fund public pensions, and the competing demands for health and aged care, will put pressure on the ability of the government to fund future public pension payments and leave retirees vulnerable to political risk.

Overall, the current payout structures of the DC retirement saving schemes in Australia and New Zealand, which lack a well-designed payout structure for retirement benefits, leave present and future retirees vulnerable to investment risk, longevity risk, and political risk, and consequently the risk that retirement benefits will not adequately replace pre-retirement income (that is, replacement risk).

4. Feasible reform measures for retirement income provision policies in Australia and New Zealand

The key deficiency in DC payout structures in both Australia and New Zealand is the short menu of retirement income products and the absence of a market for longevity products. The solution to this is quite complex and involves a more sophisticated approach than just mandating life annuities at retirement or providing incentives for annuity purchase. In both Australia and New Zealand a co-operative policy approach is required to address weak consumer demand, ineffective product distribution channels, poor policy coordination between regulators and policy departments, and the constraints faced by product providers as they seek means to hedge against interest, inflation, and mortality risks.[10]

4.1. Enhancing consumer demand for longevity products

Economic theory suggests that life annuities can substantially increase individual welfare by eliminating the financial risks associated with uncertain lifetimes and providing consumers with a higher level of lifetime consumption. However, theory is not supported by empirical evidence on annuitization, which indicates that voluntary annuity markets are very thin. In Australia and New Zealand combined, for example, fewer than 50 life annuity policies were sold in 2009.

Explanations put forward to explain this lack of voluntary annuitization include adverse selection and high prices, crowding out (due to preexisting annuitization and risk sharing in families), demand for liquidity (for bequests and unexpected expenditures), incomplete annuity markets, and, more recently, behavioral hypotheses (Brown, 2007; Brown et al., 2008; Agnew et al., 2008). Possible solutions to address deficient demand include the following.

Mandating or encouraging annuity purchase

In Australia this could be achieved by mandating life annuity purchase with accumulations resulting from the mandatory superannuation guarantee. A mandatory system would address adverse selection by ensuring that the people in the insurance pool reflect the average life expectancy in the community as a whole. Mandating purchase could apply to all accumulations, or a proportion of accumulations – determined by a requirement to achieve a pre-determined replacement rate, or perhaps a requirement to 'top up' the public pension to a pre-determined replacement rate (Evans and Sherris, 2010). Notably, the recent review of the tax and superannuation arrangements argues against mandatory annuitization and concluded that 'a mandatory system would constrain the ability of people to make their own decisions on how they use their superannuation to fund their retirement' (AFTS, 2010b, p122). Furthermore, mandatory annuitization fails to address supply side, distribution, or policy coordination issues.

A less prescriptive solution could be achieved by providing incentives for life annuity purchase, although this is difficult to achieve under the current TTE superannuation tax arrangements where retirement benefits are tax free.[11] One approach could be to follow the design of Roth IRAs and 401ks in the United States, which offer a choice between either one or both kinds of retirement saving account, one taxed under a standard EET regime and the other under a TEE regime. Subject to contribution caps, retirement savers can contribute to both standard and Roth retirement saving plans. If introduced in Australia, an alternative EET account could be established to complement the current accounts taxed under a TTE regime. Accumulations in the 'new' accounts would be reserved for the purchase of lifetime annuities (as suggested in Bateman and Kingston, 2010b). Over time contributions would grow in the 'new' accounts, and an increasing proportion of retirement accumulations would be taken as life annuities.

It is likely to be politically easier to introduce mandatory annuitization in New Zealand given the recent introduction of Kiwisaver in 2007. As noted in St John

(2007, n.p.), 'New Zealand has a unique opportunity with a tax neutral TTE regime to design an explicit subsidy to recognize the gains to society from annuitisation'. However, whether there would be widespread support for mandatory annuitization is unclear.

An alternative approach would be to make annuitization the default option for benefit take-up at retirement. This was recommended in Australia's 2010 review of the superannuation industry (Super System Review, 2010) but not supported by the government (Australian Government, 2010a).

Increasing the size of retirement accumulation available for retirement

One possible reason for the lack of annuitization is the small size of retirement accumulations. Average superannuation accumulations in Australia (with a more mature system than new Zealand) are only AUD 140,000 for men and AUD 65,000 for women, and median accumulations are much lower. It is possible that annuity demand will pick up as retirement accumulations increase over time. Australian policy has already initiated this with a proposed increase in the mandatory 9 percent contribution rate to 12 percent. However, additional changes could be made, including modifying the incentives to increase voluntary contributions or increasing the eligibility age for accessing superannuation accumulations, say to age 65.

Facilitating larger retirement accumulations is more problematic in New Zealand. The minimum contribution to Kiwisaver is only 4 percent of earnings (comprising a 2 percent employee contribution and a 2 percent employer contribution), and accumulations are compromised by the ability to withdraw from Kiwisaver for a first home purchase. Possible reforms to facilitate larger retirement accumulations include discontinuing withdrawals from Kiwisaver for first home purchase, increasing the minimum contributions to Kiwisaver accounts, and expanding the incentives for employers and employees to make voluntary contributions. A final, more extreme reform could be to make contributions both higher and compulsory.

Addressing behavioral barriers to annuitization

Investigation of sub-optimal annuitization is increasingly turning to behavioral hypotheses. Possible behavioral barriers to annuitization include complexity and financial literacy, mental accounting and loss aversion, misleading heuristics, the illusion of control, and other factors (including ambiguity aversion, avoidance, and hyperbolic discounting) (Brown, 2007). In an experimental setting, Brown et al. (2008) and Agnew et al. (2008) find that information presentation and financial literacy influence annuity demand.

This raises the possibility that inadequate annuity demand could be addressed by targeting the identified behavioral barriers. Initiatives that could reasonably be introduced on a large scale include (1) financial literacy policies targeted at retirement benefit decisions and (2) comparative product information drafted to address behavioral biases.

Australia and New Zealand have already introduced financial literacy initiatives, through the Retirement Commission in New Zealand and the Financial Literacy Board in Australia. However, surveys of financial competence show large variation in levels of financial literacy (Retirement Commission, 2010, ANZ, 2008; Bateman et al., 2011), indicating that a more targeted approach is required.

There has been some progress on information provision requirements. Australia introduced mandatory financial product disclosure requirements in 2001, and these are being refined and simplified as part of the implementation of selected recommendations of the recent Super System Review (Australian Government, 2010a). A better approach may be to coordinate information provision and financial literacy initiatives (Bateman et al., 2011).

Developing a new suite of longevity products

The menu of annuity products offered in Australia and particularly New Zealand is short and unimaginative. Absent from both are variable annuities and deferred annuities, both of which have potential appeal to consumers. A variable life annuity provides discretion over asset allocation and therefore does not require annuitants to significantly alter their portfolio allocation at the point of retirement. These products are not available in New Zealand, and while not disallowed in Australia, penal tax, transfer, and prudential regulations preclude the development of a market. In particular, an annuity with variable payments is not considered an annuity for tax (or Age Pension means test) purposes.

A deferred annuity is an annuity where payment is delayed until either a pre-specified date or a particular contingency (such as the depletion of a phased withdrawal – account-based pension – account). In Australia, deferred annuities are subject to penal tax and means test provisions, as with variable annuities, and are not offered. Nor are they available in New Zealand. An example of a deferred annuity would be the purchase of an annuity at retirement, at say age 65, which does not begin paying until age 85. Because payments commence 20 years in the future and are discounted by interest and mortality rates, they appear relatively cheap to purchase.

Other more interesting products could be developed that combine the various features of a longer menu of retirement benefits including immediate and term annuities, phased withdrawal products (account-based pensions), variable annuities, and deferred annuities. Such products could be designed to provide one or more of the following benefits: longevity insurance, capital guarantees, insurance against inflation, reversionary benefits, guarantees, etc., and, as a result, create hybrid products with consumer appeal. The final report of the review of the Australian tax system noted that it was a 'structural weakness in the Australian retirement income system' that those products are not available to cover the broad range of preferences of retirees in achieving security of income (AFTS, 2010b, p119).

Such developments are already underway in Australia but are inhibited by tax, means test, and regulatory barriers. Again, the task is greater for New Zealand, where the current menu of retirement income products is limited to term and life annuities.

Another direction in product development includes pooled annuity funds (or group annuitization products). These products provide idiosyncratic risk pooling but leave systematic longevity risk with the annuitizing cohort(s). Because longevity risk is not covered, organizations other than life insurance companies may offer these products, such as industry superannuation funds in Australia or Kiwisaver providers in New Zealand. Longevity insurance, if desired, could be achieved through bilateral relationships with life insurance companies.

The high levels of mortgage free homeownership among Australian and New Zealand retirees offer alternative vehicles for retirement income provision. Currently most reverse mortgages are paid as lump sums, but in theory homeownership does provide an asset base from which to generate a retirement income stream (including a longevity product).

4.2. Addressing supply side constraints

Potential providers of longevity products in Australia and New Zealand face a number of risks in bringing a product to market. These include interest rate (or investment) risk, inflation risk, and mortality risk. Investment rate risk is lower when a provider can more closely match long term liabilities with long term assets. Inflation risk can be reduced if the provider can purchase an income stream linked to inflation, such as an indexed bond. Longevity risk on the supply side is the risk that income streams will need to be paid for longer than expected owing to an unexpected increase in life expectancy.

Policy initiatives could be introduced to address these risks, for example, if the government were required to issue a broader range of indexed and long term bonds, or perhaps if the government invested in the development of a longevity insurance market. The final report of Australia's recent tax review did not support this initiative. Instead, it recommended that the government and private sector work together to develop a longevity index to assist product providers to hedge against longevity risk.

However, it may be the case that the government itself is in a better position than the private sector to bear longevity risk, and an option could be for it to enter the annuity market directly, alongside private insurers. This possibility was recommended in the final report of the review of Australia's tax system. Specifically, Recommendation 22 stated, 'The Government should consider offering an immediate annuity and a deferred annuity product that would allow a person to purchase a lifetime annuity' (AFTS, 2010b, p121). This could be a complete product or just a top-up to the publicly provided Age Pension (Evans and Sherris, 2010).

Similar initiatives could be applied in New Zealand. For example, retirement accumulations from the new Kiwisaver retirement saving scheme could be used to purchase a top-up to NZS.

4.3. Policy coordination between government agencies

In retirement incomes policy, responsibilities are often spread among various government bodies. In Australia, for example, financial service providers developing longevity products have been required to coordinate with up to five different government agencies – Treasury, the Australian Taxation Office, the social security department, and regulators responsible for the superannuation industry and consumer protection. Under current arrangements responsibility for policy design is spread across one or more of these bodies, but the response tends not to be well coordinated. Each of these agencies is acting in what it sees as a responsible fashion in light of its own mandate, but the overall effect may well be to restrict an appealing longevity insurance product. What is needed is a coordinated approach to the regulations and policies impacting on retirement income products so that greater longevity insurance is encouraged.

4.4. Improving distribution channels

Finally, more sophisticated distribution channels are required for the promotion and sale of longevity insurance products. In Australia, many people approaching retirement seek the advice of a financial advisor, who in many cases is naive about longevity risk and is motivated by commission incentives built around investment style products. A possible mechanism for breaking through this lies with the large superannuation funds, which do have a relationship with their members. The not-for-profit funds especially, which account for a large proportion of the workforce, may have the capacity to harness their relationships to promote products embracing greater longevity insurance than presently. Other policy suggestions, such as limiting commission payments to financial planners, may help with increasing net returns but seem unlikely on their own to address the retirement protection issue (Bateman and Piggott, 2011).

5. Concluding comments

The private DC arrangements in Australia and New Zealand are different in design and at different stages of development. Australia's superannuation guarantee is mandatory, reasonably mature, and supported by tax concessions. The New Zealand's Kiwisaver is voluntary, at a very early stage of development, and fully taxed (but subject to a government subsidy).

The differences continue into retirement, with almost all New Zealanders taking lump sums, and most Australians transferring funds to account-based pensions (i.e., phased withdrawal products). Common to both systems, however, is a very short menu of retirement income stream products and under-insurance against longevity risk. Demand for life annuities in Australia and New Zealand combined stands at around 50 policies a year.

Co-operation between the private and public sectors is required to kick-start the market for longevity products. Policy reforms must address weak consumer demand, behavioral biases, risks faced by product providers, ineffective product distribution channels, and poor policy coordination.

Overall, there is far more optimism for the development and expansion of a market for longevity products in Australia, where longevity risks are increasingly raised in the policy debate. New Zealand policymakers should be prepared to follow suit.

Notes

1 The discussion of Australia's retirement income system draws on Bateman and Piggott (2011) and Bateman (2011).
2 The Age Pension age for females is gradually being increased from age 60 to age 65 by 2014. Between 2017 and 2023 the Age Pension age will increase to 67 for both males and females (see Australian Government, 2009).
3 Mainly of the DC variety, although defined benefit arrangements comply under certain conditions.
4 Term allocated pensions (TAPs), also known as market-linked income streams, were introduced in September 2004 in response to changes in the tax, Age Pension means test, and regulatory requirements. TAPs had a similar account structure to account-based pensions but a similar term structure to a 'life expectancy' term annuity. TAPs are no longer marketed following further changes to the tax and regulatory requirements in September 2007. As well, those retiring with a defined benefit pension plan may receive a superannuation pension provided by the superannuation plan, rather than purchased in the private market.
5 A 'transition to retirement pension' is an account-based pension that is available to those with a preservation age of between 55 and 60. These products allow older workers access to superannuation benefits before retirement, provided the benefits are taken as an income stream with a maximum annual drawdown of 10 percent of assets. The overall aim was to encourage older people who would otherwise leave the labor force to work at least part time.
6 In a response to the global financial crisis the minimum annual drawdown was been reduced by 50 percent to minimize the extent to which self-funded retirees are required to draw down capital.
7 A detailed discussion of account-based pensions can be found in Bateman and Thorp (2008).
8 These were a series of reforms to superannuation and the Age Pension, announced in the May 2006 budget (and implemented throughout 2006 and 2007), with the aim of reducing complexity in retirement income provision (Australian Treasury, 2006).
9 This is an abbreviated summary of public pensions in New Zealand. For a detailed discussion of public pension reforms over the past 30 years see Retirement Policy Research Centre (2008).
10 Recommendations for New Zealand drawn from Mercer (2010).
11 For those aged 60 and above.

References

Agnew J., L. Anderson, J. Gerlach, and L. Szykman. (2008). Who chooses annuities? An experimental investigation of the role of gender, framing and defaults. *American Economic Review*, 98(2): 418–422.
ANZ Bank. (2008). *ANZ survey of adult financial literacy in Australia*. Melbourne: Author.

Association of Superannuation Funds of Australia. (2009). *Media release – budget 2009: A fork in the road*. 12 May. Sydney, Australia: Author. Available at www.superannuation.asn.au/mr090512/default.aspx.

Australian Bureau of Statistics (ABS). (2009). *Employment arrangements, retirement and superannuation, Australia*. Cat No. 6361.0. April to July 2007 (Re-issue). Canberra, Australia: Author.

Australian Government. (2009). *Secure and sustainable pensions*. 12 May 2009. Canberra, Australia: Author.

Australian Government. (2010a). *Stronger Super – government response to the Super System Review*. Canberra: Commonwealth of Australia.

Australian Government. (2010b). *Tax policy statement: Stronger, fairer, simpler – a tax plan for our future*. Canberra, Australia: Author.

Australian Prudential Regulation Authority. (2007). Celebrating 10 years of superannuation data collection 1996–2006. *Insight*, no. 2, n.p.

Australian Prudential Regulation Authority. (2011). *Annual superannuation bulletin*. June 2010 (issued January 2011). Sydney, Australia: Author.

Australian Treasury. (2006). *A plan to simplify and streamline superannuation – detailed outline*. Canberra: Australian Government.

Australian Treasury. (2010). *Australia to 2050: Future challenges*. Canberra: Australian Government.

Australia's Future Tax System (AFTS). (2009). *The retirement income system: Report on strategic issues*. Canberra: Commonwealth of Australia.

Australia's Future Tax System (AFTS). (2010a). *Report to the treasurer, December 2009, part one: Overview*. Canberra: Commonwealth of Australia.

Australia's Future Tax System (AFTS). (2010b). *Report to the treasurer, December 2009, part two: Detailed analysis (part 1 of 2)*. Canberra: Commonwealth of Australia.

Australia's Future Tax System (AFTS). (2010c). *Report to the treasurer, December 2009, part two: Detailed analysis (part 2 of 2)*. Canberra: Commonwealth of Australia.

Bateman H. (2011). Retirement income provision in Australia in the wake of the global financial crisis, in Y. Stevens (ed), *Protecting pension rights in times of economic turmoil*. Social Europe Series, vol. 26. Cambridge, UK: Intersentia: 63–91.

Bateman H., C. Eckert, J. Geweke, J. Louviere, S. Satchell, and S. Thorp. (2011). Financial competence, risk presentation and retirement portfolio preferences. Discussion paper 2011-1. Sydney, Australia: Centre for Pensions and Superannuation.

Bateman H. and G. Kingston. (2010a). The Henry Review and Super and Saving. *Australian Economic Review*, 43(4): 437–448.

Bateman H. and G. Kingston. (2010b). Tax and Super – unfinished business. *JASSA*, 4: 49–54.

Bateman H., G. Kingston, and J. Piggott. (2001). *Forced savings: Mandating private retirement incomes*. Cambridge: Cambridge University Press.

Bateman H. and J. Piggott. (2011). Developments in the Australian annuities market, in O. S. Mitchell, J. Piggott, and N. Takayama (eds), *Securing lifelong retirement income: Global annuity markets and policy*. Oxford: Oxford University Press: 81–105.

Bateman H. and S. Thorp. (2008). Choices and constraints over retirement income streams: Comparing rules and regulations. *Economic Record*, 84(September): S17–S31.

Brown J. (2007), *Rational and behavioral perspectives on the role of annuities in retirement planning*, National Bureau of Economic Research Working Paper No. 13537. Cambridge, MA: National Bureau of Economic Research.

Brown J., J. R. Kling, S. Mullainathan, and M. V. Wrobel. (2008). Why don't people insure late life consumption? A framing explanation of the under-annuitisation puzzle. *American Economic Review*, 98(2): 304–309.

Deloitte. (2010a). *SEQUAL/Deloitte reverse mortgage survey.* December 2009. Sydney, Australia: Deloitte Actuaries and Consultants.

Deloitte. (2010b). *SHERPA/Deloitte reverse mortgage survey.* December 2009. Deloitte Actuaries and Consultants.

Department of Families, Housing, Community Services and Indigenous Affairs. (2008). *Annual Report 2007–8.* Canberra: Australian Government.

Evans J. and M. Sherris. (2010). Longevity risk management and the development of a life annuity market in Australia. Australian Business School Research Paper No. 2010ACTL01. Sydney, Australia: University of New South Wales.

Harmer J. (2009). *Pension review report.* Canberra: Department of Families, Housing, Community Services and Indigenous Affairs (FaHCSIA).

Industry Super Network. (2010). ISN investigates how older Australians are using their super: Retirement intentions. November. Sydney, Australia: Industry Super Network.

Internationale Nederlanden Groep (ING). (n.d.). 'MoneyforLife'. Available at www.ing.com.au/personal/retirement/ing-moneyforlife.aspx.

Mercer. (2009). *Time to act: Risks, challenges and opportunities with New Zealand's retirement income system.* Auckland, New Zealand: Mercer. www.workplacesavings.org.nz/assets/KiwiSaver/SecuringretirementincomesAug09.pdf.

Ministry of Social Development. (2010). *Description of New Zealand's current retirement income policies.* Background paper prepared for the Retirement Commission's 2010 Review of Retirement Income Policy, July 2010. Wellington, New Zealand: Author.

New Zealand Government. (2009). *Challenges and choices: New Zealand's long term fiscal statement.* October. Wellington, New Zealand: Author.

New Zealand Superannuation Fund (NZSF). (2010). *2010 annual report, guardians of New Zealand superannuation.* Auckland, New Zealand: Author.

Organisation for Economic Co-operation and Development. (2009). *Pensions at a glance: Retirement income systems in OECD countries.* Paris: Organisation for Economic Co-operation and Development.

Plan for Life Research. (2011a). *Immediate annuity report.* Melbourne: Plan for Life, Actuaries and Researchers.

Plan for Life Research. (2011b). Pensions and annuity market research report, Issue 69, Melbourne: Plan for Life, Actuaries and Researchers.

Purcal S. (2006). *Supply challenges to the provision of annuities.* School of Actuarial Studies Discussion Paper, University of New South Wales June 2006. Wellington, New Zealand. www.business.unsw.edu.au/About-Site/Schools-Site/risk-actuarial-site/Documents/S.%20Purcal%20-%20Supply%20Challenges%20to%20the%20Provision%20of%20Annuities.pdf

Retirement Commission. (2010). *2010 review of retirement income policy.* Wellington, New Zealand: Commission for Financial Literacy and Retirement Income.

Retirement Policy Research Centre. (2008). *A condensed history of public and private provision for retirement income in New Zealand – 1975–2008.* Retirement Policy Research Centre Pension Briefing 05/2008. Auckland, New Zealand: University of Auckland Business School.

Retirement Policy Research Centre. (2010). *How much will New Zealand superannuation really cost?* Retirement Policy Research Centre Pension Briefing 2010-4. Auckland, New Zealand: University of Auckland Business School.

Robertson A. and R. Sawyers. (2009). 100 years of the age pension in Australia. Paper presented to the 17th Colloquium of Superannuation Researchers, 6–7 July, Sydney, Australia.

St John S. (2007). New Zealand's experiment in tax neutrality for retirement saving. *The Geneva Papers*, 32: 532–552.

St John S. (2009). *The annuities market in New Zealand*. Report prepared for the Ministry of Economic Development, Retirement Policy and Research Centre, University of Auckland, New Zealand.

St John S., M. Littlewood, and C. Dale. (2010). Kiwisaver, the first three years: Lessons for Ireland? Retirement Policy and Research Centre Working Paper 2010/2. Auckland, New Zealand: University of Auckland Business School.

Superannuation Industry (Supervision) Amendment Regulations 2007 (No.1), Schedule 3. Australia. www.comlaw.gov.au/Details/F2007L00820/30475d35-f533-444d-824c-128f995595c4

Super System Review. (2010). *Final report, part 1: Overview and recommendations*. Canberra: Australian Government.

5 Structuring the payout phase in a defined contribution scheme in high income countries

Experiences of Singapore[1]

Ngee-Choon Chia and Albert K. Tsui

1. Introduction

With a demographic shift in most high income countries towards a graying population and with increasing life expectancy, how to finance retirement becomes increasingly important for policy makers. Countries with pay-as-you-go defined benefits (DB) systems are gradually coming to terms with sustainability issues as there are more benefit recipients than contributors. These countries had introduced the old-age pension using the DB system when their populations were relatively young. Now with aging populations and a falling contributors–benefactors ratio, DB schemes are increasingly becoming financially unsustainable and need to be supplemented or replaced by alternative schemes. For example, Australia, Denmark, Germany, the Netherlands and Switzerland have introduced various forms of funded defined contribution (DC) as an alternative pillar to reduce the financing burden.[2] The United States, once predominated by DB plans, is now seeing a shift towards DC plans. In 1980 roughly three quarters of retirement plans were DB plans compared to 73 percent DC 401(k) plans in 2005 (Poterba et al., 2007).

Countries with DC systems enjoy a fiscal advantage because the benefit payouts are directly correlated to contributions. There are minimal effects on labor supply and early retirement. Besides being less sensitive to demographic changes, the DC system also avoids sustainability problems and averts political costs from unrealistic benefit promises. But the DC system exposes individuals to risks – longevity, interest rate, and inflation risks. Whether a DC system can successfully provide an adequate retirement income and help protect against longevity risk depends on the design of both the accumulation and the payout phases.

As retirement wealth depends on how much workers save, there are concerns about whether the accumulated savings are adequate. Adequacy of retirement income depends on contribution rates, contribution periods (higher retirement ages), inflation rates and returns to savings. Thus, macroeconomic variables influencing salary growth, unemployment episodes and rates of return will affect the size of retirement savings.

During the payout phase, institutional structure has to be put in place to support a market for de-accumulation products, such as the life annuity market. Mechanisms must be put in place to convert accumulated assets into regular payouts of fixed amounts. Pension economists, for example Milevsky (2005) and Scott et al. (2006), have studied the feasibility and efficiency of advanced life deferred annuities or delayed payout annuities to finance retirement. The questions that arise are as follows: Does such a market exist? How should life annuities be priced? What types of products are available (life versus term, nominal or inflation-indexed, the drawdown age)? Furthermore, to enable a provider to supply life annuity products, there need to be financial assets that will allow providers to hedge some risks that are associated with lifelong annuity payment promises.[3] Schich (2008) highlighted clearly the challenges facing financial intermediaries in offering de-accumulation products. There are investment challenges during the payout phase owing to asset price and interest rate fluctuations and, in addition, increasing life expectancy leads to individuals outliving the accumulated savings. However, suitable hedging products such as longevity bonds are scarce, and the market for longevity bonds remains inactive. Thomsen and Andersen (2007) attributed this to the lack of natural investors who would benefit from an unexpected rise in life expectancy, among other reasons.

This chapter examines the major issues relating to the payout phase of Singapore's Central Provident Fund (CPF) system. Singapore's pension system operates as a fully funded mandatory DC social security system. The system, which is based on individual accounts, is administered and managed by the CPF Board, which is a statutory board under the Ministry of Manpower.[4] While there are fiscal advantages to policy makers, there is an intrinsic link between the accumulation and de-accumulation phases.

The amount available to the individual during the payout phase depends on the amount accumulated during the work cycle. Thus, accumulated savings depend crucially on the CPF policy parameters. These include the contribution rate, the rates of returns and the apportionment of the contributions to the various accounts. Individual workers' wage profiles and macroeconomic variables influencing salary growth and unemployment episodes will affect accumulation.

The challenge of adequate old-age provision during the payout phase lies in the existence of annuity markets to provide financial instruments that yield a steady monthly stream of income till death. One early criticism of the adequacy of the CPF system was its lack of mandatory annuitization. In 2009 the CPF Board introduced mandatory annuitization to convert accumulated savings into a stream of retirement income under the CPF Lifelong Income Scheme (CPF LIFE). CPF LIFE insures retirees against longevity risk, so that they will not outlive their accumulated savings.

One unique feature of the Singapore's CPF system is that savings can be withdrawn to help finance housing and healthcare. To make home ownership affordable, CPF members are able to make pre-retirement withdrawals from the mandatory retirement CPF savings to pay for the down-payment, stamp duties, mortgage payments and interest incurred in the purchase. Although such pre-retirement withdrawals reduce the amount available during the payout phase, they help CPF members to accumulate assets. With retirement and housing policies so closely intertwined, we can regard the Singapore's social security system as an asset-based social security. As Singapore's prime minister Mr. Lee Hsien Loong puts it, "home, an appreciating asset in Singapore, is a nest egg. . . . It's for you to live in, it's for your investment, it's for you for your old age" (*Straits Times*, 21 February 2010). In 2009, 95 percent of the Housing Development Board (HDB) flat owners bought their flats using CPF savings, and 63 percent of homeowners (public and private homes) used CPF savings to pay for their homes (CPF Annual Report, 2009).

According to Visco (2006), while annuities are the classical answer to retirement financing during the payout phase, they are not the only one. Indeed, in Singapore almost 83 percent of the current elderly living in public housing identified the flat they lived in as their main financial asset (Singapore, HDB, 2010b, p. 154). The government has put in place several mechanisms to help these asset-rich, cash-poor Singaporeans to monetize housing as part of the de-accumulation process. These instruments include reverse mortgages, subletting, downsizing and lease buyback schemes.

The next section highlights the key determinants that influence the net accumulation of CPF savings. Section 3 assesses the financial instruments to facilitate the de-accumulation of the accumulated assets and/or CPF savings. We will first compare the monetization options available for Singaporeans to unlock their accumulated housing assets and then examine the newly implemented Lifelong Income Scheme (CPFLIFE) that will help provide steady income for life for CPF members. Section 4 explores other mechanisms that can be used to enhance adequacy of retirement savings during the de-accumulation phase, such as enhancement of housing subsidies. Section 5 concludes the analysis with some policy recommendations.

2. CPF accumulation

The CPF is mandatory for all employees, including low wage workers and the self-employed with annual trade incomes of above S$ 6,000. Contributions to CPF begin upon entry into the workforce, with no minimum age requirement. The employers' CPF contribution rate is currently set at 15 percent of the monthly salary for workers below the age of 50, while rates for workers above 50 range from 5.5 percent to 11 percent. The employee's contribution is set at 20 percent of the monthly salary for workers below 50 years of age and range from 5 percent to 18 percent for those above 50. As CPF contributions are tax deductible, to limit tax subsidies to high income earners, there is a wage cap set at S$ 4,500. This is around the 75th percentile of gross monthly earned incomes. The salary ceiling was raised to S$5,000 in 2011, which is around the 80th income percentile. Contributions by both employers and employees are exempted from the employee's personal income tax. Voluntary contributions to the CPF also offer tax relief, subject to a cap.

Table 5.1 Contribution rates and account allocations as of 1 March 2011

Employee Age (years)	Contribution (% of wage)		Total Contribution (% of wage)	% of Total Contribution Credited To:		
	Employer	Employee		Ordinary Account	Special Account	Medisave Account
35 and below	15.5	20.0	35.0	23.0	5.5	7.0
36–45	15.5	20.0	35.0	21.0	6.5	8.0
46–50	15.5	20.0	35.0	19.0	7.5	9.0
51–55	11.5	18.0	29.0	13.0	7.5	9.0
56–60	8.5	12.5	20.5	11.5	0.5	9.0
61–65	5.5	7.5	13.0	3.5	0.5	9.5
66 and above	5.5	5.0	10.5	1.0	0.5	9.5

Source: Singapore CPF *Annual Report* 2012.

Notes: Contribution rates are subject to a salary ceiling of $4,500, which was raised from $5,000 in September 2011.

2.1. CPF accounts and pre-retirement withdrawals

Savings are apportioned to three different accounts: the ordinary account (OA), special accounts (SAs) and Medisave accounts (MAs). These three accounts are designed for different uses. The OA savings can be utilized to finance housing, to invest in approved shares and stocks and to finance children's tertiary education. A unique feature of the CPF scheme is that it permits pre-retirement withdrawals for approved uses such as housing, healthcare expenses and investments. Figure 5.1 shows that housing withdrawals are the major type of withdrawals. Most CPF members finance their monthly housing mortgage installments by drawing down their OA contributions.[5] Compared to countries with DC pension systems, the overall contribution rate to CPF, at 36 percent, seems high. However, the portion set aside for retirement is well within the range of contributions in other countries, at around 6 to 8 percent.

2.2. Rates of return

CPF savings are capital-protected and enjoy risk-free returns, with a guaranteed floor rate of 2.5 percent per annum. Since savings in the OA are regarded as short-term monies, the OA interest rate is pegged to weighted market interest rates, with 80 percent based on the 12-month fixed deposit rates and 20 percent based on the savings rates of the major local banks. Higher weight is put on the fixed deposit rate to help CPF members earn more savings. However, given the currently low interest rate environment, the CPFOA rate has been set at the leg-islated floor rate of 2.5 percent. To enhance the overall returns, as of 2008, the

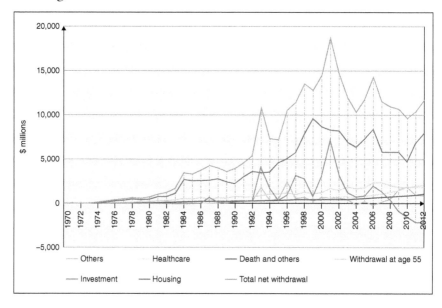

Figure 5.1 Central Provident Fund (CPF) withdrawals under various schemes
Source: CPF (n.d.). CPF Trends

first $60,000 of the combined balances in the OA and SA, with up to $20,000 in the OA, earns a rate that is 1 percentage point higher than the OA interest rate. It was estimated by the CPF Board that about 70 percent of all CPF members will be eligible for the extra 1 percent on all their CPF monies.

Savings in the special, medical and retirement accounts (SMRA) are mainly to finance old-age expenditure and are regarded as long-term money. Since January 2008 the CPF Board has departed from using fixed SMRA rates and instead benchmarks the SMRA rate to long-term bond yields. The SMRA rate is pegged at 1 percentage point above the average yield of the 10-year Singapore government securities (10 YSGS), with a guaranteed floor rate of 2.5 percent. To minimize volatility, the SMRA rate is determined by taking the average daily yields of the 10 YSGS over the previous 12 months. To help members adjust to the change, the CPF Board set the SMRA rate at the 4 percent floor rate plus 1 additional percentage point. Currently, the SMRA rate is at 4 percent.

2.3. Investment structure during the accumulation phase

It is mandatory that the first accumulated net CPF savings of $60,000 be invested in a default fund. This is considered a safe option as the monies are invested in non-tradable Special Singapore Government Securities (SSGS) with guaranteed returns. Only savings in excess of $20,000 in the OA and $40,000 in the

SA can be used for investment in CPF-approved investment products under the CPF Investment Scheme (CPFIS). The CPFIS was introduced to enhance retirement savings. However, over the years, the CPF Board has tightened the rules on the use of CPF monies for investment. The approved investments include equity funds, exchange-traded funds and investment-linked insurance products. Derivatives and hedge funds, which are considered very high risk investments, are excluded from the CPFIS. The CPF Board also sets limits on the amount of savings that can be invested in assets that have concentrated risk, such as stock counters, gold etc.

To protect the returns of savings, CPF members are also not allowed to invest in high cost funds (i.e. funds with sales charges of more than 3 percent) and funds with high expense ratios (i.e. exceeding the median for funds in their respective risk category). Since 2006 the CPF Board has progressively tightened the admission criteria in its effort to improve returns for its members, to enhance the quality of funds in its scheme and to cap costs. With stricter admission criteria, the median total expense ratio of CPFIS funds has come down. The ratio for lower risk funds dropped from 0.72 in 2006 to 0.32 in 2009. It is hoped that lower expense ratios will translate to better returns for CPF members since "an increase of one percent charge on funds over 40 years could erode returns at retirement age by 22 percent" (Tan, 2011).

Indeed, the CPF Board has reckoned that the "proliferation of choices under CPFIS in the past has not served CPF investors well" (CPF Board spokesman, quoted in Tan, 2011). After the tightening of the admission criteria, the number of funds dwindled from more than 400 funds in 2006 to about 310 funds at the beginning of 2011. This represents a fall of almost 30 percent in the number of funds. The CPF Board has fully implemented the stricter admission criteria for funds in the CPFIS, causing the number of unit trusts and investment-linked insurance plans that could meet the stricter criteria to fall further, to 195 funds.

Furthermore, to encourage prudence in investments, the CPF Board also requires members to be adequately informed through the use of a uniform set of metrics. The Lipper Leader rating system is used to provide comparative data on the costs, returns and risks of funds, the Sharpe ratio, the expense ratio etc. Based on chosen samples of unit trusts, Chia et al. (2011) found mixed evidence regarding the stock picking ability of fund managers and did not find support for the market timing ability and consistency of performance of fund managers for the evaluation periods. Table 5.2 shows the investment performance of the CPFIS-included unit trusts in which CPF monies from the OAs were invested. From fiscal years 2004 to 2009, 48 percent of the CPF members who liquidated their investment made losses. Of those who made profits, 20 percent of them enjoyed returns that beat the risk-free rate (at 2.5 percent) that the CPF Board paid on the OA account. Thirty-two percent had returns smaller than the guaranteed risk-free rate. Table 5.2 also shows that although the absolute number of CPFIS investors is increasing, the rate of increase has slowed down since financial year 2007.

Table 5.2 Performance of CPFI SOA investment: realized profits/losses for investments

	FY 2004	FY 2005	FY2006	FY 2007	FY 2008	FY 2009	Average (2004–2009)
Realized losses							
No. of CPF investors	369,591	363,124	362,129	368,054	440,063	465,724	
% of all CPF investors	50.1	47.7	45.3	43.2	49.3	52.1	48.0
Realized profits							
No. with returns that *beat* OA rate of 2.5%	127,518	147,387	179,987	239,137	173,987	112,642	
% of all CPF investors	17.3	19.4	22.5	28.1	19.5	12.6	20.0
No. with returns *less than* or *equal to* OA rate of 2.5%	240,010	250,237	257,191	244,841	278,758	314,901	
% of total CPF investors	32.6	32.9	32.2	28.7	31.2	35.3	32.0
CPFIS participation							
Total no. of CPF investors	737,119	760,748	799,307	852,032	892,808	893,267	
Growth rate (%)		3.2	5.1	6.6	4.8	0.1	

Source: Central Provident Fund (n.d.). Constructed from CPFIS Profits/Losses for the financial year ended, various years, downloaded from CPF website.

Note: The fiscal year (FY) is from 1 October to 30 September. CPFIS = Central Provident Fund Investment Scheme; OA = ordinary account.

3. Institutional structure to facilitate the payout phase

3.1. Monetizing options

All public housing in Singapore is 99-year leasehold property. This housing is provided by the HDB and made affordable through government interventions.[6] An important demand-side intervention is the CPF–HDB link created in 1968 to ease financing difficulty. Under this home ownership scheme, CPF savings can be used to finance housing. On the supply side, the government subsidizes the HDB from tax revenue and non-tax revenue from sales of state land. Furthermore, the Land Acquisition Act empowered the government to acquire land from private land owners at below-market prices. This enables the HDB to price its flats below market prices. In addition, HDB buyers enjoy subsidized mortgage loans (about 2 percent lower than the market rate).

These interventions have skewed housing tenure choices. About 85 percent of Singaporeans reside in public flats. Of these, 93 percent are flat owners (Singapore, Department of Statistics, 2008). Housing is the most important non-financial asset for most Singaporeans. The National Survey of Senior Citizens (Singapore, Ministry of Community Development, Youth and Sports, 2005, p. 31) reveals that 68 percent of those aged 55 or above felt that their home is their most important asset. For the elderly living in HDB flats, 83 percent of those aged 65 and above regarded the HDB flat they lived in as their major financial asset. For future elderly (i.e. those who are currently 55 years and above), 94 percent regarded the HDB flat they lived in as their major asset. The instruments available for homeowners to unlock their housing equity to help supplement their retirement incomes include lease buyback schemes (LBSs), subletting, downsizing and reverse mortgages (RMs). These products available during the de-accumulation phase not only help offer protection against longevity risk but also help provide liquidity and flexibility. Flat owners can choose an option that best balances their preference for retirement adequacy, aging in place and leaving a bequest.

3.1.1. LBSs

LBSs, launched in March 2009 by the HDB, provide an avenue for lower income elderly in two- and three-room flats to unlock their housing equity. They must, however, fulfill some eligibility conditions, such as having occupied the flat for at least five years. Under the LBS, HDB buys back the tail-end of the lease, leaving a shorter 30-year lease for the elderly to continue living in their flats. The longer the remaining lease, the more housing equity will be unlocked. In addition to the value of the housing equity unlocked from the shorter lease, they also receive a $10,000 subsidy from the government. Half of the subsidy received, together with the unlocked housing value, is then used to buy an annuity product under the CPF LIFE scheme. The LIFE scheme is a new feature in CPF to ensure lifelong incomes for retirees. It operates like a deferred life annuity with a refund feature, which helps to address CPF's lack of mandatory annuitization. LBS was revised in September 2014, and its provision may be broadly similar.

3.1.2. Subletting

The elderly also have the option to age in place by subletting room(s). They can also sublet the entire flat by moving in with their married children. Table 5.3 shows the housing preference of the elderly, which we can use to infer the elderly's preferences regarding upgrading to a bigger flat, downgrading to a smaller flat or maintaining the status quo and aging in place. The diagonal entries in Table 5.3 indicate that most elderly (about three-fourths) prefer to age in place, rather than upgrading or downgrading. Since October 2003 the HDB permits the entire flat to be sublet, provided that owners meet the minimum occupancy requirement. We compute the average rental incomes from subletting a room under different rental market environments over the remaining lifecycle of the elderly. For details of the computations, see Chia and Tsui (2009).

3.1.3. Downsizing

The elderly can also monetize their housing assets by selling the flats they live in and downgrading to smaller flats or to HDB studio apartments. Table 5.4 shows that on average, $79,000 or $132,000 can be cashed out by downgrading from a four-room to a three-room or two-room flat respectively (based on 2010 market values). They will be able to cash out a bigger amount if they downgrade to smaller units. Table 5.4 presents the monthly annuity payouts that are generated from unlocking housing equities.

Table 5.3 Housing preference

Housing Type Content with	1 Room	2 Rooms	3 Rooms	4 Rooms	5 Rooms
1 room	**89.3**	14.7	2.7	1.1	2.5
2 rooms	5.4	**70.6**	2.9	2.9	0
3 rooms	3.5	7.8	**77.3**	13.1	11.7
4 rooms	0.9	2.5	9.9	**71.3**	1.5
5 rooms	0.4	2.1	3.1	0.9	**71.4**

Source: Singapore, HDB (2005).

Note: The bold diagonal figures indicate the percent of people currently living in the housing type who do not prefer to either move to a smaller or larger flat.

Table 5.4 Monthly draw-downs from downsizing to smaller flats

		Downsizing from 3 rooms ($236,000) to:			
	3 Rooms	2 Rooms	1 Room	Studio (45m²)	Studio (35m²)
Unlocked Total	n/a	53,000	88,000	121,000	156,000
Male Monthly	n/a	337–352	560–586	770–806	992–1,038
Female Monthly	n/a	302–316	501–526	688–723	931–986

		Downsizing from 4-room ($325,000) to:			
	3 Rooms	2 Rooms	1 Room	Studio (45m²)	Studio (35m²)
Unlocked Total	79,000	132,000	167,000	200,000	235,000
Male Monthly	502–526	840–878	1,062–1,110	1,272–1,330	1,494–1,564
Female Monthly	450–472	751–788	950–997	1,137–1,194	1,330–1,403

Source: Authors' computations.

Note: The table presents a range of monthly drawdowns, corresponding to different interest rates (3.75 and 4.24 percent) used in the computations. These are also the rates used in the Housing Development Board's calculation.

3.1.4. RMs

RM products issued in Singapore lack the "non-recourse" feature and are similar to collateralized loans. When the accumulated payouts reach 70 percent of the property value, monthly payments stop and loans must start to be re-paid. There were two major RM providers: NTUC-Income and OCBC Bank. NTUC-Income launched its first term RM (maximum tenure of 20 years) for private properties in 1998 and extended it to HDB flats in 2006. Since its inception NTUC-Income has issued 500 such loans, but only 134 remain active. OCBC Bank offered term-based and annuity-linked RMs. However, since 2008 both providers have ceased issuing RM loans.

3.1.5. De-accumulation through monetizing HDB flats

The monetization options available to HDB owners depend on their flat types. In 2008, 4.7 percent of the elderly are in one-room flats, 5.2 percent in two-room flats, 31 percent in three-room flats, 34 percent in four-room flats and 25 percent in five-room and larger flats (Singapore, HDB, 2010a). The proportion in smaller flat types is higher than for the overall HDB resident population. Table 5.5 shows that elderly who own three-room and larger flats will have all monetization options available to them. But this is not so for the elderly in a one-room HDB flat. This is because only about 1.2 percent of HDB residents are in one-room flats, and most of these are rental units and hence cannot be monetized.

The expected present value of the income stream generated by RMs, the LBS, downsizing and subletting and the corresponding average monthly drawdowns that can be generated from the unlocked housing equity are shown in Table 5.6. The LBS

Table 5.5 Monetizing options available for HDB dwellers in different flat types

Current Flat Owned	Reverse Mortgage	Lease Buyback	Downsizing	Subletting
1-room	X	X	n/a	X
2-room	X	Y	Y	X
3-room	Y	Y	Y	Y
4-room	Y	Y	Y	Y

Source: Authors' compilation.

Notes: X means "not available," and Y means "available." The reverse mortgage scheme has now been withdrawn.

Table 5.6 Average monthly draw-downs

Flat Types	Monetization Options	Average Income Stream (S$)	Average Monthly Drawdown	
			Male (S$)	Female (S$)
2-room	Lease buyback scheme	79,200	515	462
3-room	Lease buyback scheme	109,000	709	635
	Downsizing	104,500	676	607
	Subletting one room	86,576	562	504
	Reverse mortgage*	165,200	581	560
4-room	Downsizing	157,000	783	770
	Subletting one room	86,576	432	423
	Reverse mortgage*	227,500	804	766

Source: Authors' computations.

*Including 30 percent as loading. For details on the computations, refer to Chia and Tsui (2009).

generates the highest monthly payout ($635). Subletting a room yields the lowest ($504) payouts, although the home owner gets to retain the housing asset and to age in place. Monthly payouts from downsizing ($607) and RMs ($560) for three-room flats are smaller compared to the LBS.

A recent HDB survey of the current elderly living in HDB flats reveals that the major source of retirement support is financial support from children, followed by personal and CPF savings, and then monetization of their housing assets. Almost all elderly had at least one financial source to finance their old age by 2010, up from 80 percent in 2003. Furthermore, compared to five years ago, more elderly (about 40 percent) had more than one financial source.[7] Asset-rich and cash-poor elderly Singaporean can choose from the various monetization options available to supplement their retirement income. All monetization options, except RMs, involve some kind of government subsidies. They can choose an option that best balances their preference for retirement adequacy, aging in place and leaving a bequest.

The elderly in Singapore have expressed a strong preference for aging in place. Survey results conducted on the social characteristics of the elderly (Singapore, HDB, 2005) indicated that about three quarters of the elderly prefer to age in place and that alternatives such as retirement villages and old people's homes are not popular. Subletting, the LBS and RMs are more favorable options as they allow the elderly to age in place while helping generate a steady stream of monthly payouts. However, the RM scheme is no longer available.

The survey results also show that almost 80 percent of the elderly would not consider either a RM or the LBS. Table 5.7 shows that RMs are the least preferred option. Seventeen percent of the elderly also indicated that they prefer to keep their flats as a bequest. The future elderly (those who are currently 55 to 64) have a similar preference and also demonstrated a strong bequest motive. If they have to monetize their housing asset, 10.9 percent of them prefer subletting a room; only 4.4 percent prefer to downsize or sublet the entire flat and live with their children.[8] Clearly, subletting is a more attractive option. Although it releases only part of the housing equity, it makes it possible for the elderly to keep their flats as a bequest. In addition, subletting allows them to age in place.

In the 2008 HDB survey, about 6.4 percent of the elderly are currently subletting their rooms and will continue to do so as an extra source of income (Singapore, HDB, 2010b). However, the LBS scheme has a low take-up rate as HDB owners have strong bequest motives.[9] Besides, many consider the amount that can be unlocked as too low. These views are also confirmed in the HDB survey.

3.2. Mandatory annuitization: Lifelong Income Scheme (CPF LIFE)

Before the introduction of the national annuity scheme, the CPF Board had attempted to enhance the retirement savings in the retirement account (RA)

Table 5.7 Preference for lease buyback schemes (LBSs) or reverse mortgages (RMs) among the elderly and future elderly

	Current Elderly	Future Elderly
LBS	6.6	5.0
RM	1.3	2.6
Either LBS or RM	11.8	20.3
Neither LBS nor RM	79.7	71.3
Not sure	0.7	0.9

Source: Singapore, HDB (2010b).

account by improving its rate of returns. However, the issue of longevity risk remains, and it is necessary to introduce an insurance scheme to address the uncertainty.[10] In September 2009 the CPF Board implemented a mandatory annuitization for the payout phase through the CPF LIFE scheme. The implementation of longevity insurance can be regarded as one of the main structural reforms in Singapore's social security system, as most of the earlier CPF changes were mainly parametric in nature. CPF LIFE scheme was made compulsory in 2013, starting with the 1958 cohort.[11] CPF members with at least $40,000 in their retirement accounts when they reach age 55 will automatically be included in CPF LIFE.

The main feature of the CPF LIFE is that it pools longevity risk among all annuitants – those who die younger will share the interest accumulated on their annuity premium with those who survive longer. Premiums paid to the CPF LIFE scheme are pooled and invested in government bonds (SSGS), which pay long term rates of return. CPF LIFE provides lifetime benefits with fixed monthly payouts that are not inflation indexed. The benefit is structured to match the payouts under the spend-down or phased withdrawal under the minimum sum (MS) scheme. This is to ensure that members' monthly payouts do not fall as they transit into the lifetime benefit phase under the mandatory annuity. LIFE payouts may be adjusted to reflect the investment and mortality experiences and to ensure that the scheme remains financially sustainable.

However, the implementation of mandatory annuitization was not without challenges. The scheme was first announced by the prime minister at the 2007 National Day Rally as a "longevity insurance scheme."[12] Upon this announcement, many Singaporeans expressed concerns and had misgivings that as an insurance scheme, this might imply that their contributions to a DC system would not be refunded but would be shared out in a risk-pooling structure. The idea of using one's own contribution to support another person with a longer life expectancy was not palatable. Hence, in the final form as CPF LIFE, a refundable option was provided. There was also public feedback that insurance is needed only for protection against something negative. Longevity is considered something positive and need not be insured for. Hence, in the final form, the word *insurance* was dropped and replaced with something positive, termed the Lifelong Income Scheme, or LIFE scheme.

When it was first announced, the longevity insurance scheme was to be like an advanced life deferred annuity, with payouts commencing at age 85. However, Singaporeans seem to exhibit what behavioral economists term the "availability fallacy"– i.e., instead of assessing risks based on objective data, they assess them based on subjective knowledge. They were doubtful that they would live beyond 85 although the life expectancy at birth for males and females is 79 and 83.7 years respectively. Furthermore, they expressed a preference for the drawdown age to be brought forward as 85 years old seemed too far away, as they were more concerned for the immediate future, that is, whether they were able to finance retirement at age 62. In response to Singaporeans' perception of their life expectancy at age 80, the choice that was presented to the CPF members were framed differently, in terms of "four different plans to balance their preferences." To

Table 5.8 CPFLIFE options: tradeoffs between levels of payouts and bequests

	Monthly Payouts	*Bequest*
Refundable		
LIFE Plus Plan	High	Low
LIFE Balanced Plan	Medium	Medium
LIFE Basic Plan	Low	High
Non-refundable		
LIFE Income Plan	Highest	No bequest

Source: Singapore, CPF (2011).

Note: CPF LIFE = Central Provident Fund Lifelong Income Scheme.

simplify it and to help members make choices, the CPF Board set a default option for its members. In the default option, the insurance risk-pooling element will commence at age 80. The default plan also gives a balance between the monthly payout and the amount available to be left as a bequest.

In communication to the public, the CPF Board simplifies the options available and merely informs them of the availability of four options, which will balance their preferences for the levels of retirement income and bequest.[13] The default option is the LIFE Balanced Plan, which offers a balance between the retirement income level and the amount of left as a bequest; the LIFE Plus Plan gives a higher monthly income but leaves less for the estate; the LIFE Basic Plan allows a higher bequest at the expense of a lower income; and the LIFE Income Plan delivers the highest income but leaves no bequest at all. These options are summarized in Table 5.8.

3.2.1. Design and structure of a national annuity scheme: CPF LIFE

The design of the new mandatory national annuity scheme complements the existing minimum sum (MS) scheme. Instead of replacing the MS scheme, CPF LIFE is integrated seamlessly into the MS scheme. Since the inception of the CPF Board in 1955, withdrawals from CPF are allowed at age 55, corresponding to the retirement age at that time. Subsequently, the mandatory retirement age was raised to 60 in 1993 and to 62 in 1999. Despite the lifting of the retirement age, the CPF withdrawal age is still at 55. To ensure at least a subsistence living upon retirement, at age 55 members are not allowed to withdraw the entire amount of savings but have to set aside a CPF MS in a retirement account (RA), which is created when a member reaches 55. The portion that needs to be kept in the RA is stipulated by the CPF Board, with different withdrawal rules for different 55-year-old cohorts.[14] The stipulated MS is expected to support a basic standard of living during retirement. Before the introduction of CPF LIFE, members could de-accumulate using two different phased withdrawal plans. First, the MS can be deposited with the CPF or a bank that pays a regular retirement income from age 62 for 20 years or till the sum is exhausted. Second, the MS can be used to buy a deferred life annuity. However, very few opted for the second option. Thus, the MS scheme exposed the elderly to longevity risk, i.e. that of outliving their MS. The MS scheme is thus a managed spend-down account with structured monthly withdrawals over 20 years from the retirement age of 62 to 82.[15] The MS is invested in the default fund, and in the event of the demise of the CPF members, the remaining monies are paid to their nominated beneficiaries or dependents according to the intestacy law.

CPF LIFE plans are designed to balance the CPF members' preference for meeting retirement needs and fulfilling bequest motives. The CPF Board allows individuals to choose the drawdown age (DDA), i.e. the age when the annuity payment will begin. Opting for a later DDA and refundable premiums allows the elderly to have a lower annuity level at a later date but to leave more as a bequest.

When a CPF member joins CPF LIFE, a portion of his/her cash savings in the RA is used to pay for the premium for a deferred life annuity. Under the four different options, different proportions of the RA savings are pooled, which in turn depends on the DDA, i.e. the point when the lifetime benefits will commence. The Basic option has the smallest percentage that is pooled, and hence offers the lowest monthly payouts, and the DDA is the earliest possible, at age 65. In contrast, under the non-refundable Income option, the entire retirement savings are pooled, and it thus offers the highest monthly payout, with no bequest.

Next, we describe in greater detail the structure of these four options. Table 5.9 shows the proportion of RA savings that are allocated to the annuity premium and to the managed drawdown under the different plans. Members buy the national annuity at age 55, though the payout date is deferred to age 65 at the earliest. A portion of the RA is set aside at age 55 to pay for the annuity premium, with the understanding that the first payout will be deferred till the person is age 65 or older, depending on the plan chosen. The interest from the annuity premiums of all annuitants is pooled into the Lifelong Income Fund. The remaining portion of the RA savings in the managed drawdown account will continue to earn

Table 5.9 Allocation of retirement account savings under different CPF LIFE options

| | Refundable Plans | | | Non-refundable |
	Plus	*Balanced*	*Basic*	*Income*
Managed spend-down (%)	0	70	90	0
Annuity (%)	100	30	10	100

Source: Singapore, CPF (2011).

Note: Table shows the approximate amounts allocated to the managed spend-down account and to the annuity. CPF LIFE = Central Provident Fund Lifelong Income Scheme.

interest, and the interest earned will be paid into the RA. However, the interest on the annuity premium will not accrue to the buyer but will be pooled that of the other CPF LIFE participants. The monthly withdrawals from the remaining savings are managed in a way to ensure that the payments will continue until the deferred annuity payments commence.

The amount available in the managed spend-down account, together with the life annuity, will provide monthly payouts till the member dies. The monthly payout is structured to match the payouts de-accumulated from the RA from age 62, until the DDA of the life annuity. This is to ensure that the monthly payouts in principle remain the same whether drawn from the spend-down portion of the accumulated MS or from the annuity. The annuity premium thus depends on both the amount available in the RA and the choice of the start date of the annuity benefit payout.

Figures 5.2a through 5.2c illustrate the structure of the payout phase under the CPF LIFE scheme. Figure 5.2a depicts the Plus Plan, in which the entire RA is annuitized, with the DDA at 65. As a deferred life annuity with payout at age 65, all the accumulated savings are annuitized. As this is a refundable plan, the bequest available will be the balance in the RA plus the unused annuity premium. The Income Plan also involves the full annuitization of the RA with the DDA at 65. However, it is non-refundable: no refund will be made to the buyer's

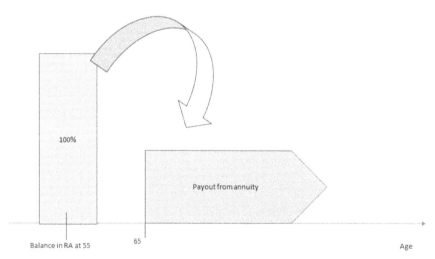

Figure 5.2 An illustration of the different CPF LIFE options, with varying degrees of annuitization

(a) Plus Plan: 100 percent risk pooling, DDA = 65

Source: Singapore, Central Provident Fund (CPF) Board. (2011). Cropped from CPF LIFE Booklet, downloaded from CPF website. http://mycpf.cpf.gov.sg/NR/rdonlyres/09EA0C05-C8E9-4705-9D91-E8BD1D12CF1E/0/LIFEBrochure.pdf

Note: CPF LIFE = Central Provident Fund Lifelong Income Scheme; DDA = drawdown age; RA = retirement account.

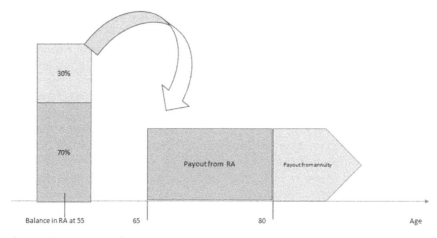

Figure 5.2 (Continued)

(b) Balanced Plan: 30 percent risk pooling, DDA = 80

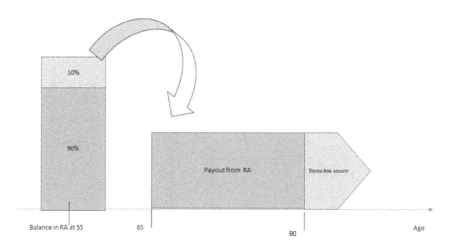

Figure 5.2 (Continued)

(c) Basic Plan: 10 percent risk pooling, DDA =90

beneficiaries upon the buyer's death even if the monthly payouts under the plan have not kicked in, i.e. if death occurs between age 55 and 65.

Figure 5.2b shows the default plan – the Balanced Plan. Under this plan, about 30 percent of the RA is annuitized, with the first annuity payout commencing at age 80. Beginning at age 65, members under the Balanced Plan will be drawing a monthly payout from their accumulated balance in the RA net of the annuity premium. The payout amount is structured so that this balance will be exhausted at age 80, and payouts from the CPF LIFE annuity will begin.

Under the Basic Plan, shown in Figure 5.2c, only 10 percent of the RA is used for pooling. The remaining 90 percent will be structured into monthly annuity payouts for the next 35 years, to age 90. Hence, the monthly payout is smaller. At age 90, the CPF LIFE annuity begins. However, if the member dies earlier than the DDA of 90, more will be left as a bequest.

Using the CPF LIFE payout estimator on the CPF website, we compute the monthly life annuity payouts for a future elderly person (currently age 53) for different levels of savings accumulated in the CPF RA. The monthly drawdowns under the various options are presented in Table 5.10. Given that the life expectancy of females is higher than for males, the monthly life annuity payouts for females are smaller than for males. The monthly payouts during the payout phase depend on the amount saved during the accumulation phase.

Under the managed spend-down or phased withdrawal under the MS scheme, CPF members are not insured against longevity risks. There is also no reduction in their accumulated savings in the RA, for both the principal and/or interest. Any unspent portion will be refunded to the member's beneficiaries. The CPF LIFE, in essence, has introduced an element of defined benefits funded by the interest on the annuity premiums paid by members in a DC system. There is thus efficiency gained from pooling of longevity risks. One concern of the CPF LIFE scheme is that the monthly payouts are not inflation indexed. Introducing an inflation-indexed payout will require a much higher annuity premium, which may not be affordable for most of the CPF members. Furthermore, unlike in a

Table 5.10 Monthly payouts of savings under different CPF LIFE options

	Male			Female		
	Plus	*Balanced*	*Basic*	*Plus*	*Balanced*	*Basic*
40,000	426	406	381	388	378	366
50,000	508	483	454	462	450	435
60,000	588	558	524	534	520	502
70,000	667	633	593	597	589	568
80000	746	708	663	676	658	634
90,000	826	782	733	747	727	701
100,000	905	857	803	818	797	767
110,000	984	931	872	889	866	833
120,000	1063	1006	942	960	935	900

Source: Monthly payouts are computed using the CPF LIFE Payout Estimator on the CPF website. www.cpf.gov.sg/cpf_trans/ssl/financial_model/lifecal/Life_Estimator.asp

Note: All amounts are in Singaporean dollars. The calculations include the LIFE bonus for eligible low income elderly living in four-room or smaller HDB flats with an assessed income of not more than $24,000 per year. CPF LIFE = Central Provident Fund Lifelong Income Scheme.

commercial life annuity scheme, the CPF Board sets the maximum amount that can be annuitized as the full MS in cash, which is currently at $123,000. The National Longevity Insurance Committee's (2008) view is that this scheme caters mainly to the average Singaporean and provides basic retirement income. As can be seen from Table 5.10, the annuity payout as a proportion of the last drawn income for higher income earners will likely be below the recommended replacement ratios, even if the RA is at the MS level. Members who wish to annuitize a larger sum may do so through the private annuity market.[16]

4. Mechanisms to enhance payments during the payout phase

We have seem that in a DC system how much can be de-accumulated during the payout phase depends on the amount accumulated during the work cycle. Moreover, in a system like Singapore's that permits pre-retirement withdrawals, CPF policy parameters that increase contribution rates and returns while reducing amounts withdrawn would increase the pot of money that can be annuitized during the payout phase. In the 2011 budget, the finance minister announced two changes that would enhance savings. First, the CPF salary ceiling would be raised from $4,500 to $5,000 per month. This will correspond to the 80th percentile of workers. The lifting of the ceiling will benefit workers with incomes above $4,500. Second, the employer's contribution rate would be raised by another 0.5 percent, from 15 percent to 15.5 percent. The additional 0.5 percent will go into the SA. Overall, it will restore the total contribution to the CPF to 36 percent. Plugging these changes into a simulation model, the present value of accumulated savings at age 55 will be higher for all income deciles.[17] However, as can be gleaned from Figure 5.3, the higher income deciles will benefit more than the lower income deciles. In this simulation model, we assume that a worker at age 25 enters the workforce with these revised changes.

Not only do CPF's policy parameters influence accumulation, but how much is accumulated by age 55 is affected by the starting wage and the wage growth rates of workers. Figure 5.4 demonstrates the impact of economic growth on accumulated

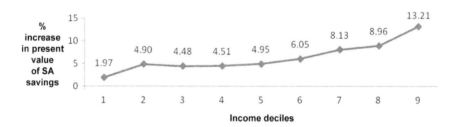

Figure 5.3 Impacts of Central Provident Fund changes on the present value of retirement savings in the special account (SA) for different income deciles

Source: Authors' computations.

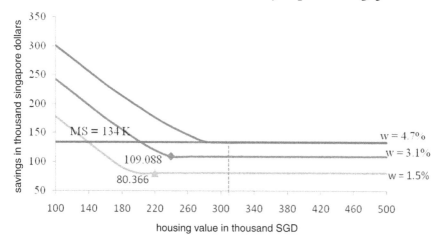

Figure 5.4 Sensitivity of the present value of savings to annual wage growth

Source: Authors' computations.

Note: MS = minimum sum; w = wage growth.

savings using the same calibrated model as in Chia and Tsui (2011). At an annual wage growth rate of 4.7 percent, an entrant worker who starts contributing to CPF at 25 years of age will have accumulated enough CPF savings to meet the targeted MS at age 55, regardless of his housing consumption. However, as illustrated in Figure 5.4, if the annual wage growth rate is slower, at 1.5 percent, the same individual will have to buy a property costing not more than $140,000 if he wants to reach the decreed MS.

Figure 5.5 shows that if he were to consume a more expensive HDB flat, the percentage deviation from the MS would widen from 17.6 percent to 40 percent. As he has withdrawn the entire available balance from the OA to finance housing, he has to use more cash to pay the monthly housing installments. The accumulated savings largely reflect the amount from the SA that cannot be withdrawn. At an annual wage growth of 1.5 percent, he will accumulate at least $80,000 in cash as the MS (figure is discounted to current dollars). This will be translated to an average of $706 per month (in present value). The de-accumulation from the CPF savings, together with incomes that can be unlocked from the accumulated asset, will provide an adequate retirement income.

4.1. Housing subsidies

Housing grants, which were first introduced in March 2006, area form of housing subsidy to make public housing more affordable. First-time buyers of HDB resale flats are entitled to a $30,000 housing grant. To encourage children to stay in the same neighborhood as their parents, if they buy a flat within two kilometers of their parents' flat, they are entitled to an additional $10,000 grant.

As part of its asset-based social security policies to make home ownership affordable for lower income households, households with incomes of less than

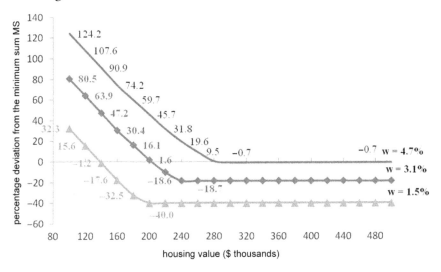

Figure 5.5 Wage growth and percentage deviation from the decreed minimum sum

Source: Authors' computations.

Note: w = wage growth.

$5,000 per month who are first-time home buyers are eligible for additional subsidy under the Additional CPF Housing Grant (AHG) scheme.[18] For these homebuyers, if they buy a new flat directly from the HDB, the AHG is an enhanced subsidy over and above the regular market subsidy they enjoy. If they buy a HDB resale flats in the secondary market, the AHG is over and above the basic CPF housing grant. The AHG ranges from $5,000 to $40,000 depending on the household monthly income. Households with a monthly income of $1,500 or less can receive $40,000 (see Table 5.11). Households with monthly incomes above $5,000 are not eligible for the AHG. The housing grant can be used only as a capital payment for the flat purchase, and the balance, if any, must be used to reduce the mortgage loan.

In the 2011 budget, the finance minister announced that the government was introducing a Special CPF Housing Grant (SHG) to help low income families. On top of the AHG, low income families with earned income of up to $2,250 per month would be entitled to an additional grant that could be used towards the purchase of a new HDB flat.[19]

Since details on the amount of the SHG had not yet been released at the time of writing, we made assumptions about the size of the housing grants and estimated the proportion of household incomes that would be released for other non-housing-related consumption.[20] An SHG of $10,000 and the existing AHG would enable low income households to increase their non-housing-related consumption by 13 percent. The proportion is increased to 15 percent if the SHG is $20,000. Figure 5.6 shows that with the existing AHG, a low income household buying a HDB flat valued at $180,000 would spend around a fifth of their

Table 5.11 Additional Central Provident Fund housing grant ($)

Average Gross Monthly Household Income	Enhanced Additional CPF Housing Grant
1,500 or less	40,000
1,501–2,000	35,000
2,001–2,500	30,000
2,501–3,000	25,000
3,001–3,500	20,000
3,501–4,000	15,000
4,001–4,500	10,000
4,501–5,000	5,000

Source: Singapore, Housing Development Board (HDB). (n.d.).

Note: The monthly income is assessed over the past one year. The grant amounts are as of February 2009.

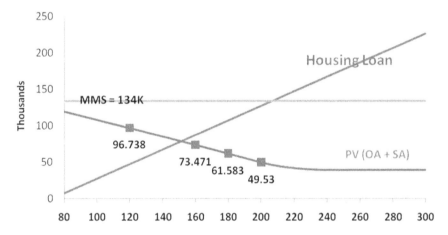

Figure 5.6 Effects of special Central Provident Fund housing grant on 2010 consumption

monthly income on housing mortgage payments and would have an accumulated savings of around $50,000 at age 55. With the additional SHG grant of $20,000, the monthly housing installment as a proportion of household income would be reduced to 17 percent. Furthermore, the present value of the accumulated savings in the OA and SA at age 55 would increase from $61,000 to $73,000 (see Figure 5.6). When this is annuitized during the payout phase using CPF LIFE, if we take the average monthly payment from the three refundable plans, the expected monthly payouts will be raised by 12 percent. The housing subsidy thus enhances retirement adequacy and reduces the gap between the accumulated savings and the decreed MS.

Supporting data for Figure 5.6

HDB	80	92	100	120	140	160	180	200	210	220	230	240	260	300
Mortgage payment (monthly)	31	85	121	212	303	393	484	575	620	666	711	756	847	1026
Mortgage payment as% of income	1.3	3.7	5.3	9.2	13.2	17.1	21.1	25	27	29	30.9	32.9	36.8	44.6

Source: Authors' computations.

Note: MMS = Medisave Minimum Sum; OA = ordinary account; PV = present value; SA = special account. The row of figures under the HDB represents the price of HDB flat in thousand dollars. The row representing mortgage payment represents monthly payout in Singapore dollars.

5. Conclusion

Singapore's experience of a DC social security arrangement has ensured individual equity, as benefits are directly linked to contributions. Both the CPF policy parameters and individuals' earning profiles and the macroeconomic environment will affect the accumulation. Unlike other DC systems, the feature of pre-retirement withdrawals to finance housing has direct implications for accumulated savings and asset-building. The Singaporean system is thus an asset-based social security system, with housing policy being interwoven with retirement policy. At the time of retirement, most Singaporeans would have accumulated housing as their major financial asset. The government has put in place monetization instruments to help Singaporeans convert some of the housing equity to support retirement. In evaluating the adequacy of CPF to provide for retirement, we have to include housing wealth as part of the retirement wealth. How housing equity can be monetized is an important consideration for the payout phase in such a DC system.

A DB system gives benefit payouts till the death of the recipients and thus protects against longevity risk. The DC system without annuitization does not have such protection. This was one of the major criticisms of the CPF system. In 2007 the government proposed to introduce longevity insurance – an advanced life deferred annuity funded from the CPF savings, with risk pooling among members. The initial proposal was not well accepted, and after much fine-tuning, a new product called CPF LIFE was hatched. In 2009 the CPF Board implemented a mandatory national annuity scheme to annuitize accumulated savings into a stream of retirement income under the CPF LIFE scheme. It offers a better way of de-accumulating retirement savings than the old MS scheme. CPF LIFE pools longevity risk among all annuitants. Those who die younger will leave the interest accumulated from their annuity premium to be shared among those who survive longer. It provides lifetime benefits with fixed monthly payouts (though it is not inflation indexed). The benefit is structured to match the payouts under the spend-down MS scheme to ensure that the monthly payouts do not fall as the elderly transition to the lifetime benefit phase. The design and structure of CPF LIFE complements the DC system to enhance retirement adequacy.

Finally, this chapter has demonstrated that policies affecting housing consumption have impacts on how much can be unlocked from housing equity upon retirement and how much can be accumulated in the CPF. There is a tradeoff between current and future consumption. A larger housing subsidy through the CPF SHG scheme not only has made housing more affordable but will also enhance retirement.

Notes

1 ERIA Working Group, Second Workshop Social Protection in East Asia – Current State and Challenges.
2 See Palacios and Pallares-Miralles (2000) for countries with alternative pillars.

3 See Antolin (2008) for a detailed discussion of the payout phase of pensions, annuities and financial markets.

4 For institutional details on the CPF, see Chia and Tsui (2003).

5 Indeed, given the intrinsic link between the CPF Board and the HDB, the monthly mortgage payment is remitted directly from the member's CPF account to the HDB.

6 Direct interventions include grants, subsidized government loans and mortgage financing loans to the HDB Board. Home buyers also enjoy direct housing subsidies such as discounted market flat prices and housing grants. These are part of the social protection policies to ensure affordable housing for Singaporeans and consequently lead to an asset-based social security. For more detailed discussion see Chia (2010).

7 HDB (2010b, p.152).

8 See HDB (2010b, p. 157).

9 One year into its implementation, HDB had received only 552 applications, of which 229 had been approved, 166 were being processed and the remaining 157 were ineligible (Singapore, My Paper, 20 May 2010).

10 From 1 January 2010, RA savings are invested in SSGS which earn a fixed coupon equal to the 12-month average yield of the 10 YSGS plus 1 percentage point at the point of issuance. The interest rate to be credited to the RA will be the weighted average interest of the entire portfolio of these SSGS, and adjusted yearly in January. The 12-month average yield of the 10 YSGS plus 1 percent works out to be 3.52 percent for the period 1 September 2009 to 31 August 2010. The current RA interest rate is at 4 percent p.a. (Singapore, *Government Monitor*, 2010).

11 The LIFE scheme is mandatory for CPF members born after 1957 who have at least $40,000 in their retirement account but is optional for members born before 1957.

12 The government appointed the National Longevity Insurance Committee to seek views from the wider public and to conduct public consultations. The committee concluded from its consultations that Singaporeans wanted a lifelong income scheme that is fair and affordable, provides a steady income for life and offers a bequest option. Although there were private sector parties who have expressed interest in offering the lifelong income product, the committee recommended that the CPF Board administers the lifelong income scheme.

13 Initially, there were 12 plans in CPF LIFE, but this was reduced to 4 plans after feedback from the public that they were confused over the many options.

14 The CPF website provides a CPF withdrawal calculator for members to calculate the cash balances they can withdraw after satisfying the CPF and Medisave MS requirements.

15 The withdrawal age has been raised to 65 for those who turned 55 in 2009.

16 Fong (2002) conjectures that the CPF institutional setting in Singapore should provide insurers with a large market for annuities; the money's worth of annuities is higher than for annuities sold in other developed countries. However, the private annuity market has remained thin. In 2006 only 8.8 percent of those turning 55 years old used the accumulated savings in the CPF to buy a private annuity.

17 This simulation model was constructed for a research project with the Risk Management Institute, Singapore. See Chia and Tsui (2011) for details on the calibration of this model. The model also incorporates the housing consumption choice of households in different income deciles.

18 The median monthly household income from work is $5,398 per month in 2009, compared to $4,495 in 2006. See DOS (2010, p.4).

19 See Singapore's *Budget Statement 2011*, delivered by the minister for finance, Mr. Tharman Shanmugaratnam, on 18 February 2011 (Singapore, Ministry of Finance, 2011).

20 The amount of SHG has subsequently been officially announced as S$ 20,000. For more information, please see www.hdb.gov.sg/fi10/fi10321p.nsf/w/BuyingNew FlatAdditionalCPFHousingGrant?OpenDocument#GrantAmt

References

Antolin, P. (2008). Aging and the payout phase of pensions, annuities and financial markets. *OECD Working Papers on Insurance and Private Pensions*, No. 29. Paris: OECD.

Central Provident Fund, Government of Singapore. (2009). *CPF Annual Report.* http://mycpf.cpf.gov.sg/CPF/About-Us/Ann-Rpt/AnnualReport_PDF_2009.htm

Central Provident Fund, Government of Singapore. (2012). *CPF Annual Report.* http://mycpf.cpf.gov.sg/CPF/About-Us/Ann-Rpt/AnnualReport_PDF_2012.htm

Central Provident Fund, Government of Singapore. (n.d.). http://mycpf.cpf.gov.sg/NR/rdonlyres/BA17D1C5-2C82-4DD4-B7C3-4C036A942BE5/0/CPFISProfitandLossReport.pdf

Chia N.C. (2010). Social protection in Singapore: Targeted welfare and asset-based social security, in M.G. Asher, S. Oum and F. Parulian (ed). *Social protection in East Asia – Current state and challenges.* Jakarta: Economic Research Institute for ASEAN.

Chia N.C., P. Fei, and A. Tsui. (2011). *Enhancing retirement savings through the central provident fund investment scheme.* Manuscript in progress.

Chia N.C. and A. Tsui. (2003). Life annuities of compulsory savings and income adequacy of the elderly in Singapore. *Journal of Pension Economics and Finance*, March, 41–65.

Chia N.C. and A. Tsui. (2009). Monetizing housing equity to generate retirement incomes. *SCAPE Working Paper*, No. 2009/01. National University of Singapore, Economics Department. Singapore: Singapore Center for Applied Policy and Economics.

Chia N.C. and A. Tsui. (2011). *Accumulation of retirement savings through the CPF savings scheme.* Research report to be submitted to National University of Singapore: Risk Management Institute, mimeo.

Department of Statistics (DOS). (2010). Key Household Characteristics and Household Income Trends. Singapore: Department of Statistics.

Fong, W.M. (2002). On the cost of adverse selection in individual annuity markets: Evidence from Singapore. *Journal of Risk and Insurance*, 69(2), 193–207.

Milevsky, M. (2005). Real longevity insurance with a deductible: Introduction to advanced-life delayed annuities (ALDA). *North American Actuarial Journal*, 9(4), 109–122.

Palacios, R. and M. Pallares-Miralles. (2000). *International patterns of pension provision.* Washington, D.C.: World Bank.

Poterba, J., Rauh, J., Veni, S., Wise, D. (2007). Defined contribution plans, defined benefit plans, and the accumulation of retirement wealth. *Journal of Public Economics*, 91(10), 2062–2086.

Schich, S. (2008). Challenges for financial intermediaries offering decumulation products. *OECD Working Papers on Insurance and Private Pensions*, No. 29. Paris: OECD.

Scott, J.S., J.G. Watson, and W. Hu. (2006). *Annuitization with delayed payout annuities.* http://ssrn.com/abstract=932145

Singapore, Central Provident Fund (CPF) Board. (2011). *Understanding your CPF LIFE plan.* Singapore: Central Provident Fund Board.

Singapore, Central Provident Fund Board (2009). *Annual report.* Various years. http://mycpf.cpf.gov.sg/CPF/About-Us/Ann-Rpt/Ann_Report

Singapore Department of Statistics. (2008). *Yearbook of statistics.* Singapore: SNP.

Singapore, *Government Monitor.* (2010). Singapore extends 4 percent floor rate for all SMRA monies. 20 September. www.thegovmonitor.com

Singapore, Housing Development Board (HDB). (n.d.). *Annual report.* Various years. SNP. www.hdb.gov.sg/fi10/fi10320p.nsf/w/AboutUsAnnualReports?OpenDocument

Singapore, Housing Development Board (HDB). (2005). *Public housing in Singapore: Residents' profile and physical aspects.* Singapore: SNP.

Singapore, Housing Development Board (HDB). (2010a). *Public housing in Singapore: Residents' profile, housing, satisfaction and preferences.* [HDB Sample Household Survey 2008.] March. Housing Development Board, Research and Planning Department. Singapore: SNP.

Singapore, Housing Development Board (HDB). (2010b). Public housing in Singapore: Well-being of communities, families and the elderly. *HDB Sample Household Survey 2008.* March. Housing Development Board, Research and Planning Department. Singapore: SNP.

Singapore, Ministry of Community Development, Youth and Sports. (2005). *The national survey of senior citizens in Singapore 2005.* www.mcys.gov.sg/MCDSFiles/Resource/Materials/NSSC%202005.pdf

Singapore, Ministry of Finance. (2011). *Budget statement 2011.* 18 February. Singapore, Author.

Singapore, National Longevity Insurance Committee. (2008). *Report by the National Longevity Insurance Committee.* Singapore: Ministry of Manpower. http://mycpf.cpf.gov.sg/Members/Gen-Info/CPF_LIFE/NLIC.htm

Tan, L. (2011). CPFIS tightening = Steadier returns. *Straits Times,* 9 January.

Thomsen, J. and J.V. Andersen. (2007). Longevity bonds – a financial market instrument to manage longevity risk. *Denmark National Bank Monetary Review,* 4th Quarter, n.p.

Visco, I. (2007). Longevity risk and financial markets. In M. Balling, E. Gnan and F. Lierman (eds), "Money, Finance and Demography: The Consequences of Ageing"; SUERF: Vienna, 2007, 9–30.

6 Civil service pension arrangements in India, the Philippines, and Thailand

An assessment

Mukul G. Asher and Friska Parulian

1. Introduction

There has been increasing anxiety among policymakers, members of pension organizations, and other stakeholders about the credibility and sustainability of pension promises globally, including in many low- and middle-income Asian countries (Asher, 2010a). In the aftermath of the 2008 global crisis, the notion of sovereign default risk is no longer unthinkable. As fiscal stringency becomes the norm in most countries, the fiscal costs of civil service pensions and equity aspects (particularly differences between private and public sector pension benefits and risk mitigation) are receiving greater attention. Among the high-income countries, these concerns are exemplified by the Hutton Commission's report on civil service pensions in the United Kingdom (Independent Public Service Pensions Commission, 2011)[1] and reforms of public sector pension arrangements in high-income countries (*The Economist*, 2011a).

Traditional civil service pensions have been of the defined benefit type, in which the benefits to be paid are defined. In many countries, particularly in Asia, civil servants either are not required to contribute to their pensions or contribute a relatively small share of the total costs.

There has been little pressure on these pension schemes, once designed, to be subjected to parametric or systemic reforms. While the fiscal stringency arising from the 2008 global financial crisis is forcing high-income countries to re-examine civil service pension arrangements, in low- and middle-income countries, there has been relatively less urgency in reforming civil service pension systems.

There is, however, a need to re-examine civil service pension schemes in these countries as well. It is in the above context that this chapter analyzes civil service pensions arrangements in three middle-income Asian countries: India, the Philippines, and Thailand. The premise of the chapter is that parametric and systemic reforms of civil service pensions could help allocate total national resources devoted to the elderly more equitably and efficiently. Both inter-generational and intra-generational equity issues are relevant.

This chapter is structured as follows. In Section 2 a brief overview of the demographic trends and fiscal indicators for the three countries is provided. This is followed by an analysis of the current civil service pension arrangements in the three countries. It also contains suggestions for reforming the current systems in these countries. The final section provides the concluding observations.

2. Demographic trends and fiscal indicators

This section provides a brief overview of demographic trends and fiscal indicators in the three countries. Ideally, these are the demographic trends relating to civil servants in each country. There is evidence that civil servants as a group usually have a longer life expectancy then the population average. However, as such data is not available for the three countries, demographic trends using population averages are provided (Tables 6.1a and 6.1b).

The following observations may be made from the data in Tables 6.1a and 6.1b.

a) The three countries are expected to exhibit more rapid aging than the global average between 2005 and 2050. Thus, for the world, the proportion of persons over 60 years of age will be 2.1 times higher in 2050 than in 2005, but the corresponding figures for India (2.6 times), the Philippines (3.0 times), and Thailand (2.6 times) are higher.

b) The number of elderly will increase from 90 million in 2005 to 330 billion in 2050 in India, from 5 to 25 million in the Philippines, and from 7 to 20 million in Thailand.

To the extent that civil servants live longer, the burden implied by their pension (and health care) benefits will be even higher than implied by the population averages. In all three countries, there is a need to construct more comprehensive, timely, and disaggregated databases for civil servants and their compensation structures, including pensions.

2.1 Fiscal indicators

In 2011 the ratio of the public debt to the gross domestic product (GDP) was 55.5 percent in India, 55.4 percent in the Philippines, and 49.2 percent in Thailand (*The Economist*, 2011b). These levels, while not alarming, do suggests that the three countries have only modest fiscal space for expanding government expenditure, including civil service pensions.

In 2010 the fiscal deficit as a percentage of the GDP was 6.7 percent in India, 3.9 percent in the Philippines, and 3.8 percent in Thailand (Asian Development Bank, 2010). The fiscal deficit in India is on the high side, suggesting very limited fiscal space. The national average may, however, hide the fact that for several fiscally weak provinces, meeting future pension liabilities arising from the promises already made would be a challenge.

Table 6.1a Selected demographic trends in India, the Philippines, and Thailand

Country/area	Total population (million)		Average annual rate of change in population (%)		Total fertility rate		Median ages (years)		Life expectancy at birth (years)	
	2007	2050	2005–2010	2045–2050	2005–2010	2045–2050	2005–2010	2045–2050	2005–2010	2045–2050
World	6,671.2	9,191.3	1.17	0.36	2.6	2.0	28.0	38.1	67.2	75.4
India	1,103.4	1,592.7	1.55	0.30	3.0	1.8	24.3	38.7	63.1	75.9
Philippines	87.9	140.5	1.90	0.50	3.2	1.8	21.8	36.3	71.7	78.7
Thailand	63.9	67.4	0.66	−0.27	1.8	1.8	32.6	44.3	70.6	78.1

Source: United.

Table 6.1b Selected demographic trends in India, the Philippines, and Thailand

Country/area	Life expectancy at age 60, 2000–2005		Percentage of total population aged 60 and above		Population aged 60 and above (millions)	
	Male	Female	2005	2050	2005	2050
World	n/a	n/a	10.3	21.8	672.8	2005.7
India	17	19	8.0	21.0	89.9	329.6
Philippines	17	19	6.0	18.2	5.1	25.5
Thailand	17	22	11.3	29.8	7.1	20.1

Source: United.

3. Civil service pension arrangements

This section analyzes the civil service pension arrangements in India, the Philippines, and Thailand.

3.1. India

The structure of retirement schemes for the estimated 22 million civil servants at the central, state, and local government levels is broadly similar. The civil servants constitute 4.4 percent of the labor force but nearly one-third of those in the formal organized sector to which traditional social security schemes are applicable.

Civil servants are provided with three types of retirement benefits. They receive a non-contributory, unfunded, defined benefit pension, which is indexed for prices and has fairly generous commutation provisions and survivors' benefits. The benefits for the central government employees are computed at around 1/60 or 1.7% of wages for each year of service subject to a benefit rate cap at 50 percent. The pension benefits are roughly half the wages in the last 10 months of employment.

Commutation provisions permit a civil servant to take up to 40 percent of the pension benefits as a lump sum (without paying income tax) at the time of retirement. There are also survivor's benefits, usually around 30 percent of full pension benefits.

In addition, each employee is mandated to contribute a percentage of his/her salary to a Government Provident Fund (GPF) scheme. Finally, civil servants also receive a lump-sum gratuity benefit based on their period of service and the salary level, with a maximum ceiling of INR 1 million.

In principle, each state has the freedom to design pension plans for its civil servants. In practice, states usually adopt the pension schemes followed by the central government with relatively minor modifications. As a result, states with different fiscal capacities end up having similar pension schemes, a practice that severely affects the ability of the poorer states to meet their wage and pension liabilities and still leave enough resources for meeting social and infrastructural needs.

Over the years, many implementing rules and regulations concerning commutation (that is, the proportion of the total pension value that can be taken as a lump sum), family pension benefits, etc. have been introduced on an ad hoc basis. Substantial efficiency, equity, and cost savings are possible through parametric reforms in the existing civil service pension schemes. Such reforms involve altering the parameters of the existing pension scheme, such as the commutation formula, indexation method, eligibility criteria for family pension, etc. These reforms can help as over the years many ad hoc provisions have been added, whose rationale may need re-examination. Thus, as the provident fund, gratuity, and leave encashment allowance are all provided in a lump sum at retirement, the rationale for commutation as a method to provide for a lump sum of cash has become extremely weak.

The fiscal costs of the civil service pension schemes are high. The civil servants constitute 4.4 percent of the labor force, but their retirement benefits are already equivalent to nearly 2 percent of GDP. There is also a high level of longevity and inflation risk protection as the benefits are indexed to prices and to wages.

Every 10 years there is a provision for the Pay Commission to review civil service salaries. This review also includes adjustments to the pensions of those who have already retired in line with salary revisions. Thus, many Indian civil servants end up receiving pensions that are several times their last drawn salary, adding to fiscal costs. Such costs are particularly challenging for fiscally weak states. These arrangements underscore the strong dualism between the pension arrangements for civil servants on the one hand and for the rest of the population on the other.

In addition to fiscal costs, there are also governance and transparency issues that need to be addressed. The civil servants are the beneficiaries of the schemes, but they also are the key actors in formulating and implementing the civil service pensions. There is no independent regulator that oversees these schemes. This is contrary to good governance practices.

3.1.1. New Pension Scheme

To reform its civil service pension system, the Government of India introduced in January 2004 the New Pension Scheme (NPS) – a defined contribution scheme with distinct mandatory and voluntary components. The NPS architecture consists of Central Recordkeeping Agency (CRA), auctioning of investment mandates, and points of presence, which act as distribution and collection agents.

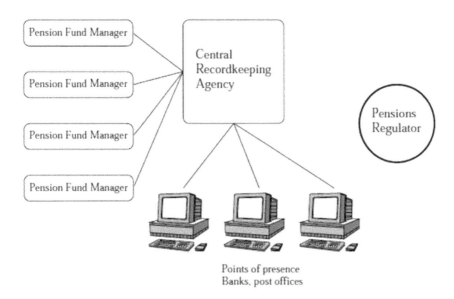

Figure 6.1 An illustration of the New Pension Scheme architecture
Source: Sane and Shah (2011).

The design and architecture of the NPS are much more in tune with international pension best practices.

The mandatory component was made fully operational from 1 April 2008. Mandatory membership covers those central government employees (except armed forces personnel) who commenced employment on or after 1 January 2004. The total contribution rate for the mandatory NPS is 20 percent of monthly earnings, split equally among the employee and the government (as the employer). Members have a limited choice of investments, with life cycle funds as a default choice. Under the mandatory NPS, the pension is paid at age 60, and pre-retirement withdrawals are not permitted. By 2011, all except three states/union territories in India had introduced NPS-type schemes. An estimated 1.1 million government employees out of the current 22 million have become members of the mandatory NPS (Table 6.2).

The voluntary component of the NPS is open to all citizens between the ages of 18 and 55. It became operational on 1 May 2009. A minimum annual contribution of INR 6,000 is required. The voluntary NPS has limited pre-retirement withdrawal provisions and flexible contributions. The 2010 budget has introduced an initiative called Swavalamban for low-income individuals, under which the central government would contribute INR 1,000 per year to each voluntary NPS account opened in financial year 2010–2011. This applies only to those accounts where the minimum annual contribution is INR 1,000 and the maximum is INR 12,000. This scheme will be available for five years.

Over 0.4 million have joined the Swavalamban Scheme (as of January 2011). The 2011–2012 budget relaxed the exit norms. Its members can exit at the age of 50 years instead of 60 years, or after a minimum tenure of 20 years, whichever is later. In view of rising longevity, this relaxation is unwarranted. The 2011–2012 budget estimated that total membership will be 2.0 million by March 2012. In the 2011 budget speech, the Finance Minister announced that the Pension Funds Regulation and Development Authority (PFRDA) Bill would be introduced in Parliament that year. Parliament, however, passed the PFRDA Bill in September 2013.

Table 6.2 New Pension Scheme membership as of January 2011

Member type	Number	% of total
Central government	670,843	60.7
Central gov. autonomous bodies	11,621	1.1
State governments	404,677	36.6
Outside of government	18,367	1.7
Total	1,105,508	100.0

Source: Pension Funds Regulation and Development Authority
PFRDA (2012), Annual Report. http://pfrda.org.in//MyAuth/
Admin/showimg.cshtml?ID=50

The NPS offers well-considered investment choices, including a default option that automatically reduces the risk levels of asset class exposure with age. The equity exposure in all cases is only through indexed funds. The investment management is auctioned to the lowest bidders. In the latest round, the lowest bid by asset fund managers was only nine basis points, or INR 9 for every INR 100,000 worth of assets under management. This is much lower than the average cost of a mutual fund, which is 2 percent (INR 2,000 per year per INR 100,000) and 1.5 percent (INR 1,500) for a standard unit-linked insurance plan (Halan, 2009). The Initial membership cost and operating cost of the NPS are also relatively low (Table 6.3).

The EEE (Exempt contributions, Exempt investment income, Exempt withdrawals at retirement) tax treatment proposed for the NPS in the Discussion Paper of the Direct Taxes Code (Prakash 2013) will level the playing field and allow the NPS to compete with other tax-advantaged retirement income instruments in India. The following three refinements to the well-designed NPS scheme and its architecture merit serious consideration.

Table 6.3 NPS costs, 2010

Head	Service charge
Central Recordkeeping Agency	
Account opening	INR 50
Annual maintenance	INR 280
Charge per transaction	INR 6
Points of Presence	
Initial subscriber registration and contribution upload	INR 40
Any subsequent transaction	INR 20
Trustee bank	
Transaction from a RBI location	INR 0
Transaction from a non-RBI location	INR 15
Custodian	
Asset servicing charges	0.0075% p.a. for electronic segment
	0.0500% p.a. for physical segment
Pension Fund Management	
Investment management fee	0.0009% p.a.

Source: Sane and Shah (2011).

Note: RBI = Reserve Bank of India , which is India's Central Bank, p.a. = per annum

Reconsideration of the Mandatory Annuity Requirement: The current design of both the mandatory and the voluntary NPS mandates that at age 60 a member can withdraw 60 percent of the accumulated balances as a lump sum, but at least 40 percent must be annuitized. It appears that this design feature was incorporated without detailed consideration of its appropriateness for the Indian context.

There is merit in exploring various phased withdrawal program options.[2] Under such a program, a member retains the annuity component (40 percent) of the accumulated balance in a special interest-bearing account or invests it in a senior-citizen bond. This arrangement does not require an individual to join an insurance pool but retains the balances under his or her own name. Unlike annuities, balances remaining under such a program can be inherited by the designated nominees when a person dies.

Under the phased withdrawal, there is no insurance pool, so the member retains the ownership of balances, and therefore nominees benefit in the event of the member's death. The PFRDA should encourage research and policy dialogue on phased withdrawal options appropriate for the NPS. For India, the phased withdrawal option may represent a workable compromise between a lump-sum withdrawal and a life annuity.[3]This can also benefit micro-pension and occupational pension plans as they could adapt phased withdrawal plans to suit their requirements and context. The design of the plans should be kept simple, and only limited options should be permitted.

Both empirical and theoretical research in this area also need to be encouraged. The PFRDA, in coordination with the Insurance Regulatory and Development Authority, should have a well-designed, user-friendly, and up-to-date website to provide information on annuities. Any annuity requirement would, however, require strong prudential regulation of insurance companies.

Flexible Age of Exit from the NPS: There is a strong case for making the age of exit from the NPS more flexible. Thus, a member could choose to partially withdraw the accumulated balances as a lump sum (60 percent), purchase a mandatory annuity, and, as proposed above, invest in a phased withdrawal plan at any time between the ages of 60 and 70.

This would have several advantages. First, it would permit individuals to enter the NPS even between the ages of 55 and 60 and still have sufficient time to accumulate retirement funds. Second, it would provide flexibility to individuals to choose the macroeconomic conditions, particularly the interest rate conditions, under which to purchase annuities and participate in the proposed phased withdrawal program. For greater flexibility the withdrawal of a lump sum and the purchase of an annuity (and phased withdrawal program) could be separated in time. Thus, a person could withdraw a lump sum at age 60 but purchase the annuity anytime between 60 and 70 years of age. Third, flexibility in timing of annuity purchases would better enable suppliers of annuities and bonds, such as life insurance companies, to match their assets and liabilities and would help manage uncertainties in longevity trends. Last, as individuals continue to engage in paid economic activities even after formal retirement,[4] such flexibility in the age of exit would enable them to better achieve life-time consumption smoothing.

Communication and Financial Literacy Initiatives: A voluntary pension scheme does not attract large numbers, even if tax, regulatory, and other measures are favorable. For the voluntary NPS to become more widely accepted, it will need to be popularized as a concept through the help of a variety of groups, such as the cooperative societies, trade unions, non-governmental organizations, and others. India's decentralized society is well suited for such partnerships.

a)   The NPS architecture is well suited for realizing economies of scale (as suggested by the negative relationship between membership size and fees) and economies of scope (as suggested by the use of its architecture for the voluntary NPS available to all citizens). Given the need to economize on the scarce expertise in negotiating Central Recordkeeping Agency contracts and auctioning of investment mandates, the states and other public sector organizations should be encouraged to use the NPS architecture.

b)   It is also essential that the relatively low life-time administrative costs of the current NPS arrangements be sustained, and in particular that distribution costs be minimized.

The current civil service pensions at all levels of government require parametric, administrative and record-keeping, and governance reforms. Civil servants are beneficiaries of pension schemes as well as being formulators and implementers of the schemes. This is against good governance principles, and, predictably, the transparency and accountability of civil service schemes have been low. Many current practices, such as overly generous commutation benefits based on outdated morbidity and mortality data, linking of pensions with wage revisions for current government employees, etc., reflect the above arrangements.

The government's cash accounting system does not permit the recording of accrued pension (and health care) liabilities. In the private sector, accounting regulations already require companies to reflect such accrued liabilities in their profit and loss statements and in their balance sheets. Listed government enterprises will need to follow such practices. Moreover, for purposes of proper accounting, all government and quasi-governmental organizations must recognize such liabilities and clearly specify their plans for meeting them.

Currently, even the GPF and gratuity contributions are not accumulated in separate funds; instead, they are paid from current revenues. This practice must be changed, and sinking funds arrangements must be instituted to meet future liabilities in an orderly manner. The current arrangements unduly encourage soft budget constraints at all levels of government. The fiscal capacities of states vary greatly – those with weak fiscal positions and those disinclined to undertake fiscal reforms will find it particularly challenging to meet their pension and other liabilities. If they do meet these liabilities, the opportunity costs, in terms of limited fiscal flexibility and lower growth, will be high.

3.3. The Philippines

3.3.1. Introduction of the Philippines government service

The Philippines bureaucracy had an estimated total of 1,312,508 government employees in the second quarter of 2010. This figure is 1,030 lower than the number of government personnel in year 2008, and 163,191 lower than the number of government personnel in year 2004, which means an 11 percent decrease in government personnel between 2004 and 2010.

The Philippines government personnel can be classified into three major subdivisions: the National Government Agencies (NGAs), the Local Government Units (LGUs), and the Government Owned and Controlled Corporations (GOCCs). In 2010, employees in the NGAs (including state universities and colleges [SUCs]) comprised 63.6 percent, or 834,327 personnel, while the GOCCs had a total of 94,759 personnel, or 7.2 percent. The total personnel complement in the LGUs reached 383,422, or 29.2 percent.

3.3.2. The geographical distribution and major subdivisions of the Philippines government service employees

The latest data available on the geographical distribution of the Philippines bureaucracy is for the year 2008. The National Capital Region (NCR) has the biggest number at 506,103, or 38.5 percent of the total workforce, followed by Regions 3 and 4 with 104,354 (7.9 percent) and 100,758 (7.7 percent) employees respectively. In contrast, the smallest government workforces were recorded in Caraga (23,186) and Region 2 (23,258).

3.3.3. Categories of service and levels of position

The Philippines government personnel have two categories of service: the career service and the non-career service government officers. The career service is further classified into four categories based on the level of position: first level, second level, executive/managerial (third level), and non-executive career officers. According to the 2008 inventory of government file, the career service accounted for 88 percent of the total personnel, while the non-career service accounted for 12 percent (Figure 6.2).

As of the first quarter of 2010, career personnel totaled 1.15 million, of which the first level made up 30.3 percent, the second level 67.4 percent, and the third level 1.1 percent, while non-executive career personnel accounted for 1.2 percent (Figure 6.3).

The non-career personnel are categorized into five types: the coterminous staff, casual staff, contractual staff, elective officials, and non-career executives. Of the 161,350 non-career personnel, 12.2 percent are coterminous staff, and 60.8 percent are casual employees, while 13.2 percent are contractual personnel. Elective officials total 12.8 percent, while non-career executives reached 1 percent of the total number of non-career personnel (Figure 6.4).

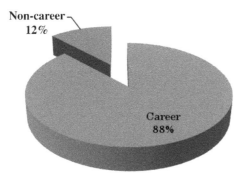

Figure 6.2 Distribution of Philippine government officials

Source: Civil Services Commission, Government of Philippines (2010)

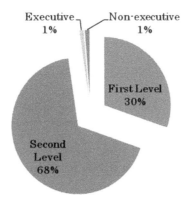

Figure 6.3 Career service government officers by position (quarter 1:2010)

Source: Civil Services Commission, Government of Philippines (2010)

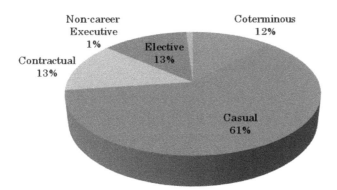

Figure 6.4 Non-career service government officers by position (quarter 1:2010)

Source: Civil Services Commission, Government of Philippines (2010)

3.3.4. Classification by gender

By the end of 2008, the total number of male government personnel was almost equal to the number of female employees (Figure 6.5). Male employees dominate the NCR with a total figure of 295,190, while the total number of female employees in the same region is 206,169. In contrast, female employees dominate Region 4 with 60,116 compared to a total of only 39,861 male employees.

There is a greater number of females than males in the career service: 583,045 females compared to 531,040 males (Figure 6.6). The non-career service,

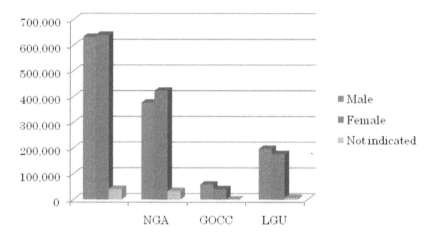

Figure 6.5 Number of government personnel by sex and subdivision

Source: Civil Services Commission, Government of Philippines (2010)

Note: GOCC = Government Owned and Controlled Corporations; LGU = Local Government Units; NGAs = National Government Agencies.

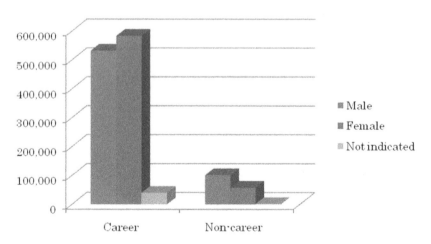

Figure 6.6 Number of government personnel by sex and category of services

Source: Civil Services Commission, Government of Philippines (2010)

however, is dominated by males with 101,084 and only 57,259 females. This data shows that females prefer jobs that provide better opportunities and ensure security of tenure.

3.3.5. *The Philippines Government Service Insurance System (GSIS)*

Introduction of the GSIS: The Philippines GSIS was created by Commonwealth Act No. 186,whichwas passed on 14 November 1936, and was later amended under Republic Act No. 8291, dated 24 June 1997. The GSIS, as designed in its charter, is a social insurance institution under a defined benefit scheme. It insures its members against the occurrence of certain contingencies in exchange for their monthly premium contributions.

The social security benefits available for all GSIS members are compulsory life insurance, optional life insurance, retirement benefits, disability benefits for work-related contingencies, and death benefits. In addition, the GSIS is entrusted with the administration of the General Insurance Fund by virtue of Republic Act (RA) 656 of the Property Insurance Law. It provides insurance coverage for assets and properties that have government insurable interests.

The GSIS covers all government workers irrespective of their employment status, except for members of the Judiciary and Constitutional Commissions, who are covered by separated retirement laws; contractual employees who have no employee–employer relationship with their agencies; and uniformed members of the Armed Forces of the Philippines and the Philippine National Police, including the Bureau of Jail Management and Penology and the Bureau of Fire Protection.

Benefits and Services: The principal benefits package of the GSIS consists of compulsory and optional life insurance, retirement, separation, and employee's compensation benefits. Active GSIS members are entitled to the following loan privileges: salary, policy, emergency, and housing loans, subject to the cross-default policy of the Claims and Loans Interdependent Policy (CLIP) system.

Retirement Benefits: The retirement benefits of government employees depend on the mode of retirement chosen. Although the compulsory retirement age from government service is 65, a government employee may apply for any of the following four retirement modes as soon as he/she meets the corresponding eligibility criteria, which include length of service, age, and date of entry into the service. The value of the benefit, for each type of benefit, is anchored on the basic monthly pension (BMP), which is computed as follows:

- 37.5 percent of the average monthly basic compensation in the last three years;
- plus 2.5 percent of the AMC in the last three years for each year of service in excess of 15 years.

However, in no case shall the BMP exceed 90 percent of the AMC.

A member who retires from the service is entitled to retirement benefits if:

a) he/she has rendered at least 15 years of service;
b) he/she is at least 60 years of age at the time of retirement; and
c) he/she is not receiving a monthly pension because of permanent total disability.

Retirement from government service is compulsory at age 65. The retirement benefit is equal to either

- a lump-sum payment equivalent to 60 months of the BMP payable at the time of retirement *plus* an old-age pension benefit equal to the BMP payable monthly for life starting upon the expiration of the five-year guaranteed period covered by the lump sum; or
- a cash payment equivalent to 18 months of the BMP *plus* a monthly pension for life payable immediately equivalent to the BMP.

Survivorship Benefits: Beneficiaries of a member or pensioner who was in the service or had rendered at least three years of service at the time of his/her death (RA 8291, Sec. 20–22) are eligible for survivorship benefits. The benefits include the following:

a) A survivorship pension that consists of the basic survivorship pension, which is 50 percent of the BMP payable to the spouse for life or until he/she remarries, and a dependent children's pension not exceeding 50 percent of the BMP, to be paid until the age of majority, marriage, employment, or death of the child;
b) A survivorship pension plus a cash payment equivalent to 100 percent of his/her Average Monthly Compensation (AMC) for every year of service if the deceased was in the service at the time of his/her death with at least three years of service;
c) A cash payment equivalent to 100 percent of the employee's AMC for each year of service but not less than PHP 12,000. RA 8291 also provides for a funeral benefit of at least PHP 12,000 (RA 8291, Sec. 23). The amount was increased to PHP 20,000 as of January 2000.

Disability Benefits: Members who suffer disability for reasons other than any of the following conditions, namely, grave misconduct, notorious negligence, habitual intoxication, or willful intention to kill oneself or another, and who meet the other eligibility requirements of the GSIS, are entitled to disability benefits. The disability benefits may include a monthly income benefit for life, an additional cash payment, or a cash payment to be determined by the GSIS. The benefits vary according to the schedule of disabilities prescribed by the GSIS, as follows:

a) For permanent total disability,[5] a monthly income benefit for life equal to the BMP effective from the date of disability plus an additional cash payment equivalent to 18 times the employee's BMP or a cash payment equivalent to 100 percent of his/her AMC for each year of service he/she paid contributions but not less than PHP 12,000;

b) For permanent partial disability,[6] a cash payment in accordance with the prescribed schedule of disabilities;

c) For temporary total disability,[7] 75 percent of a member's current daily compensation but not less than PHP 70 per day for a maximum of 120 days in a year after exhausting all leave credits, and an extension not to exceed a total of 240 days if more extensive treatment is required beyond 120 days;

d) For non-scheduled disability or injuries or illnesses resulting in a disability not listed in the schedule of partial/total disability, the benefits are to be determined by the GSIS based on the nature of the disability (RA 8291, Sec. 15–19).

Separation Benefits :Members of the GSIS who separated from government service before the retirement age but have rendered at least three years of service and are below 60 years of age are entitled to separation benefits in the form of cash payments. For members who have rendered at least 3 years but less than 15 years of service, the cash payment is equivalent to 100 percent of the AMC for every year of service but not less than PHP 12,000, payable upon reaching the age of 60 or upon resignation or separation, whichever comes later. For members who have served the government for at least 15 years, the cash payment is equivalent to 18 times the BMP payable upon separation plus an old-age benefit pension for life starting at age 60. An unemployment or involuntary separation benefit, also in the form of a cash payment, is granted to permanent employees who have rendered less than 15 years of government service and have been paying contributions for at least one year but who separated involuntarily owing to the abolition of their office or position, usually arising from reorganization. The cash payment is equivalent to 50 percent of the AMC payable for a period of two to six months depending on the length of contribution, ranging from 1 year to less than 15 years before unemployment or involuntary separation.

Life Insurance: All government employees except for members of the Armed Forces of Philippines (AFP) and Philippines National Police (PNP) are automatically covered by compulsory life insurance, in particular, a Life Endowment Policy for those who entered the service before 1 August 2003 and an Enhanced Life Policy for those who entered the service after 31 July 2003 and members whose policies have matured. The life insurance benefits include, among others, policy loans and annual dividends. The GSIS also offers its members an optional insurance and/or pre-need coverage for life, health, hospitalization, education, memorial plans, and such other plans as may be designed by the system, with premiums payable by the insured or his/her employer and/or any person acceptable to GSIS.

Lending Program: The GSIS also provides service loans to its members and pension loans for the retirees.

GSIS Mutual Fund Program: The GSIS Kinabukasan Fund is a balanced fund[8] managed by Philam Asset Management Inc., a member of the Philam Group of Companies, starting in 1998. It was intended to provide affordable investment options for government employees. The minimum investment requirement is PHP 1,000 for members and PHP 5,000 for non-members (optional). The mutual fund registered an annual return on investment as high as 21.92 percent in 2007. As of February 2010, the year-to-date return is 1.58 percent.[9]

Contribution Rates and Base: The monthly contribution rate is equal to 21 percent of the member's total monthly base compensation. The total contribution is divided between the employee (9 percent) and employer (12 percent). The employer's share includes a 4 percent premium for life insurance. Members of the Judiciary and constitutional commissioners contribute 3 percent of their monthly compensation, while the government pays a corresponding 3 percent share of their life insurance coverage.

Organization and Recent Membership: The governing and policy-making body of the GSIS is the Board of Trustees, the members of which are appointed by the President of the Philippines. The GSIS workforce consists of 3,104 employees, 52 percent of whom are in the head office while the remaining 48 percent are in the branches. To date, the GSIS has 15 regional offices, 25 branch offices, and 18 satellite offices nationwide. In 2005 the estimated membership of the GSIS was 1.5 million, and it was disbursing 32.4 billion pesos per year in benefits.

GSIS Asset Allocation and Investment Performance: The funds of the GSIS that are not needed to meet the current obligations may be invested under such terms, conditions, rules, and regulations as may be prescribed by the Board of Trustees. The investments shall satisfy the requirements of liquidity, safety/security, and yield in order to ensure the actuarial solvency of the funds of the GSIS. Furthermore, the GSIS is required to submit an annual report on all investments made to both Houses of Congress of the Philippines, under investment instruments mentioned below:

a)   interest-bearing bonds or securities or other evidence of indebtedness of the government of the Philippines;
b)   interest-bearing deposits or securities in any domestic bank doing business in the Philippines:
c)   direct housing loans to members and group housing projects secured by first mortgage, giving priority to the low-income groups and short- and medium-term loans to members such as salary, policy, educational, emergency, stock purchase plan and other similar loans: Provided, That no less

than 40 percent of the investable fund of the GSIS Social Insurance Fund shall be invested for these purposes;

d)　bonds, securities, promissory notes or other evidence of indebtedness of educational or medical institutions to finance the construction, improvement and maintenance of schools and hospitals;

e)　real estate property including shares of stocks involving real estate property and investments secured by first mortgages on real estate or other collaterals acceptable to the GSIS: Provided, That such investments shall, in the determination of the Board, redound to the benefit of the GSIS, its members, as well as the general public;

f)　debt instruments and other securities traded in the secondary markets;

g)　loans to, or in bonds, debentures, promissory notes or other evidence of indebtedness of any solvent corporation created or existing under the laws of the Philippines;

h)　common and preferred stocks of any solvent corporation or financial institution created or existing under the laws of the Philippines listed in the stock exchange with proven track record of profitability over the last three years and payment of dividends at least once over the same period;

i)　domestic mutual funds including investments related to the operations of mutual funds;

j)　foreign mutual funds and in foreign currency deposits or foreign currency deposits or foreign currency-denominated debts, non-speculative equities and other financial instruments or other assets issued in accordance with existing laws of the countries where such financial instruments are issued: Provided, That these instruments or assets are listed in bourses of the respective countries where these instruments or assets are issued: Provided, further, That the issuing company has proven track record of profitability over the last three years and payment of dividends at least once over the same period.

As one of the benefits of the GSIS program, GSIS Mutual Fund, Inc. gives opportunity to its members to obtain affordable investments. The investment objective of the fund is described as capital growth with returns and inflows derived from investments in both equity and fixed income securities. The fund considers a medium- to long-term investment horizon for its shareholders. The fund is positioned to compete directly with other balanced mutual funds and unit investment trust funds offered by commercial banks.

The GSIS Mutual Fund Assets are divided almost equally between equity and fixed income securities. (Figure 6.7). Equity investments include companies listed in the primary and secondary boards of the Philippines Stock Exchange. Fixed income investments consist of domestic fixed income instruments, including but not limited to treasury bills, Bangko Sentral ng Pilipinas (BSP) Certificate of Indebtedness, other government securities or bonds, and such other evidences of obligations issued by the BSP or guaranteed by the Philippine government.

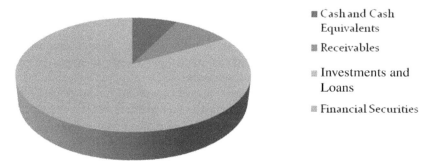

Figure 6.7 Government Service Insurance System (GSIS) asset allocation

Source: GSIS (n.d.).

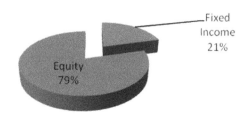

Figure 6.8 Government Service Insurance System (GSIS) mutual fund allocation as of March 2011

Source: Philam Asset Management, www.philamfunds.com.ph

However, the fund manager may, at its discretion, and when in its judgment the conditions so warrant, invest a substantial amount of the fund's assets in equity securities up to the maximum allowed under prevailing Philippine laws or up to 100 percent in fixed income securities (i.e., liquid or semi-liquid assets), subject to any existing liquidity requirements as may be required by law. In addition, as a defensive strategy, the manager, at its discretion, may elect to invest up to 100 percent of the fund's assets in cash and/or other liquid assets, again subject to any existing liquidity requirements as may be required by law. Securities and Exchange Commission (SEC) Memorandum Circular 7 Series of 2005, or the "Guidelines on the Evaluation of Foreign Investments by Mutual Fund Companies," allows mutual fund companies to invest up to 100 percent of their assets in foreign securities.

Compared to the bank deposit rate, which varies between 1.64 percent and 2.56 percent, and the inflation rate, at 4.3 percent in February 2011, the GSIS Mutual Fund provides an attractive alternative for investment (Figure 6.8). The GSIS is also the first fund in the Philippines with the capability of allocating up to 20 percent of its portfolio in global investment opportunities.

3.3.6. Assessment and challenges of the GSIS

Coverage and compliance. In 2007 the GSIS had 1.4 million members accounting for 92 percent of the total civilian public sector employees. Together the GSIS and the Social Security System (SSS, the private sector pension) covered 28 percent of the total employed population and 22 percent of the total population who were at least 65 years old in 2007. Thus, the coverage of the social security system in the Philippines (i.e., GSIS plus SSS) is one of the lowest in the region. The coverage rate of the GSIS and SSS is lower than for the social security systems of Thailand, Malaysia, Singapore, and South Korea but higher than that of Indonesia.

It is recognized that poor compliance will persist if the incentives for evasion are engendered by the very design of pension benefits and contributions (Holzmann et al., 2000). For instance, both the Organisation for Economic Co-operation and Development (2009) and Holzmann et al. (2000) argued that the minimum pension provision and the provision that pensions are computed on the basis of salaries in the last five years of service tend to result in the evasion of the payment of appropriate premiums. In other words, these two provisions create incentives for workers and employers to collude by either (i) under-reporting earnings until the last five years of their working life and/or (ii) artificially boosting the pay that is reported to the pension system in the last five years of their working life.

On the other hand, the lack of sanctions for employers who either under-report or do not remit the contributions they withhold from their employees obviously results in a reduction in the amount of contributions that actually reach the system. In addition, it also reduces the credibility of the system and discourages other workers from participating in the system.

Equity. Equity may be assessed in terms of the relationship between the value of the benefits received and the accumulated contributions made on behalf of the workers, as well as the manner in which the various covered classes are treated relative to each other. This measure, however, has to be taken in relation to the objectives of the pension program. Redistribution, as one of the objectives of the defined benefit program, is expected to result in decreasing benefit to contribution ratios with increasing wage levels. The defined contribution program, on the other hand, is based on equity, resulting in a one-to-one relationship between benefits and contributions. Estimated ratios of the present value of benefits at retirement (also known as pension wealth in Organisation for Economic Co-operation and Development terminology) to the accumulated contributions for the defined benefit programs are shown in Table 6.4 for both GSIS and SSS for comparison. The effect of the 13th-month pension is an additional 8 percent more than on the presented values based on 12 months' pension.[10]

These benefit values will further increase when the effects of the survivors' benefits and the longer life span of the increasing number of females are considered. The additional ratios for the private sector program resulting from RA 7641 are shown in Tables 6.4 and 6.5.

Table 6.4 Ratio of present value of benefits to accumulated contributions

	Monthly wage levels (PHP)					
	1,993	3,986	7,972 (average)	15,944	23,916	Ceiling
SSS	25.00%	50.00%	100.00%	200.00%	300.00%	Ceiling = 15,000
Benefit / contribution	2.4	1.58	1.56	1.55	1.55	× 1.08 with 13 months
PV benefit / actual wage	14.4	9.49	9.33	8.72	5.81	Pension
GSIS	25.00%	50.00%	100.00%	200.00%	300.00%	Ceiling = 16,000
Benefit / contribution	NA	0.87	0.87	0.87	0.87	× 1.08 with 13 months
PV benefit / actual wage	NA	10.55	10.55	10.55	7.06	Pension
GSIS	25.00%	50.00%	100.00%	200.00%	300.00%	No Ceiling after 2003
Benefit / contribution	NA	0.87	0.87	0.87	0.87	× 1.08 with 13 months
PV benefit / actual wage	NA	10.55	10.55	10.55	10.55	Pension

Source: Reyes (2010).

Note: GSIS = Government Service Insurance System; SSS = Social Security System, PV = Present Value. Monetary amounts are shown in Philippine pesos, and the percentages are those of the average wage of 7972 pesos.

Table 6.5 Estimated ratio of present value of benefits to accumulated contributions under Republic Act 7641

	Monthly wage levels, as a percentage of average wage					
	25.00%	50.00%	100.00%	200.00%	300.00%	No Ceiling
5 years of service before retirement						
Benefit/ contribution	1.00	1.00	1.00	1.00	1.00	12 months pension
PV benefit/actual wage	0.37	0.37	0.37	0.37	0.37	Equivalent only
20 years of service before retirement						
Benefit/ contribution	1.00	1.00	1.00	1.00	1.00	12 months pension
PV benefit/actual wage	1.47	1.47	1.47	1.47	1.47	Equivalent only

Source: Reyes (2010).

Table 6.6 SSS and GSIS pensioners data

	SSS pensioners and average pension				GSIS average pension
Year	Male	Female	Total number	Average monthly pension (PHP)[1]	Average monthly pension (PHP)
2007	534,806	714,385	1,249,191	2,962	7,200
2008	572,246	757,977	1,330,223	3,109	7,800
2009	610,872	803,201	1,414,073	3,080	n/a

Source: SSS, Complied from SSS Republic of Philippines Annual Reports various years. www.sss.gov.ph/sss/appmanager/pages.jsp?page=annualreport

Note: Average exchange rates of PHP versus USD have been as follows: 2007: USD 1 = PHP 46.1484; 2008: USD 1 = PHP 44.4746; and 2009: USD 1 = PHP 47.6372. GSIS = Government Service Insurance System; SSS = Social Security System.

Another equity issue also appears between the benefit values of SSS and GSIS. The average monthly pension of SSS pensioners for 2008 and 2009 is much lower than those for the GSIS (Table 6.6). Since 2000 the GSIS pension fund has increased its monthly pension benefit by as much as 84 percent (GSIS, 2008). Unlike the SSS, the GSIS has lifted its ceilings on the basis of benefits and contributions.

The release of the ceilings (caps) under the GSIS program in 2003 gave undue advantage only to the high income groups, resulting from additional benefits over those based on the original PHP 16,000 ceiling. This effectively increased government support in terms of additional counterpart contributions beyond the original ceiling. Private sector firms cannot afford to follow this move as the increased contribution would already be relatively higher than what these firms are likely willing to bear. If the ceiling were restored, the released government counterpart could be put to better use for poverty alleviation. High income members could always turn to supplementary programs to channel their extra income.

The current use of the three- or five-year average rather than the career average as the basis for computing pension benefits could result in a perverse redistribution in favor of the high income group, who usually have steeper salary increases near retirement. This is even more pronounced in programs where ceilings have been lifted. Near-retirement promotions and the use of the monthly base and longevity pay of the next higher grade as the wage base (in the case of the Armed Forces of the Philippines Retirement and Separation Benefits System) could be subject to abuse and make actuarial evaluation difficult.

Financial sustainability. The GSIS operates partially funded defined benefit pension schemes; i.e., they pay pensions that are related to the earnings of their members during their working lives. As such, the financial sustainability of the pension system is largely related to any discrepancy between contributions and benefits (Table 6.7). At present, the replacement rate (i.e., the value of the pension

Table 6.7 GSIS and SSS contribution and benefit payments, 2007

	GSIS	SSS	Total
Total contributions (PHP billions)	43	61.9	104.9
Social insurance (PHP billions)	40.8	60.8	101.6
Employees Compensation Program (PHP billions)	2.2	1.1	3.3
Total benefit payments (PHP billions)	32.4	93.2	125.6
Social insurance (PHP billions)	32.3	92	124.3
Employees Compensation Program (PHP billions)	0.1	1.2	1.3
Total contributions as %of GDP	0.6	0.9	1.6
Total benefits as %of GDP	0.5	0.9	1.4
Ratio of contributions to benefits	1.33	1.02	1.13
No. of contributing members (millions)	1.4	8.0	9.4
As %of potential members	91.90	28.90	32.10

Source: GSIS (n.d.) and SSS annual report.

Note: GSIS = Government Service Insurance System; SSS = Social Security System.

payment as a percentage of the earnings of members during their working lives) ranges from 37.5 percent to 90 percent for the GSIS. The average replacement rate of the GSIS in the 1990s was estimated to be equal to 70 percent based on a sample of retirees (Asher, 2000). In contrast, the mandatory contribution to the GSIS is equal to 17 percent of the monthly compensation of members, not including the 4 percent contribution for the life insurance premium.

The growth of contributions to the GSIS lagged behind that of benefits payments in 2000–2007 (Table 6.8). In specific terms, total benefits payments made by the GSIS grew by 10 percent annually, from PHP 17 billion in 2000 to PHP 32.3 billion in 2007. At the same time, member contributions rose from PHP 35 billion in 2000 to PHP 41 billion in 2007, reflecting a 2 percent increase yearly (Table 6.4). Thus, the ratio of contributions to benefit payments declined continuously from 2.1 in 2000 to 1.3 in 2007. This occurred despite the abolition of the ceiling on the AMC in reckoning members' contributions to the GSIS in 2003, perhaps because only 5 percent of GSIS members are affected by this change.

In recent years, the GSIS intensified the collection of the premium arrears of various government agencies. At the same time, it was able to improve the yield on its investments. With the enactment of amendments to the GSIS law in 1997, the GSIS was authorized to invest part of its funds in foreign assets so as to diversify its portfolio and secure better returns given the lack of local investment instruments.[11] In line with its global investment program, the GSIS obtained the services of a professional global fund manager. It has also adopted an absolute-return strategy for its international investments. Specifically, as part of this

Table 6.8 Total premium contributions and total benefits paid by the GSIS and SSS, 2002–2007 (PHP billion)

	2002	2003	2004	2005	2006	2007
GSIS						
Premium contributions	39.9	40.4	39.2	40.4	39.1	40.8
Benefit payments	24.5	25.9	30.9	29.9	30.6	32.3
Ratio of contributions to benefit payments	1.63	1.56	1.27	1.35	1.28	1.26
SSS						
Premium contributions	33.7	38.6	43.1	46.6	51.6	60.8
Benefit payments	39.6	41.6	43.7	45.2	51.1	59.7
Ratio of contributions to benefit payments	0.82	0.93	0.98	1.03	1.01	1.02

Source: GSIS (n.d.) and SSS annual report.

Note: GSIS = Government Service Insurance System; SSS = Social Security System.

strategy the GSIS requires a minimum annual US dollar return of 8 percent and a maximum portfolio volatility of 7 percent. Thus, the actuarial life of the GSIS reserve fund is estimated to be good up to 2055, as of 2007, an improvement from the 1999 actuarial valuation, when the GSIS reserve fund was estimated to run out in 2041.

However, the continuous slide in the ratio of contributions to benefit payments made by the GSIS in 2000–2007 indicates the need for intensified efforts to improve its financial sustainability. The GSIS also embarked on the installation of a computerized information system to manage members' service records, contributions, payments, and other data. This is much needed by the GSIS management for the monitoring of its day-to-day operations, its actual actuarial situation, and the performance of its investment portfolio, among others. This information system is also critical for the GSIS to actually operationalize the premium-based policy that was adopted recently (which calls for the proper matching of premium contributions with the amount of benefits to be received) and for it to be able to service its members' requirements efficiently and effectively. *Improvement of the protection provided to pensioners.* There is also a need to further improve the protection provided to pensioners. At present, pensions are adjusted in an ad hoc manner over time. The value of pensions may be better protected from erosion resulting from inflation if pensions are adjusted in a systematic manner through inflation indexation. At the same time, the GSIS allows pensioners to get their benefits as a lump sum at the time of retirement. The withdrawal of benefits in such a chunky manner rather than in the form of annuities tends to reduce the welfare of beneficiaries as they run the risk of outliving their retirement savings.

Greater emphasis on fiduciary responsibility of social security institutions and improved management of their investment portfolios. Holzmann et al. (2000) and Asher (2008) emphasized the need to strengthen corporate governance and promote accountability in the social security institutions so as to help them perform their fiduciary responsibility more effectively (i) to preserve the value of the pension fund and (ii) to maximize the returns on investment. They also pointed out that the fiduciary role of pension funds is sometimes given less emphasis in favor of the pursuit of other domestic policy goals (like financing of infrastructure investment, foreign exchange management, and even outright political intervention) as these pension funds manage their investment portfolios.

There are many examples of the politicization of the SSS and GSIS in the past. Palmiery (2002) notes that the government has influenced the use of public pension funds to attain a variety of public policy objectives. Given the large pool of funds, it is often tempting for government bodies to direct the investment of a portion of these assets for specific domestic political purposes such as low-income housing, financing of start-up businesses, and development of the capital market, among others. While well intended these economically targeted investments normally lead to lower than market rates and thus deviate from the fiduciary principles. For instance, at the behest of the Marcos government, the GSIS funded the construction of numerous hotels that later on became non-performing loans in the mid-1980s. At about the same time, it also took over the ownership of the Philippine Airlines. More recently, both the GSIS and SSS acquired substantial shares in a commercial bank at the behest of President Estrada in support of a crony's take-over of that bank.

Reduction in administrative costs. Holzmann et al. (2000) found that the administrative costs of running the GSIS are high relative to those of social security systems in other countries. For instance, the operating expense of the pension fund in Malaysia is 2 percent of total contributions, while that of the pension fund in Singapore is 0.5 percent of total contributions. In comparison, the operating expense of the GSIS was equal to 15 percent in 2007, even higher than corresponding ratio in 1996 (10.8 percent).

Avoidance of using the pension fund for political and other purposes. Governments around the world are responding to the weakness in their own economies and those of their major trading partners with countercyclical fiscal spending. But precisely because tax revenues tend to be co-variant with the overall growth of the economy, the use of pension funds to partially finance the fiscal stimulus package may appeal to some policy makers. For instance, the GSIS and SSS are reportedly going to finance PHP 50 billion of large infrastructure projects under the Economic Resiliency Plan of the government. This situation is not unique to the Philippines. Malaysia did the same in the wake of the Asian financial crisis in 1998 (Holzmann et al., 2000). However, there is a need to resist the temptation to dip into the pension funds for the purpose of priming the pump of the domestic economy as this will likely not match the primary objective of the fund to protect the old-age income of its members.

3.4. Thailand

3.4.1. Government Pension Fund

Before 1997 government officers received a defined benefit pension upon retirement, the amount of which depended on their level of income in the last month before retirement and the number of years worked. The formula used to calculate the monthly pension was (1/50) × (level of income in the *last month* before retirement) × (the number of years worked as a government official). This pension was financed from the national budget.

The current program, consisting of a budget financed defined benefit pension plus a defined contribution accumulation known as the Government Pension Fund (GPF), was established on 27 March 1997 following enactment of the Government Pension Fund Act B.E. 2539, promulgated in September 1996. The reform was therefore not motivated by the 1997 financial crisis.

The GPF is currently Thailand's largest institutional investor, serving more than one million members. Twelve categories of employees are covered, including civil, judicial and university officials; teachers; and police officers and military officers.

Employees hired after 24 March 1997 are required to participate in the GPF program. Government employees who were employed before the fund's inception were required to choose between remaining in the pre-1997 defined benefit pension scheme or participating in a combination of

- a defined benefit component based on a modified formula using compensation averaged over the final 60 months of government service and capped at 70 percent of average compensation, plus
- accumulations in the GPF.

The defined benefit component (which requires completion of 25 years of service) can be paid either as an annuity or as a lump sum, with additional GPF contributions being credited for those who choose an annuity. Currently, GPF member accounts may be withdrawn, in one lump sum, only upon the termination of membership, which occurs upon retirement or other termination of government service or at the age of 60, or at death. The law does not provide for portability or annuity payments from someone's GPF defined contribution account.

Under the GPF program, government officials contribute 3 percent of monthly wages, and the government contributes 3 percent of monthly wages. Upon retirement, GPF members receive a traditional pension (under the revised, less generous formula) together with a lump-sum retirement allowance. This allowance is based on the value of accumulated contributions, which, in turn, comprise three to five contribution components, depending on an individual's situation:

a) the employee's 3 percent contributions;
b) the government 3 percent employer contributions;

c) 2 percent of monthly income contributed by the government in addition to (b) (but credited only to those who choose to receive their pension as an annuity);

d) lump-sum endowment fund (incentive scheme for a person who was employed before 27 March 1997 and chose to participate in the GPF program);

e) investment returns.

GPF members receive generous tax treatment. Member contributions of up to THB 300,000 per year are tax deductible. The returns on contributions accumulated with the fund are fully tax exempt. Sums withdrawn after age 50 are tax free. However, members are not allowed to contribute above the mandatory 3 percent, and their accounts may be withdrawn, in one lump sum, only upon the termination of membership. Additionally, the fund offers housing loans from both the member's and the employer's contribution accounts as well as life insurance benefits.

At end 2008, there were 1.19 million GPF members, equivalent to 3.2 percent of the 2008 labor force. As of December 2010, the total net assets of the GPF were baht 483 billion, equivalent to 5.3 percent of the 2009 GDP. Its investment mandate is to maximize returns for members. However, as it is controlled by the Ministry of Finance, it needs to adhere to certain policy directions, such as supporting and helping to deepen the local stock market.

The investment performance of the GPF for the 1997–2009 period is summarized in Figure 6.9. The data suggest that for the 1997–2009 period, the real rate of return (nominal rate of return – inflation rate) averaged 3.97 percent per year. This compares favorably with the corresponding annual return of 0.54 percent for the bank deposits.

The investment policy for the GPF complies with Finance Ministry rules. There is an investment sub-committee to review and recommend investments to the Board of Directors. The ministerial rules state that investments must consist of more than 60 percent low-risk (i.e., credit risk) assets and less than 40 percent higher-risk assets. In 2009 GPF's investment was managed 70 percent in-house and 30 percent by external fund managers.

Figure 6.10 provides a summary of asset allocation of Thailand's GPF as of June 2010. The asset classes are well diversified, though Thai fixed income assets dominate, as they constitute nearly 70 percent of the total assets. The GPF invests both domestically and abroad, with foreign allocation accounting for nearly 14 percent of the total assets.

Two aspects of the current civil service pension arrangements merit reconsideration. First, there is a lack of incentive upon separation from one's employer to keep saving until retirement age because members must take the lump sum payable at the time of separation. Generally, fund membership must be promptly terminated upon separation from service, and tax law encourages taking one's accumulated benefit as a lump sum. Also, there is no vehicle to rollover the benefit to another retirement savings funds (Brustad, 2012). Second, the laws discourage

	1997	1998	1999	2000	2001	2002	2003	2004	2005	2006	2007	2008	2009
Net Rate of Returns to member %	10.96	16.51	9.42	6.41	7.22	8.21	11.84	2.02	6.83	3.44	9.22	-5.17	8.92
Average Bank Deposit Rate %	8.54	9.81	5.09	3.82	3.13	2.56	1.50	1.00	1.29	3.68	2.78	2.52	0.93
Inflation Rate	5.60	8.10	0.31	1.55	1.65	0.60	1.82	2.73	4.56	4.64	2.23	5.47	-0.85

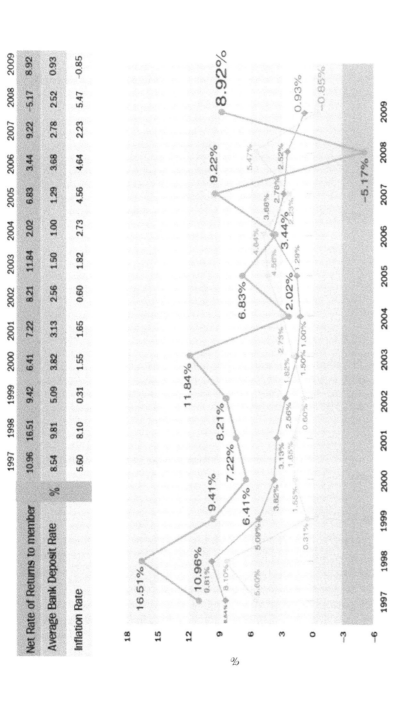

Figure 6.9 Nominal and real returns for Government Pension Fund members, 1997–2009

Source: Government Provident Fund, Thailand, Auditors Report and Financial Statements (various years). www.gpf.or.th//eng2012/financstat.asp and www.gpf.or.th/cgi-bin/CMS/Budget/budget_s_7.pdf

Before the reforms in 1997, the replacement ratio received by government employees was around 70 percent of the last drawn salary. The replacement rate under the new government pension arrangements remains unclear at this stage but is expected to be comparable to that under the old system. In addition, those receiving pensions are also eligible to receive survivors' benefits and non-contributory medical benefits until death.

As of June 2010

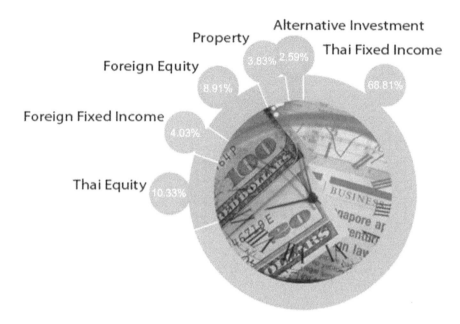

Figure 6.10 Asset allocation of Thailand's Government Pension Fund

Source: Government Provident Fund, Thailand , Auditors Report and Financial Statements various years the web link for 2008 paper is www.gpf.or.th/eng2012/financstat.asp www.gpf.or.th/cgi-bin/CMS/Budget/budget_s_7.pdf

a high level of savings even for those who are inclined to do so. GPF members are not allowed to make contributions above 3 percent of compensation.

4. Concluding remarks

Except for the Philippines, there is a dualism in the philosophy concerning retirement benefits for government employees, on the one hand, and private sector employees, on the other. The coverage is also much higher for the government employees, and so are the risks covered and the replacement rate.

Nevertheless, the details of the pension design and implementation aspects, as well as the extent to which the existing pension systems are fiscally sustainable, vary greatly among the sample countries. In particular, non-contributory (on the part of the employees) civil service pension systems will also put considerable stress on the fiscal systems.

The investment policies and performance in those countries where the systems are partially or fully funded remain in need of substantial reform. In particular, there appears to be a mismatch between assets and liabilities, as well as insufficient diversification among asset classes. In none of the sample countries are the funds invested abroad, and thus they do not benefit from international risk diversification.

In the three sample countries, there is substantial scope for improving record keeping for, administration of, and compliance with the civil service pension's schemes. The transparency concerning civil service pension schemes is low and requires urgent attention. There is also a need to statutorily require periodic actuarial review of the schemes and their wide dissemination.

There appears to be very little capacity for, interest in, or official encouragement of research on civil service pension reform by the academic and research institutions in the sample countries. The issues raised by civil service pension reform are important areas of public policy and require a much wider but informed debate and discussion, which has not been the case so far. While the data constraints are severe, efforts must be made to overcome them.

In conclusion, the issues raised by civil service pension reform are very similar to those of pension reform in general. An important difference, however, is that financing of health care benefits must be considered an integral part of civil service pension reform, as these benefits are often provided to civil servants and their families during their retirement in the sample countries with only nominal contributions from the beneficiaries.

Notes

1 The report of the Independent Public Service Pensions Commission (known as Hutton Commission) [2011] is available at www.nhsbsa.nhs.uk/Documents/Pensions/hutton_final_100311.pdf
2 Under a phased withdrawal plan, a member may choose a period (for example, 15 years) over which regular withdrawals of accumulated balances plus investment income are permitted, in such a way that the total is exhausted. As there is no risk pooling the trade-off is that, in contrast to a life annuity, longevity risk is inadequately addressed (Mackenzie, 2006). For India, the phased withdrawal option may represent a workable compromise between a lump-sum withdrawal and a life annuity, especially if social pension programs, such as the Old Age Pension Scheme, are strengthened and their coverage extended.
3 If social pensions, such as the Old Age Pension Scheme, currently financed jointly by the central government and states but administered by the latter, are strengthened, the longevity risk could be substantially mitigated (Asher, 2010).
4 Increasing life expectancy, and consequent lengthening of the period for which individuals must finance retirement, has made it even more essential for individuals to learn some skills (e.g. sewing, cooking, repairing of plumbing, teaching) that could be used to generate part of their resources during retirement. Society should create an enabling environment for this such as by lowering statutory provident fund and related contributions for economic activities during old age.
5 Permanent total disability arises when the likelihood of recovery from impairment is medically remote. Injuries resulting in any of the following are deemed as permanent total disability: complete loss of both eyes, loss of two limbs at or above the ankle or wrist, permanent complete paralysis of two limbs, brain injury resulting in incurable imbecility or insanity, and such other cases as may be determined by the GSIS (RA 8291, Sec.16).

6 Permanent partial disability arises when there is functional loss of any part of the body, despite which gainful occupation can still be pursued. The following are disabilities deemed as permanent partial disability: complete and permanent loss of the use of any finger, any toe, one arm, one hand, one foot, one leg, one or both ears, hearing in one or both ears, or sight of one eye and such other cases as may be determined by the GSIS (RA 8291, Sec. 17).

7 Temporary total disability arises when a person can be rehabilitated from a mental/physical impairment or restored to normal function.

8 A type of mutual fund that combines a stock component, a bond component, and sometimes a money market component in a single portfolio.

9 Derived from https://philamfunds.com/InformationController?action=InformationInvestFundProducts

10 The mandatory 13th-month pay to workers is not subject to tax or contributions to the pension systems and could thus not offset the effect of the 13th-month pension of the retiree.

11 Similarly, the 1997 amendments to the SSS law also allowed the SSS to invest its funds in foreign assets.

References

Asher, M.G. (2000). *Reforming civil service pensions in selected Asia–Pacific countries.* Washington, D.C.: World Bank. http://info.worldbank.org/etools/docs/library/76548/march2000/proceedings/pdfpaper/week1/asher1.pdf.

Asher, M.G. (2008). Pension reform in India. In Jha, R. (Ed.) *The Indian economy sixty years after independence,* pp. 66–93. London: Palgrave McMillan.

Asher, M.G. (2010a). Making pension promises more credible in Asia–Pacific economies. In the Japan Institute of International Affairs (ed.), *Towards a more resilient society: Lessons from economic crises,* pp. 25–43. Tokyo: Pacific Economic Cooperation Council (PECC). www.pecc.org/resources/doc_view/1544-towards-a-more-resilient-society-lessons-from-economic-crises.

Asher, M.G. (2010b). *NPS: Some suggested refinements.* CFO Connect. Guragaon, India: International Market Assessment India Pvt. Ltd.

Asian Development Bank. (2010). *Economic and financial indicator.* Manila: Asian Development Bank.

Brustad, O.D. (2012). Thailand. In D. Park (Ed.) *Asian Development Bank's pension systems in East and Southeast Asia: Promoting fairness and sustainability.* Mandaluyong City, Philippines: Asian Development Bank.

Civil Service Commission , Government of the Philippines. (2008). *Social Security System 2008 Annual Report.* Quezon City, Philippines: Civil Service Commission.

Civil Services Commission, Government of the Philippines. (2010). Inventory of Government Personnel. http://excell.csc.gov.ph/cscweb/statisti.html

The Economist. (2011a). Public sector pay and pensions: A bad habit continues. 21 February. www.economist.com/blogs/buttonwood/2011/02/public_sector_pay_and_pensions/print.

The Economist. (2011b). Tackling the intractable. 10 March. www.economist.com/node/18338792.

Economist Intelligence Unit (EIU). (2009). *Global debt comparison.* London: Author. http://buttonwood.economist.com/content/gdc?source=hptextfeature.

Government Service Insurance System (GSIC). (n.d.). Annual Report: 2007, 2008, 2009 edition. Manila: Government Service Insurance System.

Halan, M. (2009). *Is the new pension system really that cheap?* LiveMint (Mumbai), 6 May. www.livemint.com/

Holzmann, R., I.W. Mac Arthur, and Y. Sin. (2000). *Pension systems in East Asia and the Pacific: Challenges and opportunities.* Social Protection. Discussion Paper Series 0004. Washington, DC: World Bank.

Independent Public Service Pensions Commission. (Known as Hutton Commission) (2011). *Independent Public Service Pensions Commission: Final Report.* www.nhsbsa. nhs.uk/Documents/Pensions/hutton_final_100311.pdf. London: Author.

Mackenzie, G. (2006). *Annuity markets and pension reform.* Cambridge: Cambridge University Press.

Palmiery, R. (2002). *Investment of social security funds: The Philippine experience.* Address to the Board of the ASEAN Social Security Association (ASSA). www. asean-ssa.org/Material/BM_22Mar2002_1.pdf.

Prakash P (2013) Direct taxes code : a discussion paper. Centre for Budget and Governance Accountability. www.cbgaindia.org/files/recent_publications/ Direct%20Taxes%20Code-%20A%20Discussion%20Paper.pdf

Reyes, E. (2010). *The Philippine pension system: Overview and reform direction.* Paper prepared for Asian Development Bank, Manila.

Sane, R. and A. Shah. (2011). *Civil service and military pension in India.* Paper present at the Workshop on Civil Service and Military Pension Arrangements in the Asia-Pacific. http://cis.ier.hit-u.ac.jp/Japanese/society/conference1101/shah

United Nations. (2008). *World population prospects: The 2008 revision.* http://esa. un.org/unpp.

7 Strengthening sustainability and extending the pension coverage in China

Yuwei Hu

1. Introduction

1.1. Socio-economic background

Since initiating the economic reform and open-door policy in the late 1970s, China has witnessed a tremendous transformation. A once centrally planned and impoverished country was gradually transformed into a market-oriented economy and became in 2010 the second largest economy after the United States of America.

This impressive economic expansion is shown in the socio-economic statistics in Tables 7.1 and 7.2. Table 7.1 shows that as of 2009 the annual growth rate of the gross domestic product (GDP) was 9.1 percent in China, compared to –0.1 percent in East Asia and the Pacific region, –1.9 percent at world level and –2.5 percent in upper middle-income economies. Using five-year average time series data, the trend is also quite clear. As revealed in Table 7.2 in all periods (except 1961 to 1970) during the past five decades, China performed much better than most other countries. This is particularly the case since the late 1970s, when China started its economic reform and opening-up policy. The average growth ratio between 1981 and 2009 was 10.1 percent, much higher than that in most other economies, e.g. 3.7 percent average in Asia and the Pacific region and 2.4 percent in upper middle-income countries, as shown in Table 7.2. Turning to the level of GDP per capita, China performed relatively well compared to other low-income economies. For example, as of 2009, the GDP per capita at constant 2000 prices was USD 2,206 in China, while it was USD 332 on average in low-income economies, as shown in Table 7.1. When PPP (Purchasing Power Parity) is used, the Chinese GDP per capita rose to USD 6,200,[1] higher than in both low-income economies and lower middle-income economies, albeit still lower than the world average.

In terms of education indicators, compared to all others, China was also in a favorable position, as indicated by higher literacy rates than in most other developing countries. Meanwhile, China witnessed improvements in health and demographic indicators as well: as of 2009 life expectancy at birth was 73.1 years in China, compared to 57.0 years in low-income economies. With regard to the

Table 7.1 Comparison of selected socio-economic development indicators, as of 2009

	China	East Asia and Pacific	Low income	Lower middle income	Upper middle income	World
Economy						
GDP growth (annual, %)	9.1	−0.1	4.8	6.8	−2.5	−1.9
GDP per capita (constant 2000 USD)	2,206	4,948	332	1,378	4,151	5,842
GDP per capita, PPP (constant 2000 US$)	6,200	8,144	1,053	4,299	10,799	9,514
Population and demographics						
Population growth rate (annual, %)	0.5	0.7	2.2	1.2	0.9	1.2
Population aged 65 and above (% of total)	8.1	8.4	3.5	6.1	7.7	7.5
Mortality rate, infant (per 1,000 live births)	16.6	20.4	75.7	42.7	18.8	43.2
Life expectancy at birth (years)	73.1	73.2	57	67.8	71.2	68.9
Education						
Literacy rate, adult total (% of people ages 15 and above)	93.7	93.2	66.1	79.9	93.3	83.4
Literacy rate, youth total (% of people ages 15–24)	99.3	98.2	75	88.8	97.9	89
Health						
Health expenditure, total (% of GDP)	4.3	6.2	5.1	4.3	6.4	9.7
Improved sanitation facilities (% of population with access)	55	63	35.5	50.3	84.1	60.6

Source: World).

Note: GDP = gross domestic product; PPP = purchasing power parity.

Table 7.2 GDP annual growth rate (%) by aggregate group, five-year average

	China	Asia and Pacific	Low income	Lower middle income	Upper middle income	World
1961–1965	1.9	8.3	3.7	4.8	5.2	5.4
1966–1970	7.4	10.4	3.8	5.5	5.9	5.3
1971–1975	5.9	4.8	1.1	5.0	6.1	3.8
1976–1980	6.6	4.8	2.8	5.6	4.7	3.9
1981–1985	10.8	3.9	2.0	5.7	1.4	2.6
1986–1990	7.9	5.5	3.4	5.9	1.9	3.7
1991–1995	12.3	3.5	1.5	6.7	1.3	2.3
1996–2000	8.6	2.7	4.0	5.9	3.1	3.3
2001–2005	9.8	3.5	4.8	7.5	3.6	2.8
2006–2009	11.4	3.3	6.0	8.8	3.5	1.9
Average a	8.3	5.1	3.3	6.1	3.7	3.5
Average b	10.1	3.7	3.6	6.8	2.4	2.8

Source: World.

Note: a. average between 1961 and 2009; b. average between 1981 and 2009. GDP = gross domestic product.

demographic structure, China was older than all other countries (but slightly younger than the Asia and Pacific region), highlighted by a higher old-age dependency ratio (i.e. population above age 65 as a percentage of the total). The population growth rate was lowest in China compared to other country groups.

Against this background of impressive growth, however, the Chinese economy is still associated with a number of key problems that remain to be solved (Organisation of Economic Co-operation and Development [OECD], 2010). Among others are widening income inequality between regions and sections of society (UNDP, 2008[2]), a weak pension system (Asher and Newman, 2002; Herd et al., 2010) and a rapidly increasing trade imbalance and consequently rapid accumulation of foreign exchange reserves (Hu, 2010a; Oksanen, 2010b). Failure to tackle any of these problems may well have a devastating impact on the Chinese economy.

1.2. Demographic background

Aging is being observed around the globe, although the process varies across countries. Table 7.3a gives statistics concerning the varying aging profiles between China and selected other Asian countries over the 100-year period from 1950 to 2050. With regard to the old-age dependency ratio, China has witnessed a slow aging process over the past decades, with the ratio increasing from 7 percent in

1950 to 8 percent in 1980; however, it is expected to increase more rapidly in the following decades, i.e. from 12 percent in 2010 to 39 percent in 2050. This implies that by the middle of this century 1 elder Chinese person would be supported by 2.5 workers on average. In comparison, the aging profile is more severe in more advanced economies. For example, the old-age dependency ratio in Hong Kong was only 4 percent in 1950, which increased to 18.3 percent by 2012 is expected to rise further to 58 percent by 2050.[3] The grayest picture is expected to be observed in Japan, which will witness the ratio increasing to 74 percent by 2050. Countries with a similar profile include Korea and Singapore. By contrast, the aging process is slower in other countries, i.e. India, Indonesia, Malaysia, the Philippines and Thailand. For example, India as the second most populated country in the world is expected to see the ratio increase to 21 percent by 2050; i.e. on average one older person will be supported by five workers.

In addition to the old-age dependency ratio as above, another aging indicator, i.e. the population aged 65 and above as a percentage of the total population, is also often used in the literature. As given in the middle panel of Table 7.3a, all countries are forecast to witness a continued rise of the ratio over the observation period, albeit with differing magnitudes. For China the ratio was 4.5 percent in 1950, which reached 12.7 in 2012 and was expected to be 22.2 percent in 2040 and 23.7 percent in 2050. Again Japan is facing the most severe aging process, while some countries (e.g. India and the Philippines) are expected to remain relatively younger by 2050.

The aging process gives rise to an increase of the older population. However, the impact differs between groups of the older population. One consequence could be that the older population (i.e. those aged 80 and above) grows faster than the "younger" older group (i.e. those aged 65–79). If this is true, it will have important policy implications in that the older population is more fragile – financially and physically – than the other groups and therefore needs more attention from the government and society alike.

Table 7.3a shows that in 1950 only 0.3 percent of the total Chinese population was aged 80 and above. However, increased to 1.4 percent by 2010 and is expected to reach 4.6 percent by 2040 and 7.3 percent in 2050. In other words, over the 100-year period, the ratio is forecast to witness a more than 20-foldincrease. In comparison, the increase is approximately 5–6 times for the Chinese old-age dependency ratio, and the ratio of population aged 65+ as a percentage of the total over the same period, as discussed above. The trend (i.e. faster growth of the older population than for other groups) is similar for all other countries, as shown in the table. For example, Hong Kong had the same proportion of older people as mainland China in 1950 (i.e. 0.3 percent), but it increased to 0.8 percent in 1980 and 3.6 percent by 2010, with the expectation that it will increased to 13.5 percent by 2050.

As in other countries, the aging process in China is caused by a number of combined factors, particularly a lower mortality rate, longer life expectancy and decreased fertility rate. Table 7.3b shows that the Chinese infant mortality rate dropped significantly from 195 deaths per 1,000 births in 1950 to 37.8 in 1980,

Table 7.3a Comparison of key demographic indicators between China and other selected Asian countries, 1950–2050

	China	Hong Kong	India	Indonesia	Japan	Korea	Malaysia	Philippines	Singapore	Thailand
Old-age dependency ratio (%)										
1950	7	4	5	7	8	6	9	7	4	6
1980	8	9	6	6	13	6	6	6	7	7
2010	12	17	8	9	35	16	7	7	14	12
2040	36	51	16	22	65	52	20	15	59	34
2050	39	58	21	29	74	65	25	19	59	38
Population aged 65+ (as % of total)										
1950	4.5	2.5	3.1	4.0	4.9	3.0	5.1	3.6	2.4	3.2
1980	4.7	6.5	3.6	3.4	9.0	3.8	3.7	3.2	4.7	3.8
2010	8.4	12.5	5.3	6.1	22.5	11.3	4.8	4.2	10.1	8.7
2040	22.2	30.2	11.3	14.7	34.9	30.5	13.2	9.9	32.5	21.2
2050	23.7	32.6	14.5	18.6	37.7	35.1	16.3	12.9	32.8	23.3
Population aged 80+ (as % of total)										
1950	0.3	0.3	0.4	0.3	0.4	0.2	0.6	0.4	0.4	0.4
1980	0.4	0.8	0.3	0.3	1.4	0.4	0.5	0.3	0.5	0.5
2010	1.4	3.6	0.8	0.8	6.3	1.9	0.7	0.5	2.0	1.6
2040	4.6	10.3	2.2	2.5	13.9	8.8	2.8	1.7	10.9	5.3
2050	7.3	13.5	3.1	4.0	15.5	12.7	4.0	2.6	14.8	7.0

Source: UN Population Database (2008).

Table 7.3b Comparison of key demographic indicators between China and other selected Asian countries, 1950–2050

	China	Hong Kong	India	Indonesia	Japan	Korea	Malaysia	Philippines	Singapore	Thailand
Infant mortality rate (deaths per 1,000 births)										
1950	195	78.5	165.7	201.2	50.6	115	98.8	134.2	66	118.1
1980	37.8	9.6	94.7	88.8	6.5	23	28	61.2	8.4	34.5
2010	20.5	3.6	48.8	21.3	3.1	4	8	19.3	3	9.5
2040	11.1	3	25.4	9.4	2.7	3.4	5.3	9.3	2.8	5.8
2050	10.1	2.9	23	8.8	2.6	3.3	5.1	8.7	2.8	5.5
Life expectancy at birth (years)										
1950	44.6	64.8	40.2	39.9	66.8	52.7	52.1	51.3	63.2	53.6
1980	65.5	75.5	56.6	56.2	76.9	67.1	68	62.1	71.8	64.6
2010	74	82.8	66.6	72.2	83.5	79.6	75.2	72.9	80.6	71.7
2040	78.7	86.2	74.7	78	86.6	83	79.5	78.1	84.1	77.3
2050	79.3	86.7	75.6	78.6	87.1	83.5	80.1	78.7	84.6	78.1
Total fertility (children per woman)										
1950	6.22	4.44	5.91	5.49	2.75	5.4	6.83	7.29	6.4	6.4
1980	2.55	1.8	4.5	4.11	1.76	2.23	4.24	4.95	1.69	2.85
2010	1.78	0.99	2.54	2.01	1.27	1.21	2.37	2.89	1.29	1.85
2040	1.85	1.29	1.85	1.85	1.55	1.49	1.85	1.85	1.59	1.85
2050	1.85	1.34	1.85	1.85	1.6	1.54	1.85	1.85	1.64	1.85

Source: UN Population Database (2008).

and it is expected to decrease further to 10.1 by 2050. Similarly, other countries also witness a continued decrease in the mortality rate over the observation period. For example, Korea's infant mortality rate was 115 in 1950, which, however, had declined to 23 in 1980 and is forecast to decrease further to 3.3 by 2050.

Life expectancy has also witnessed a steady improvement for China. The age cohort born in the 1950s were expected to live up to 44.6 years, while this increased to 65.5 years in 1980. By 2050 it is forecast that the life expectancy will be 79.3. In other words, a person who is born in 2050 is expected to live 35 years longer than a person who was born in 1950. By comparison, the more advanced economies in the region, e.g. Japan, Korea and Singapore, will witness the longest life expectancy. For Japan, for example, life expectancy at birth in 2050 is forecast to be 87.1.

The continued drop in the fertility rate in China obviously contributes to the rapid aging process in the country. In 1950 a woman, on average, gave birth to 6.22 babies. This reduced to 2.55 in 1980 and is expected to decline further to 1.85 by 2050, which is largely a result of the one-child policy in China. By comparison, the other selected Asian countries had higher fertility rates at the beginning of the observation period. However, over time all countries are expected to witness a decline in the fertility rate. For example, for Hong Kong, China, the rate dropped from 4.44 in 1950 to 1.8 in 1980 and is expected to decline further to 1.34 by 2050.

1.3. Pension crisis in China?

The data above clearly shows that China is aging. The major question, however, is how to respond to the rapidly aging population in terms of old-age income provision and to ensure that pension policies are sustainable in the long run. This chapter seeks to address this issue.

The structure of the remaining part of this chapter is as follows. Section 2 provides an overview of the Chinese pension system between 1949 and 2008. Section 3 presents the latest pension reforms (i.e. between 2008 and 2010) that have been implemented in China. Section 4 identifies problems associated with the current pension system. Section 5 proposes some policy recommendations based on the analysis in the previous sections. Section 6 concludes with a summary of results.

2. Historical overview of China's pension system (1949–2008)

2.1. Urban pension system

2.1.1. 1949–1997

After the new socialist China was established in 1949, the authorities promulgated Regulations on Labor Insurance in 1951. The regulations, as the first labor social security rules, served as the framework for the provision of cradle-to-grave benefits to urban employees. The urban population covered under this law included employees of SOEs (state owned enterprises) and large COEs (collectively owned enterprises), civil servants, and people working in other public institutions, e.g. universities, hospitals, etc. The system was run on a pay-as-you-go (PAYG) basis and solely funded by enterprises, at a rate of 3 percent of the wages paid; a 3 percent contribution rate was very low but feasible given the young population at that time. Pension funds were administered by local trade unions at the municipal level. In 1954 the All China Federation of Trade Unions was set up by the central government and took responsibility for pension fund administration at the national level. In other words, pension funds were pooled across the country, and thus pension provision could be optimized across regions with different demographic features by involving intra-national transfers. Ironically, the first established formal pension system in China was quite advanced in terms of pooling risk; the system, however, was abandoned when the Cultural Revolution took place in 1966.

Given the youthful age structure of the Chinese population at that time, the PAYG system worked well, but it lasted only 15 years, until 1966, when the Cultural Revolution started. This unforgettable disaster in Chinese contemporary history stopped economic growth and threw the whole country into ceaseless political battles and social chaos. Under these circumstances, trade unions – which had been responsible for pension administration and provisions – were abandoned and dismantled. In consequence, pension fund surpluses accumulated at both local and national levels during the previous years were eroded and/or embezzled for other purposes.

In 1978 China started its economic reform and opening-up policy. With continuous economic and social reforms, after several years' trial in the late 1980s, the Chinese government decided to deepen its pension reform with the aim of establishing a multi-pillar system more able to cope with the aging population. This was marked by the passing of state council resolution number 33 on pension reforms for Enterprise Employees, a legal formalization of several provisional regulations. This resolution called for significant contributions from individual workers. Previously, pension funds had mainly relied on contributions from enterprises, with any pension deficits met by the state. It was stipulated that employees should make contributions of not more than 3 percent of their wages to the first pillar, and these were expected to rise along with wage growth, given that the contribution rate is a percentage of wages.

2.1.2. 1997–present

In 1997 a milestone pension regulation, i.e. the *State Council Document No. 26 Establishment of a Unified Basic Pension System for Enterprise Employees,* was published. The regulation – largely influenced by recommendations from the World Bank (World Bank, 1997) – required the establishment of a multi-pillar system. Based on the new model, China was to establish a unified pension system by 2000 on a national level. The system should cover all employees working in cities and towns, regardless of the ownership of enterprises or the organizations with which employees were affiliated. Previously, pension reform mainly covered the SOE and COE workers, in addition to workers in other public sectors.

Starting from 1997 through to 2008, China's pension system underwent continuous changes. For example, in 2006 benefits from the social pooling part were not subject to a ceiling any longer, while the replacement rate increased by 1 percent for each year's contribution.

The current urban pension system consists of three pillars and four components, as described below (see Table 7.4 for details):

- Pillar 1A. This pillar is run on a PAYG basis and serves as a social pooling mechanism. The contributions are made solely by the employer, while the contribution rate is 20 percent of payroll. The expected replacement rate is approximately 35 percent of the average local wages with 35 years of contributions.
- Pillar 1B. This pillar is a mandatory individual account, designed to be fully funded. The contribution is 8 percent of employees' salary, which is contributed solely by employees. The expected replacement rate is about 24.2 percent. To receive benefits from pillars 1A and 1B, certain vesting requirements need to be met, notably a minimum of 15 years of contribution, a retirement age of 60 (men) and 55 (women), etc.
- Pillar 2. This is often referred to the enterprise annuity (EA) scheme in China, which is the equivalent of occupational pension schemes in Western countries. Participation in this pillar is voluntary. So far it has been mainly established by the large SOEs, and the contribution rate varies between enterprises.
- Pillar 3. This refers to the voluntary individual saving/pension schemes and is designed to meet the needs of the population who want to receive a higher income after retirement.

2.2. Rural pension system

Compared to urban residents, the rest of the Chinese population – principally the rural population – had no formal pension system till recently. For this group, family support plays a pivotal role.

The first central guidance related to the Chinese rural pension system was released by the Ministry of Civil Affairs in 1992, i.e. "Temporary Rules on Rural Social Insurance at the County-Level". This regulation includes details concerning contribution rates, benefit levels and payment methods, among others. Following the release of this regulation, a rural pension system aiming for national coverage started to be implemented across the country; it was reported that by 1997 accumulated funds amounted to approximately RMB 10.7 billion, while the number of contributors was around 82.8 million (Leisering, et al 2002).

Table 7.4 Existing urban pension system in China

Pillar	Mode	Mandatory (M) or voluntary (V)	Contribution	Benefit	Tax relief	Main regulator
Pillar 0	Social assistance	N.A.	State budget	Minimum living standard	N.A.	Ministry of Civil Affairs and MOHRSS
Pillar 1a	Social pooling and pay-as-you-go	M	20 percent of salary	59 percent of average local salary	Fully deductible	MOHRSS
Pillar 1b	Individual account	M	8 percent of salary	Fully deductible	MOHRSS	
Pillar 2: Enterprise annuity	Individual account	V	Varies	Varies	Very limited; only up to 5 percent of payroll	MOHRSS
Pillar 2: Others	Individual account	V	Varies	Varies	Very limited	N.A.
Pillar 3	Insurance products	V	Varies	Varies	Only selected insurance products	China Insurance Regulatory Commission
Pillar 4	Informal family support	N.A.	Family members	N.A.	N.A.	N.A.
NSSF	Strategic reserve fund	N.A.	State budget; transfer of state ownership in SOE; lottery income	N.A.	N.A.	Ministry of Finance and MOHRSS

Source: Herd et al. (2010); Hu and Stewart (2009a).

Note: MOHRSS = Ministry of Human Resources and Social Security; NSSF = National Social Security Fund; SOE = state owned enterprise.

In 1997 a thorough assessment of this trial rural pension system was conducted by the State Council, which largely resulted from discontent and disputes from local governments and central ministries, as well as farmers themselves. As a result of this assessment, it was found that the economic and financial conditions at that time were not adequate to support this system; therefore, the State Council decided to rectify the system, which in effect terminated the trial schemes in rural areas. As a consequence, pension arrangements under the old system were either transferred to insurance companies or taken over by the local governments. The main reasons leading to termination of the trial system, among others, included financial unsustainability, insufficient matching contributions from (local and central) governments, a great burden on farmers and lack of flexibility in terms of participation.

Since then there has been no (major) pension system initiated by the central government in rural areas. All the existing rural pension systems are mainly legacy schemes of the 1990s trial, with some new systems initiated by the local government. As of 2007, there were 51.7 million participants in the rural system, while the system was operating in 1,805 out of 2,000-plus counties in China (*Caijing Magazine*, 2008). As of 2006, the accumulated amount of funds was approximately RMB 34.1 billion. Meanwhile, as of 2006, pensioners in 1,484 out of 1,947 counties in China received pensions, on average less than the minimum rural living standards, which amounted to 88 percent of the total 3.3 million rural pensioners. Among them, 1.2 million rural pensioners, or 36 percent of the total rural pensioners, received less than RMB 10 per month.

The schemes mentioned above were primarily designed to cover the general rural population, particularly those rural residents whose main income source was farming. However, with rapid industrialization and urbanization of the Chinese economy, two new groups have emerged within the rural population, which has important implications for the Chinese pension system. The first group is immigrant workers, i.e. farmers who work and live in urban areas, while the second group consists of those farmers who lost their land with urbanization. With this, two issues remain unanswered, which will be addressed in depth below.

2.3. National Social Security Fund

In addition to the above urban and rural pension arrangements; the Chinese pension system has another important component, i.e. the National Social Security Fund (NSSF). The NSSF was established in 2000 by the central government in view of the increasing aging population and the expected looming fiscal pressure in the coming decades. The National Council of the Social Security Fund, the supervisory and management body of the NSSF, was established concurrently. In nature, the Chinese NSSF is similar to the national pension reserve funds in some Western countries, e.g. Norway's Government Pension Fund and the Irish National Pensions Reserve Fund (Blundell-Wignall et al., 2008), but different from the provident funds established in Singapore, Malaysia and Hong Kong.

Inflows to the NSSF mainly come from four sources. These are fiscal transfers from the central government budget, equity asset transfers from state share sales in SOEs, national lottery income and investment income. The principal asset source is the central government fiscal transfer. For example, in 2000 there was a RMB 20 billion transfer as set-up capital, and in 2009 this rose to RMB 82.6 billion – accounting for approximately 50 percent of the total assets. The second largest source is the transfer of revenues from state share sales in SOEs. Based on international experience, China decided in 2001 to transfer a portion of the state shares in SOEs to the NSSF in order to build up the NSSF. Specifically during the IPOs (initial public offerings) in both domestic and overseas stock exchanges, 10 percent of the state shares in SOEs were to be sold on the market, and the resulting revenue transferred to the NSSF.

Regarding fund management, it is stipulated that the NSSF can be invested by in-house teams or outsourced to specialist fund managers. Investment by in-house managers is limited to bank deposits, government bonds and other financial instruments with high liquidity and security, as well as private equity related products as initiated recently. For those funds invested by outsourced fund managers, a number of quantitative investment restrictions apply. The minimum investment limit for bank deposits and government bonds is 50 percent, of which at least 10 percent should be invested in bank deposits. Investments in non-government bonds, i.e. corporate bonds and other financial bonds, should not exceed 10 percent of the total assets. In addition, the limit on shares and investment securities is a maximum of 40 percent. As of 2007, the upper limit on investment in foreign markets is 20 percent of the total assets.

3. Recent reforms, 2008–2010

Despite progress achieved on China's pension system over the past decades, it is still associated with various fundamental problems. The Chinese government has been aware of these issues and has continued its efforts to fix the problematic pension system in recent years. In 2008 the central government outlined the direction and objective of China's social insurance system reform – including (basic) pensions. It aims to provide national pension coverage by 2020 in both rural and urban areas, with the reformed system to satisfy four major criteria: (a) broad coverage, (b) a low and reasonable minimum benefit, (c) a multi-layered structure, and (d) sustainability. Various reforms have been implemented to meet this objective.

3.1. Social Insurance Law

The most prominent development is the enactment of China's first ever Social Insurance Law on 28 October 2010 in the Chinese top legislature –the National People's Congress (NPC). Already in 1994, the NPC had included finalization of this law as one of its legislative priorities. However, for various reasons this law could not be passed until 16 years later, i.e. in 2010. This milestone law opened a new page in the history of China's social insurance. It mandated participation in basic social insurance schemes in China, while in the past it was just regulated by guidance from the MOHRSS or administrative decrees from the State Council, which contributed to wide participation evasion and a low compliance rate. Meanwhile, it stipulates that the pooling level of China's pension system should be elevated from the county or city level directly to the national level, rather than via an interim stage at the provincial level, which risks a prolonged national pooling process resulting from well-observed bureaucratic gaming between the central and local governments in China.

3.2. New rural pension scheme

Despite the large rural population in China (over 50 percent of the national population lives in the countryside according to 2008 data; UN Population Database, 2008), a formal pension system had been practically non-existent till recently. In June 2009 the central government announced the introduction of a new voluntary rural pension scheme after various local experiments. The key features are as follows (see Table 7.5 for details):

- A flat-rate pension of RMB 55 per month will be paid.
- An individual account will be created to which contributors can choose to pay between RMB 100 and 500 annually, in increments of RMB 100. The local government must pay at least RMB 30 per year to the account. Contributors must pay into the individual account for 15 years to obtain a pension from the account and the flat-rate pension, or if older than 45 at the inception of the scheme they must make one extra contribution at age 60 in order to have a total of 15 years of contribution.
- The monthly pension from the individual account will amount to the account balance divided by 139 and is payable for life by the local government.
- People over age 60 at the introduction of the scheme can draw a pension if their children (aged 18 and older) join the scheme.
- In the central and western provinces the entire cost of the flat-rate pension will be paid by the central government, whereas in the east the provincial governments will pay half. Local governments are free to add to the basic pension and make payments to the individual accounts.
- The pension from the individual account will be paid by the local government, which is responsible for any shortfall in the cash flow from the individual account of the pension.
- The balances of the accounts must be invested in bank deposits, the return on which will be credited to the individual accounts.

As seen above, the new rural pension scheme is in line with the basic structure of urban enterprise pension system; i.e. it consists of two pillars: one social pooling and the other an individual account. The main consideration favoring an aligned

Table 7.5 Rural pension system in China

Pillar	Mode	Mandatory (M) or voluntary (V)	Contribution	Benefit	Tax relief	Main regulator
Pillar 0	Social assistance	N.A.	State budget	Min. living standard	N.A.	Ministry of Civil Affairs and Ministry of Agriculture
Pillar 1a	Social pooling and pay-as-you-go	V	State and local government budget	Min. RMB 55 per month	Fully deductible	Ministry of Human Resources and Social Security
Pillar 1b	Individual account	V	Individual; local government and village	10 percent of average local income	Fully deductible	Ministry of Human Resources and Social Security

Source: Herd et al. (2010); Hu and Stewart (2009a).

structure rests on the planned eventual convergence and integration between rural and urban pensions systems in China in the future.

3.3. Migrant workers

With economic development in China, an increasing number of rural (young) farmers have been leaving their land to work in urban areas. It was estimated that as of 2009 there were approximately 250 million migrant workers, while at the same time there were still around 150 million surplus laborers in rural areas. Because of the dualism of the Chinese economy these migrant workers are not covered by the urban social welfare system and therefore are not entitled to the related benefits – including pensions – despite the fact that they work and live in a city. However, it is worth noting that in some localities, for various reasons (e.g. pension coverage expansion, pressure from the central government, increasing awareness of improving social welfare for the poor), migrant workers have been allowed and encouraged to participate in the urban pension system. In this context, for the purpose of incentivizing participation the contribution rate is normally lower than the standard rates. For example, the employer contribution rate could be as low as 10 percent of payroll, while the employee contribution rate is normally 8 percent. A recent estimate (MOHRSS, 2009) shows that, as of 2008, 17 percent of the migrant workers participated in the urban pension system.

Meanwhile, in order to better protect the interests of migrant workers the MOHRSS released the "Rules on Migrant Workers' Participation on the Basic Pension Insurance" in early 2009 for public consultation. The key parameters include lower contribution rates for employees (4 to 8 percent of wages) and employers (12 percent of payroll). All contributions are deposited in migrant workers' individual accounts. Meanwhile, when migrant workers move between provinces, pension records are kept at localities till their normal retirement age. In other words, all contributory history at different locations is recognized for the purposes of pension payment, which aims to solve one of the most difficult problems in China, i.e. portability between provinces. The benefit consists of two components, i.e. social pooling and an individual account, similar to the urban pension system. However, if they retire in rural areas and join the new rural pension system, the pension accumulation would be transferred to the local insurance bureau in rural areas, and they would be entitled to the relevant benefits. If they retire in rural areas and do not join the new rural pension system, funds in individual accounts would be paid to migrant workers as a lump sum.

3.4. Landless farmers

China is a country witnessing rapid industrialization and urbanization, the pace of which has been accelerating over the past 10 years or so. China's urban population as a percent of total population increased from 49% in 2010 to 54% in 2014, an increase of five percentage points. In 1950 , the corresponding urban population share was only 13%. (UN Population Database 2008). One main consequence of this trend is the increasing number of farmers who have lost their land. It was estimated (OECD, 2010) that between 1998 and 2006 approximately 18.9 million farmers lost their land. Other sources note that by 2007 approximately 40 million people had lost their land, while 1 million or 2 million farmers are expected to become landless annually in the foreseeable future. This development has important implications for China's pension system, largely because Chinese farmers in the past have traditionally relied heavily on their land to support them in their old age. In this regard, the national government has encouraged local governments to experiment according to the conditions in their own area. Based on five pilot schemes, the following patterns have emerged:

- The systems are similar in design to the urban system: a PAYG part and an individual account. The PAYG part is financed by contributions from city and county governments. Contributions from villages go to either component.
- Typically, one-third of the cost of the system is financed by the local government, one-third by the village collective and one-third by the employees.
- If landless farmers join the urban pension system they cannot join the township scheme, but in some cases those who are members of the 1992 rural pension system can remain in that scheme as it was voluntary in nature.
- There are regulations concerning the minimum number of contributions, the minimum pensionable age and benefit payment methods.

3.5. *The informal sector*

Compared to workers in the formal sector – who normally join either mandatory or voluntary pension systems, or both – those in the informal sector are typically not covered well (in many cases not at all) by modern structured pension systems (Hu and Stewart, 2009b). They do not have access to pension plans organized or run by employers, they may change jobs frequently, and they often live and work in rural areas where financial infrastructure is poor or non-existent. These workers may also come from lower-income and less educated groups, meaning that their knowledge and understanding of pension and saving products are limited, and their resources for long-term saving scarce. Hence, gaining access to a structured pension system is a challenge for these workers. This problem also exists in China, particularly in light of the increasing share of the informal sectors in the national economy.

In China, in principle participation in the urban enterprise pension system should be compulsory for both the formal and informal sectors. However, owing to lax regulation and a low compliance rate, very few employees in the informal sector join these schemes. To encourage participation, more flexible terms are applied in some provinces (it should be noted that local governments have the authority to revise the rules related to pension contribution rates according to specific local situations and conditions). For example, in many cases the contribution rate for the self-employed is reduced from 28 percent (of which 20 percent is paid by the employer and 8 percent by the employee) to 20 percent, of which 8 percent is credited to individual accounts.

3.6. Pensions for the Public Service Unit (PSU) sector

The current civil servant and Public Service Unit (PSU)[4] pension system in China allows employees to enjoy up to a 90 percent replacement rate, in comparison to 60 percent for a standard urban enterprise old-age pension. It is an unfunded PAYG system, which has mainly been financed by either the state or the employer, while employees normally do not contribute. Fiscal costs arising from the current civil servant and PSU pension system have been very high, and the burden is expected to keep increasing in the next decades.

Starting in 2008 the central government has decided to reform the PSU pension system given its financial unsustainability against the background of overall reform in the PSU sector in China. The objective is to bring the PSU pension system alongside the current urban enterprise pension system. After discussion and experimentation, the new model preferred by the MOHRSS is a system that is more or less consistent with the current urban pension system, i.e. social pooling plus an individual account. Meanwhile, the contribution rate and level of benefits would be similar to those of the urban pension system too. Given that the after-reform benefits level (60 percent) would be lower than the current level (90 percent), the government has been discussing the importance and necessity of promoting (voluntary) occupational pension schemes in order to keep the overall after-reform level around 90 percent.

In February 2009 five provinces were selected by the MOHRSS to implement the pilot PSU pension schemes, namely Shanxi, Shanghai, Zhejiang, Guangdong and Chongqing. It is noted that the exact design of the pilot schemes is not detailed and thus subject to the discretion of local governments, which reflects the typical gradualist reform approach frequently adopted by the Chinese government.

3.7. Private pensions

Private pensions in China exist in two main forms, namely enterprise annuities (EAs) and group pension insurance. In 2004 the MOHRSS released two EA decrees, which served as a catalyst to the rapid growth of the EA market over the period 2005–2007. However, for various reasons the market has not been developing as fast as expected since then. In response to this issue, the MOHRSS has been trying to stimulate the development of the EA market through a range of reforms. However, as Impavido , Hu and Li (2009) note, ". . . the current investment regulation is very conservative and based on holdings and some concentration quantitative limits that are mainly aimed at controlling market risk. However, no credit quantitative limits are prescribed to control for credit and liquidity risk".

In addition to EAs, group pension insurance is another type of supplementary private pension arrangement in China, purchased by sponsors from insurance companies on behalf of their employees. A key difference between EAs and group pension insurance is their tax treatment. For the latter, pension contributions are not subject to tax relief, although insurance companies that offer such life insurance products (to be approved by the State Taxation Administration) are allowed to deduct such contributions from business tax (but not corporate tax). For the former, pension contributions by the employer are tax deductible up to a limit of 5 percent of payroll, which, however, is lower than the maximum contribution limit (i.e. 1/12 of payroll) set by the MOHRSS. This market is subject to regulation and supervision by the insurance regulator, i.e. the China Insurance Regulatory Commission (CIRC), while in this context there has been some competition between the MOHRSS and CIRC. Notably, in December 2009 CIRC released a regulation on pensions, the *Notice on Trust Management of Pension Funds*, a regulatory initiative widely interpreted as competing with the two EA regulations of the MOHRSS.

3.8. The NSSF

As China's pension reserve fund as well as the largest institutional investor, the NSSF has undergone continual transformation and reform. Most recently it was observed that its investment strategy has been moving from traditional, conservative investments towards more liberalized investments. For example, the NSSF is the only pension fund in China that is allowed to invest abroad, while the upper limit is as high as 20 percent of the overall portfolio. So far all the foreign investment is outsourced to overseas financial institutions, with total assets of USD 1.6 billion. As of 2009, 12 foreign asset managers shared the total outsourced funds, under five different types of mandates, namely (a) global stocks (excluding US stocks), (b) US stocks, (c) Hong Kong stocks, (d) global bonds and (e) cash. Note that at the end of 2009, the NSSF selected another 12 overseas financial institutions to manage more assets. Over the period 2009–2010, another interesting observation is that the NSSF has been becoming more interested in private equity and venture capital investments, largely because of their high absolute returns.

To further increase the size of the NSSF, the Chinese government restarted its process of transferring 10 percent of state shares in the listed SOEs to the NSSF. In June 2009 the *Notice on Transferring Partial State Shares in Domestic Listed SOEs to Strengthen the NSSF* was jointly issued by the Ministry of Finance, the State-Owned Assets Supervision and Administration Commission, the China Securities Regulatory Commission and the NSSF. The market viewed it as positive news, thus facilitating a smooth transfer. It is expected that the total amount of transferred assets could be up to RMB 65 billion.

4. Assessment of China's pension system and reform

In the preceding sections we provided an overview of China's pension system in general, and particularly recent developments. In this section we will critically review and assess the system, aiming to find out what the main problems are and where they are.

4.1. Insufficient coverage in rural areas

Pension coverage in China is largely limited to urban employees working in the public sector of the economy. The rural pension system is specially designed for rural areas and is quite different from and much less generous than those operating in urban areas. Pension participation is voluntary, and the practical issues, e.g. how to make contributions to the pension system, are left to the local government. Despite the development of rural pension system particularly as detailed in previous section, the current coverage is still not sufficient. Table 7.6 gives rural pension coverage statistics over the period 2005–2010. As of 2010 it was estimated that the coverage rate was approximately 18.6 percent (an increase from 9.5 percent in 2005); i.e. one rural resident was covered out of every five to six people. Some argue that China is still a developing country and the rural population is large, and therefore the reform process (i.e. the pace of coverage extension) should be conservative rather than aggressive in light of the potential huge fiscal burden. OECD experiences, however, show that this argument might not be plausible. Table 7.7 indicates that as of 2009, i.e. the year of the introduction of the new pension scheme in China, China was already more advanced than some of the then OECD countries when the latter introduced their rural pension scheme. For example, with regards to the agricultural workforce relative to the whole economy, the ratio was 40.8 percent for China, compared to 52.7 percent for Portugal and 55.3 percent for Greece. Meanwhile, Chinese farmers were wealthier than those in some OECD countries were when those countries first introduced their

Table 7.6 Coverage in the rural pension system over the period 2005–2010

	Participants (millions)	Rural population (millions)	Coverage rate (%)
2005	54.4	574.9	9.5
2006	53.7	567.8	9.5
2007	51.7	560.2	9.2
2008	55.9	555.4	10.1
2009	86.9	547.7	15.9
2010	100	539.0	18.6

Source: National Bureau of Statistics (2010); MOHRSS (2009).

Note: "Rural population" refers to those older than 15 years of age.

Table 7.7 Economic structure when rural pension system was introduced in OECD countries and China

	Date of introduction	Agricultural workforce (as % of whole economy)	Agricultural value added (as % of whole economy)	GDP per capita in year of introduction in USD
Early adopters		40.3	26.9	4,725
Portugal	1919	52.7	n.a.	1,958
Denmark	1891	44.9	37.0	2,778
Spain	1947	48.8	41.0	3,711
Sweden	1913	46.2	23.0	4,230
Greece	1961	55.3	23.0	6,527
United Kingdom	1946	5.1	7.0	6,543
Italy	1957	29	17.0	7,331
Late adopters				
France	1952	27	13.0	9,450
Germany	1957	13.4	7.0	9,523
Netherlands	1957	10.7	11.0	11,379
Belgium	1967	5.5	5.0	12,914
Ireland	1988	15.4	10.3	15,314
United States	1950	12.2	6.8	16,946
Memorandum				
China	2009	40.8	11.3	5,919

Source: OECD (2010).

Note: OECD = Organisation for Economic Co-operation and Development.

rural pension system, as indicated by the GDP per capita. Therefore, we believe that China could afford to extend the new rural pension system at a faster pace.

4.2. Uneven coverage in urban areas

The current urban pension system largely favors the state sector of the economy, particularly employees in the SOEs. In the recent period, pension coverage in the SOE sector has achieved a good result. Figure 7.1 shows that up to 85 percent of the workforce in the SOE sector is covered. However, for employees in other sectors the coverage rate is much lower. This is particularly the case for the self-employed and those who work in domestic private enterprises; for the latter approximately 10 percent are covered by formal pension arrangements.

Various reasons contribute to this uneven coverage depending on the enterprise ownership in urban areas. The most prominent factor is the high contribution rate in China. As given in Table 7.8, the overall contribution rate in China's social

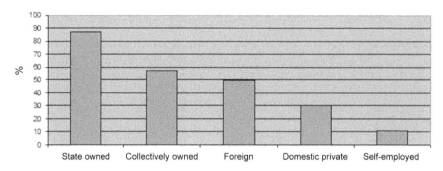

Figure 7.1 Pension coverage rate (%) of urban enterprises
Source: OECD (2010).

Table 7.8 Contribution rates in China's social insurance system (% of payroll/wages)

	Pensions	Unemployment insurance	Medical insurance	Work injury insurance	Maternity insurance	Housing provident funds	Total
Employers	20	2	6	2	1	8	39
Employees	8	1	2	0	0	8	19
Total	28	3	8	2	1	16	58

Source: MOHRSS (2009).

insurance system could be as high as 58 percent, of which 39 percent is paid by employers and 19 percent by employees. Fifty-eight percent is very high by international standards (Hu and Davis, 2009). Meanwhile, the pension parameters originally designed for formal sector employees are not attractive to those in the informal sector. For example, the strict vesting requirements are not attractive to migrant workers, the self-employed or other employees working in the informal sector, since they are relatively young and mobile and therefore see distant pension benefits as (much) less valuable than cash received at the present time; thus, they lack incentives to join the urban pension system. Ironically, participation in the urban enterprise pension system is in principle mandatory, but in reality, as the data shows, employers and employees try to avoid contributing. China's revised Social Insurance Law took effect on July 1, 2011. This law has provisions for participation in social insurance schemes by the expatriates. It is expected that this law will better address evasion and low compliance problems more effectively.

4.3. Fragmentation of the current pension system

China's pension pooling is heterogeneous across the country, both vertically and horizontally. The main benefit of pension pooling is to spread the risk among the population. In principle, to achieve a full risk sharing, the size of the basic pooling unit should be as large as possible. Indeed, in many countries the whole national population serves as the pooling base. In China, however, the pooling unit at the vertical level is quite small, at best at the provincial level. It is typical and still common today that pension pooling is arranged within a county or city., The central government has recognized this issue and, as of 2010, it was claimed that in more than half of the 34 provinces in China provincial pooling had been achieved. However, a deeper analysis indicates that the so-called provincial pooling is not genuine but rather just an administrative arrangement.

Horizontally, pension systems vary by sector. For example, employees working in urban enterprises participate in the urban enterprise pension scheme. However, those who work for the government and certain PSUs are covered by the separate, non-contributory pension system. And it becomes even more complicated: those working in certain other types of PSUs normally participate in the urban enterprise pension systems. Meanwhile, migrant workers and landless farmers always face a dilemma regarding which pension system to join: the common urban system, the new rural pension system or the stand-alone migrant work pension system.

The problem of fragmentation and variation in the current system largely results from the gradualist approach adopted by the pension reformers. In other words, the central government, through its relevant ministries – principally the MOHRSS – issues directives or operational guidelines and makes changes in policy from time to time. The nature of the directives is such that only rough guidance is provided. In this context, policy implementation is left to the lower levels of government, and local governments are allowed to adapt the general guidance to their specific local conditions. The underlying logic is justifiable in that it meets local demands for flexibility. In practice, however, it creates a great deal of variation and fragmentation.

4.4. Unsatisfactory investment returns

China's pension funds are managed according to different rules (Impavido et al., 2009).

a) Funds in the public pillar, i.e. pillars 1A and 1B, are managed by local social insurance agencies and are normally invested in bank deposits and government bonds.
b) Funds in the EA system have been managed by authorized private financial institutions since 2004.
c) Funds in the NSSF are managed by the NSSF council and either invested via an in-house team or outsourced to external financial institutions.

Table 7.9 provides statistics regarding how the returns of pension funds in China vary. The worst performers were funds accumulated in pillars 1A and 1B. Over the period 2001–2009, the return varied between 2 percent and 4 percent, which is not surprising if one takes into account the fact that bank deposits and government bonds have been the only investment vehicles. In comparison, returns for

Table 7.9 Investment return of China's pension funds by type

	Pillar 1, average %	Pillar 2, average %	NSSF, average %	Inflation rate, average %
2001	2.6	n.a.	1.73	0.7
2002	2.0	n.a.	2.59	0.8
2003	2.2	n.a.	3.56	1.2
2004	2.4	n.a.	2.61	3.9
2005	2.8	n.a.	4.16	1.8
2006	2.8	9.6	29.01	1.5
2007	3.2	24.5	43.19	4.8
2008	4.0	–1.8	–6.79	5.9
2009	3.0	7.8	16.12	–0.7
Average (2006–2009)	3.3	10.0	20.4	2.9

Source: Pillar 1: average of returns on bank deposits and government bonds. Pillar 2: Impavido et al. (2009). NSSF: NSSF website: www.ssf.gov.cn/Eng_Introduction/201206/t20120620_5603.html. Inflation rate: National Bureau of Statistics. www.stats.gov.cn/english/

Note: NSSF = National Social Security Fund.

pillar 2 (i.e. EAs) and the NSSF were much higher. Over the period for which data is available the average return on EAs was 10 percent, while it was 20.4 percent for the NSSF. When returns are compared to the inflation rate, the superior performance of funds in EAs and the NSSF is clear.

The poor performance in pillar 1 is worrying in the sense that assets within this pillar have been accumulating rapidly over the past years. As of 2010, it is estimated that the total pillar 1 funds could be as high as RMB 1.4 trillion, while those within the whole social insurance system would be up to RMB 2 trillion. If pillar 1 funds were invested in a more diversified and liberalized manner, like EA and NSSF funds, the returns would be much higher, therefore lowering the fiscal burden of the government. A simple calculation indicates that the total pension pot in China could increase or decrease by more than RMB 10 billion for every 1 percentage point difference (plus or minus) in the investment return.

4.5. Poor collaboration between ministerial agencies

China's pension system is mainly supervised by the MOHRSS. The MOHRSS is in charge of supervising pensions related to both private and public sectors (including those of civil servants), and it is responsible for issuing legislation and/ or guidelines on pension-related issues. In addition to the MOHRSS, three other financial regulators, i.e. the China Banking Regulatory Commission, the CIRC and the China Securities Regulatory Commission also play an important role in supervising the private pension market. Regarding private pensions in the form of insurance products (group or individual), the CIRC is the principal regulator and supervisor.

The Ministry of Finance and State Taxation Administration also have influence over the private pensions market in China, which mainly stems from their power in setting tax policies and collecting pension contributions. Meanwhile, the State-Owned Assets Supervision and Administration Commission also plays an important role in approving large SOEs to set up EA schemes.

Given the above regulatory structure it is important to ensure a working collaboration mechanism between the relevant authorities in China. However, such mechanisms are not really in place at the moment. In fact, a lack of cooperation between ministries and authorities has been observed to be actually hindering the development of the EA market.

5. Policy recommendations

As critically reviewed above, it is clear that the existing structure of China's pension system, in spite of its progress in the past, is not able to address the challenges it faces. Therefore, in this section we aim to propose policy recommendations in order to improve the system and thereby make the system more sustainable in the long run (see Table 7.10).

5.1. The modified new structure

A. **Pillar 0:** a universal old-age social assistance system. All urban citizens – regardless whether they have contributed to the system over their career life – are entitled to such benefits. The main purpose of this is to establish a universal system in which all citizens would not fall into poverty after retirement. Note that it is a non-contributory scheme, i.e. is entirely financed by general tax revenues, as it is now. It is recognized that the current social assistance system (i.e. Dibao, which covers the elderly poor) provides a floor of protection against poverty for the elderly in China. Therefore, given that it has increasingly been playing a positive role, and is supported by governments at different levels and widely welcomed within China, fundamental changes are not necessary, we believe. However, further improvements are still needed so as to tackle various related weaknesses. First, a well-functioning monitoring and evaluation mechanism should be in place to ensure a fair and transparent system, which could be achieved by increasing resources in terms of financing and staffing of the authorities, particularly at local levels. Meanwhile, the adjustment of old-age related Dibao subsidies over time should be based on clearly prescribed rules that take into account fiscal constraints (at both central and local government levels), wage growth and economic development, among other factors. At the moment the adjustment mechanism is rather opaque and is thus subject to political risk,

Table 7.10 Proposed new (urban) pension structure in China

Pillar	Funded vs. non-funded	Mode	Purpose	Mandatory (M) or voluntary (V)	Contribution	Benefit
Pillar 0	Non	Social assistance	Poverty relief	N.A.	State budget	Min. living standard
Pillar 1a	Non	Social pooling and pay-as-you-go	Income distribution	M	10 percent of salary (employer)	30 percent of average local salary
Pillar 1b	Non	Notional defined contribution	Actuarial fairness	M	5 percent of salary (employee)	15 percent
Pillar 2: Enterprise annuity	Funding	Individual account	Decent post-retirement life	V	10 percent of salary, split equally between employer and employee	20–30 percent
Pillar 3	Funding	Insurance products	More comfortable post-retirement life	V	Varies	Varies
Pillar 4	n.a.	Informal family support	n.a.	N.A.	Family members	N.A.
NSSF	n.a.	Strategic reserve fund	n.a.	N.A.	State budget; transfer of state ownership in SOEs; lottery income	N.A.

Source: Author.

potentially putting the benefits of the elderly at risk. Second, better ministerial collaboration is needed. In China the social assistance program is the responsibility of the Ministry of Civil Affairs, while pension issues are mainly under the MOHRSS. However, there is often overlap between their responsibilities, particularly for this component of the overall old-age provision system in China. For example, in some localities local governments (i.e. on the MOHRSS side) have experimented with some pilot programs, e.g. an old-age allowance (i.e. every resident older than 65 is allowed to receive a certain amount of benefits); this is apparently a similar scheme to Dibao, leading to an overlap. Consequently, the Ministry of Civil Affairs and the MOHRSS should establish a mechanism so as to better accommodate collaboration, thus avoiding unnecessary conflict of ministerial interests.

B. **Pillar 1:** mandatory urban pension system. The basic structure is the same as for the existing one; i.e. it consists of two components, and participation is mandatory. However, pillar 1B would be transformed into a notional defined-contribution scheme, while pillar 1A would still be run on a PAYG basis. In principle, it is mandatory for all salaried workers who work in urban areas, including regular urban workers, immigrant workers and informal sector workers. In other words, this pillar aims for as wide a target group as possible, consequently a less fragmented system. The ultimate objective is to achieve national pooling.

i) *Pillar 1A*, as a PAYG pillar, aims to cover basic pension needs for those who have contributed and meet other relevant vesting criteria. The contribution rate could be around 10 percent, or even lower, depending on fiscal constraints at both central and local government levels. We believe that it is important to reduce the current high contribution rate, which has been observed to be one of the key obstacles to including firms, particularly small and medium enterprises (SME), into the system (Hu and Stewart, 2009a). Meanwhile, by international standards, the current contribution rate of 28 percent is very high for the replacement rate. In practice, it has greatly discouraged firms from joining the system. This reality is unfortunate, in that the current age profile of this population group is typically (much) younger than the national average. Therefore, excluding them from the system prevents the government from taking advantage of the large cash surplus that could otherwise have been arisen. Meanwhile, without formal pension coverage this population group will surely have difficulties when they retire in 30 or more years, not least because of the much larger elderly population and smaller younger population to support them at that time. The benefit level would be set around 30 percent of the average local wages. Of course, given characteristics of the political economy between central and local governments in China, this level could vary according to the local fiscal conditions. However, the minimum level should be 25 percent across the country, in order to provide a basic living for pensioners. Meanwhile, this pillar would serve the function of a typical social welfare system, i.e. income redistribution across groups of the population, given that benefits are based on average local wages rather than individual wages. In this way lower-income earners receive proportionally higher benefits, and vice versa.

b) For *Pillar 1B*, one main innovation of our model is to transform the current pillar 1B (which by design is fully funded) into a notional defined-contribution pillar. A similar approach has been advocated by Nicole Barr and Peter Diamond, among other renowned pension experts (Development and Reform Center of the State Council, 2005). The contributions could be made mainly by employees, at the level of 5 percent of their salary. The expected replacement rate would be 15 percent, which, however, is subject to an automatic balancing mechanism according to varying and changing situations. The reasons for this change arise from both economic and financial judgments. Economically, the current "empty" individual accounts are backed by an implicit government commitment to pay a certain pension when a person retires. If the individual accounts are filled, then they will have tradable government debt. The swapping from implicit debt to tradable debt makes no difference to the overall government balance sheet. Financially, the current "back-filling" pilot in 13 provinces has encountered a dilemma. On the one hand, central and local governments have spared no effort to mobilize financial resources to back-fill the individual accounts, which, however, are currently deposited in banks or invested in government bonds and therefore face value depreciation in the long run. On the other hand, local governments in most of the reforming provinces are experiencing greater financial constraints in terms of making pension payments to current retirees, largely because much financial resources have been used to back-fill the above-mentioned individual accounts, thus putting local government budgets in a worse fiscal situation.

Based on a typical notional defined-contribution model, such as that in Sweden (Holzmann and Palmer, 2006), the modified pillar 1B account in China should be able to reduce fiscal pressures on both central and local governments, without distorting the labor market at the moment by closely linking contributions and benefits. Meanwhile, some balancing mechanism should be in place to match contributions and benefits in a more sustainable manner from the long-run perspective. The balancing mechanism is mainly used to address increasing longevity in China, particularly over the next decades, as shown in Tables 7.3a and 7.3b. As is well known, one of the main weaknesses of the notional defined-contribution model that is often cited in the literature is its negative impact on the saving rate, given its de facto PAYG status. However, we believe that this shortcoming is of less relevance in the Chinese context, given that China already has one of the highest saving rates in the world, and this trend is expected to continue for the next 30 years or more. Meanwhile, the notional defined-contribution model is not linked to the development of financial markets, which we believe is also of less relevance in China, largely owing to consideration of risk diversification. In other words, according to financial theory and in view of the current financial crisis, it is always wise to utilize both unfunded and funded systems. The existing Chinese pension model relies heavily on the latter: the system has (in principle) a fully funded pillar 1B, a defined-contribution-based EA, and individual savings, while only 1A is a PAYG system. Therefore, from the perspective of risk diversification, and given the (realistic) assumption that over the foreseeable future it is very likely that the Chinese economic growth, leading to wage growth, will be greater than investment returns, a notional defined-contribution model should be superior to a funded system. Hence, the benefits of the model are (a) respecting the fact that most pillar 1B accounts are currently operated as notional accounts, thus mitigating resistance from reforming local governments at different levels; (b) reducing fiscal constraints for both central and local governments, which in reality have almost brought further extension of the pilot program across the country to a standstill; and (c) achieving a better balance between PAYG and funded systems within an overall pension system, not least given the expected economic and demographic evolution of Chinese economy in the next 30 or more years.

C. **Pillar 2:** EA. This pillar would be the same as the current EA, i.e. voluntary, fully funded, trust based and professionally managed. However, some changes are needed to strengthen the role of the EA pillar in the system and promote the development of a Chinese EA market. Despite massive losses incurred in the private pension market in the OECD countries during the recent financial crisis, it is still argued that from the long-run perspective, particularly given financial considerations, the role of private pensions should be strengthened in order to close the gap between the (proportionally decreasing) benefits paid out from public pensions and the benefits needed to maintain a decent life for pensioners (Whitehouse and Stewart, 2007).

The contribution rate is variable, subject to the fiscal conditions of individual firms. However, the government could set up guidance regarding contribution levels, e.g. 10 percent of wages, which could be split equally between employers and employees. Thus, the expected replacement rate would be 20–30 percent, depending on investment performance over time. In this context it is important to allow tax relief for the EA contributions. At the moment only contributions from the employer up to 5 percent of payroll are entitled to such relief, while employee contributions do not receive tax relief. This has been argued to be one of the reasons holding back further development of the EA market in China. However, to avoid increasing income inequality in China via the social security system, (i.e. having wealthier employees in SOEs or other profitable enterprises become richer when they retire), in that low-wage earners in the informal sector and SMEs do not participate in the system, the government should first set a limit on the level of tax relief, i.e. a capped contribution towards the purposes of tax redemption. Meanwhile, collective pension funds should be designed in an affordable, efficient and convenient manner. We believe that given our proposed reforms to pillars 1A and 1B (especially the lower contribution rate) it would be much easier to encourage SMEs to set up EA schemes via collective pension funds compared to in the existing regime.

Meanwhile, the development of the EA system would facilitate reforms in other parts of the system. For example, one highly debated issue in China is how to reform pensions for employees working in the PSUs (Hu, 2010b). The current PSU system allows employees to be entitled to a 90 percent replacement rate. In 2008 the central government decided to reform the PSU system given its financial unsustainability as well as the overall reform of the PSU sector in China. The objective is to bring the PSU pension system in line with the current urban enterprise pension system. After discussion and experimentation the new model preferred by the MOHRSS was a system that is more or less consistent with the current urban pension system, i.e. social pooling plus an individual account. Meanwhile, the contribution rate and level of benefits would be similar to those for the urban pension system too. Given that the after-reform benefit level (60 percent) would be lower than the current level (90 percent), the government has been discussing the importance and necessity of promoting (voluntary) occupational pension schemes in order to keep the overall after-reform level around 90 percent. Therefore, an improved EA system will assist with experimenting with PSU reform in China, which has received strong resistance since its introduction as a pilot program in five provinces in February 2009.

D. **Pillar 3:** commercial life insurance products. Again, this will be the same as in the current system. This pillar is mainly relevant for the population group who aim for higher incomes, e.g. because of their higher income over their career life and thus higher expectation for their standard of living after retirement. This pillar in practice has a close interaction with pillar 2, i.e. the EA, for two reasons. First, given that the current EA system mainly relies on professional companies for investment management, insurance companies have been playing an important role in this context. For example, statistics show that as of 2010 over half of EA assets have been entrusted to insurance trustee companies. Second, because current life insurance products cannot enjoy as many tax benefits as EA assets, in the government's efforts (by the MOHRSS) to promote the EA system, it has been observed that traditional life insurance products previously managed by insurance companies have been reorganized into EA assets.

Meanwhile, it has been reported that insurance companies and local governments in Shanghai have been studying the possibility of providing insurance products that are entitled to tax relief like EA schemes. The prospect of this type of new products largely results from the recent decision by the central government to promote Shanghai as an international center in the areas of finance and shipping.

5.2. The rural pension system

As reviewed in this chapter, the current Chinese pension system has largely left the rural pension system out of the formal arrangements, at least at the national level. It is noted that any reform options for the Chinese rural pension system should take into account the following key characteristics of China, among others.

First, one fundamental difference between rural and urban regions in China is related to land. In rural China, which still accounts for more than 50 percent of the whole population, land is distributed to farmers. In terms of social protection, farmers have traditionally been viewed as advantaged compared to urban citizens, in that the former own the last resort for obtaining a livelihood or the means of production, i.e. the land, which is still owned by the state/village.

Second, the income stream is (much) less stable for farmers than urban employees. This is largely due to the economic structure of the two economies. In rural areas the main income source is farming. In this context, how many agricultural goods are produced, and therefore how much income is generated, largely depends on weather conditions, pest problems and other unexpected issues. Meanwhile, the level of income in rural areas is (much) lower than that in urban areas, while the growth of income is also lower in the former than in the latter.

Third, China in the past three decades has experienced rapid industrialization and urbanization. This fact has three implications for the pension system. First, a large number of immigrant workers have worked in urban areas and in the Town and Village ownership Enterprises (TVEs), and the population group in the first category typically moves around within the country. Second, a large number of landless farmers have emerged, and this is expected to accelerate in the foreseeable near future. Third, the urbanization rate in China is currently around 45 percent and will continue to rise over this century, expected to reach 73 percent by 2050 (UN Population Database, 2008).

For the purposes of including the rural population in the system we propose the following reforms.

A. **Pillar 0:** universal social assistance program. It is basically the same proposal as that for the urban system. The main purpose is to provide a floor of protection for the elderly in rural areas. It should fit well in the current rural Dibao and Wubao systems. The means-testing approach should be followed, rather than the universal benefit approach, given its lower fiscal burden on the government budget. The scheme would be non-contributory, and the benefits should be able to meet basic living needs in local rural areas.

B. **Pillar 1:** voluntary pension system. Given features related to China's rural economy as described above, it would be more appropriate to introduce a national voluntary retirement saving scheme, rather than mandatory occupational schemes, in the rural areas. However, it should be noted that this mainly refers to farmers whose main income source is from farming, i.e. agricultural produce. Immigrant workers (including both types of migrant workers) should join the modified new urban pension system. However, if they move back to countryside for whatever reason, a mechanism should be in place to facilitate transferring accrued benefits between urban and rural areas.

This voluntary rural pension system should be financed by contributions from individuals, villages and various levels of local government. The contribution rate could be calculated either as a percentage of local average revenues or as a fixed amount, as is currently the practice in the new rural pension schemes. In either case, it should be around 20 percent of local average revenues. Of course, regarding sharing of the 20 percent, it will largely depend on the fiscal conditions of all parties involved. For some areas, if the village community has a sound fiscal position, individual farmers could make no contributions to the schemes at all, as is observed in some pilot schemes. Meanwhile, local governments at different levels – typically town, county and city – should provide a significant part of the contributions. In this context it is useful to take into account the compensation fund arising from confiscation of land by local governments. Given that landless farmers in fact become urban residents and typically do not have sufficient knowledge and skills to find jobs in urban areas (particularly those who are middle-aged and older), they should be allowed to participate in the urban system or to use the consequent compensation fund to help them have secure old-age protection in the new rural pension system. In this context it is important to establish a sound budgetary mechanism to ensure that fiscal subsidies from various levels of local governments are stable, rather than subject to the discretion of local officials. In this regard, it would be helpful if such fiscal subsidies could be included in the annual budgets of local governments.

In addition to the larger subsidies from the government, flexible terms in terms of contribution, vesting criteria and withdrawal provisions could be designed for the purposes of encouraging participation (Hu and Stewart, 2009b). For example, given the irregularity of income for farmers, contributions should be allowed to be made in a more flexible manner, e.g. monthly, quarterly, or annually as well as one-off payments. Meanwhile, if significant financial needs arise, e.g. for medical care or education, early withdrawals should be allowed. Furthermore, reform of the new rural pension system could be considered as an integrated part of developing the rural economy. For example, given Chinese government's current priority of increasing farmers' income it might be useful to allow farmers to make contributions in the form of agricultural goods, which is in practice realistic in that Chinese farmers are obliged to sell a certain amount of their produce to the state on an annual basis. This arrangement could lead to two benefits. First, it helps stabilize and effectively increase the incomes of farmers. Second, it incentivizes farmers to engage in agricultural activities, thus energizing the rural economy. Meanwhile, it is worth noting that the combination of the two issues together would be useful, and much needed, in that it would have a higher possibility of receiving a strong commitment from the central government, thus making implementation of the reform across the country easier.

C. **Pillar 2:** voluntary retirement saving. This, in principle, would be the same as the urban life insurance schemes. In this context farmers would join commercial life products by themselves and would receive additional old-age protection when they retire. Note that life insurance companies, as encouraged and promoted by the CIRC, have recently been increasing their presence in rural areas, mainly aiming to cover the gap between the current insufficient state old-age protection if any and the level needed to support a basic life.

5.3. Reforms of the regulatory and supervisory framework

To effectively implement our recommended proposals as above, it is equally important to improve the current regulatory and supervisory framework related to old-age provision issues. The improvement is necessary in that any well-designed reform proposals would be in vain if the proper institutional structures do not exist, which is particularly relevant in China, not least because of the current political economic reality, as highlighted by the conflict between central and local governments, as well as that between ministries.

Against this background we propose the following suggestions, aiming to consolidate the current regulatory framework and thereby facilitate the implementation of the new pension system and achieve the associated positive effects.

A. Improve the regulatory framework

Successful implementation of the recent Social Insurance Law could serve as a catalyst to speed up Chinese pension reform and provide a legal framework for provision under a national pension system. In this context, any evasion of the system would be against the law, and so enforcing the law is expected to increase participation and coverage rates. In addition, passing such a law demonstrates the government's determination to bring about pension reform at the national level, increasing public confidence in the system. Nevertheless, a reading of the Social Insurance Law indicates that the text still suffers from a number of shortcomings that should be better addressed. For example, the description of the current version is too general and leaves too many details to complementary ministerial regulations that will be released separately later. Some (e.g. policy makers) argue that treating the details separately and focusing only on principles is reasonable, in that it facilitated passing of the law.

It should be noted that principles are indeed important, in that they set the tone and direction of the reform. However, it is equally important that the description of the law should not be too general or loose because if that is the case, it is very likely that local governments and/or the ministries in charge would make any modifications in the name of meeting regional and/or ministerial needs while in fact undermining the national interest. As a consequence, 30 years or more from now, the future pension system in China will be as fragmented as it is now.

B. Strengthen the supervisory framework

In light of the current level of staffing within the MOHRSS, it is very difficult to achieve an efficient and effective supervision, which is reflected in two dimensions, i.e. the number of staff and the level of expertise. As noted in an earlier section, the total number of staff in the Department of Supervision of the MOHRSS (approximately 20 staff in Beijing) at the national level is extremely low by international standards. The Chinese authorities should therefore seek to increase the number of oversight staff, bringing the pension system in China to a level that is consistent with the market needs (which will mean increasing staff levels considerably). Meanwhile, pension fund supervision is a complex task, involving knowledge and understanding in a range of fields. Therefore, if a properly supervised pension industry is the goal, the pension supervision team should collectively have the necessary skills, with relevant experts (in finance, investment, law etc.) being targeted for recruitment.

In this regard it is important to speed up the "Gold Social Security" project, or "Jinbao" project, to use the Chinese term. This project aims to provide a national information technology platform with a networked system through three levels of government: central, provincial and municipal. Under the system all information is stored in a centralized database to which the local offices of the MOHRSS input data regularly. This should allow the MOHRSS to monitor the market in a more efficient manner, thus strengthening the supervisory framework.

Meanwhile, the MOHRSS could consider introducing a risk-based supervisory structure as in some OECD countries, e.g. Australia and the United Kingdom. Based on this new approach, a risk profile for supervisory entities can be derived using a pre-specified model (which typically incorporates both levels of risk, and the likelihood that the risk will occur in the near future). Supervisory resources can then be prioritized and allocated to the entities that pose the most immediate and significant risk to the pension market and system. This is of particular relevance given the low level of staff within the MOHRSS. Interestingly, the CIRC has recently introduced the risk-based supervisory approach, as recommended in Hu and Stewart (2009a).

C. Closer collaboration between ministries in China

Pensions are a complex issue, so not surprisingly they are always under the supervision of several different governmental agencies in most countries. China is no exception; however, the situation is indeed more complicated in China than in many other countries, as highlighted below. First, as noted earlier, two central ministries are in competition in providing old-age provision benefits, i.e. the social assistance program is run by the (Ministry of Civil Affairs) and the other program by the MOHRSS. This is kind of unique in that in many OECD countries, these two issues are the responsibility of one ministry, which is normally in charge of social welfare issues. Second, given that financial institutions have played an important role in managing private pensions in China and are supervised by three separate industry regulators in addition to the MOHRSS, this market appears to have been over-regulated. Third, given that the current pension arrangements have been established by SOEs, particularly relating to voluntary pension schemes, another ministry, i.e. the State-Owned Assets Supervision and Administration Commission, also plays an important role. Last but not least, it is also of importance in having support from MOF/SAT (State Administration of Taxation) in that tax policy has been considered as one of the crucial factors in promoting development of a (private) pension market in OECD countries.

Unfortunately, a well-functioning cross-ministry cooperation mechanism does not exist in China, which is partially reflected by the incidence of tax disputes between MOF/SAT and the CIRC/Tianjing government, as noted in Hu and Stewart (2009a). Therefore, to promote the development of the pension system in China, it is necessary to establish a closer working relation between the MOHRSS and the various governmental agencies. This could be done via formal or informal agreements between them. If such an agreement could be struck in China, it not only would indicate the agencies' efforts to cooperate but also (most importantly) would serve as a pro-market message to the industry, therefore encouraging development of the pension market.

D. Strong commitment from the central government

This is one of the most important factors determining the future successful implementation of the new pension system in China. It is largely due to the political economic reality in China, i.e. the conflict between central and provincial governments.

In theory China is a centralized country with 31 provinces, in which four different levels of local government exist, i.e. province, prefecture, county and town. In reality, however, China is operated on a de facto federation system. In other words, local governments (particularly provincial governments) in China are as powerful and independent as a US state. This point has important implications for pension reform, in that when central ministries issue any guidance regarding various aspects of pension system, it is often the case that local governments either are not cooperative owing to their concerns for the local economy and competitiveness or modify the guidance in a way that benefits local interests while undermining national interests. Therefore, in this context, if a successful reform is desired, the central government has to show strong commitment to the reform. The central government should at least mobilize all resources necessary to demonstrate serious commitment to reform of the pension system, as they have done relating to the recent health care reform. Otherwise, based on the current institutional structure, the MOHRSS does not have the capability of implementing reform options across the country, which has been clearly shown by difficulties in terms of reforming various aspects of the Chinese pension system in the past.

5.4. Pension reform in a broader context

Pension reform is nothing but complex, which might be particularly so in China's case. Therefore, in this context, in order to successfully execute our reform proposals and maximize the benefits of the new system, it would be helpful to observe the evolution and reform of other parts of the economy and to view pension reform from a broader perspective.

5.4.1. Preservation of traditional values: family support

A large proportion of people in developing countries are not covered by any formal system and mainly rely on family support to care for the elderly. China, as the largest developing country, is no exception. Indeed, most people not covered by any social security system in China are supported by the younger generations in the family. With rapid social change and economic growth in China, however, the extended family network is breaking down. Is the traditional family support out-dated, then, and no longer appropriate in a more modernized society? Our answer is no, at least in the short and medium term. The reason is that in some respects family "insurance" is less costly and more efficient than a formal pension system. For example, the smooth running of a formal pension system incurs non-trivial transaction costs. At the very beginning, the government needs to design a set of rules or regulations after rounds of consultation with the public and professionals, and local governments would then be required to implement these regulations; if they find some particular rules or regulations inappropriate, a feedback mechanism between the central and local governments is needed; and, last, a supervisory team or committee needs to be set up to oversee the implementation of the regulations. In addition, record keeping of receipts and payments is also an essential component of the social pension system. This is not free, and the costs associated could be very significant. By comparison, a family support mechanism is largely free from such transaction costs since the operating unit is a family, which is much smaller than a country. Therefore, the implicit inter-generational contracts in some senses are less costly and more sustainable.

In addition, raising children to care for their aged parents in retirement is the norm and is deeply rooted in Chinese culture, i.e. Confucianism. By learning from a wide range of sources, e.g. TV programs, personal experience etc., the younger generation feels they have a moral duty to take care of their parents when they are too old to work. Leaving elderly parents alone or destitute is poorly regarded in China. Meanwhile, this informal mechanism has been strengthened by the Family Support Law (1981), which gives the younger generation the legal obligation to support their parents if their parents are not able to live alone by themselves.

5.4.2. Urban and rural integration, particularly Hukou and land reform

The process of urbanization and specifically reform of the Hukou (or residence permit) system can have far-reaching implications for pension reform. The main reason is that the current and the proposed pension systems are largely based on the assumption that Hukou exists, under which regime a rural Hukou holder can join the urban pension system and receive urban pension benefits (which are normally more generous than those of the rural system). However, if the Hukou regime is abolished or significantly loosened in the future, it would greatly reduce the complexity of the pension system. For example, if there is no restriction on Hukou, a separate pension scheme targeting migrant workers, which is being discussed, will prove unnecessary.

Land reform in rural areas can also impact on the pension system. The reason is that if in the future farmers are allowed to rent out their land in the market, they will be able to receive a more stable income stream. It will make it easier for them to contribute regularly to the system. It might also increase the income of farmers in general, thus helping to increase farmers' financial capacity and ultimately increasing participation in rural areas.

5.4.3. Income distribution

According to various studies, income inequality has been increasing over the past 15 years or so, and such trends do not seem to be reversing. It has been a concern for the government, not least because of its potential negative impact on social and therefore political stability. In this context, it has been argued that some central ministries, e.g. the National Development and Reform Commission, have been lukewarm about promoting the development of the EA system in China because of their concerns about the resultant increasing income inequality, given that so far EA schemes have been mainly established by large SOEs rather than SMEs in China.

Therefore, if the income distribution among population groups in China could be more equal, it would facilitate establishing consensus among policy makers in China, thus potentially stimulating the pension system's development.

5.4.4. Disposable income

A related point is that many firms and employees themselves in China are not very enthusiastic in participating in the pension system, even the mandatory schemes, because they have low disposable incomes. As a result, they view take-home cash at the present time as (much) more valuable than pension benefits promised in the distant future. Therefore, the current reform of the Chinese remuneration system goes in the right direction, and it is hoped that the gradual increase in the disposable income of the general population, particularly of the current low-income earners, will boost pension participation.

5.4.5. The financial market

Research has been conducted to look at the linkage between the financial market, economic growth and pension reform (Davis and Hu, 2006). One of the general views is that a more developed financial market could facilitate pension reform, particularly the funding part of the system. This argument is relevant in China, specifically against the background of the increasing role of professional management companies in China's private pension system. Although the financial market in China, particularly the stock market, has grown rapidly over the past 20 years, it nonetheless still suffers from various fundamental weaknesses, e.g. dominance by SOEs, strict control by the government and extreme volatility. Therefore, a more properly functioning financial market in China will greatly help in increasing investment returns, thus ultimately contributing to higher pension benefits.

5.4.6. Tax policy

Tax policy has been argued to be one of the most important components in the overall pension system, largely owing to the tax relief benefits. This is particularly the case where private pensions are concerned. In China the current tax policy does not really facilitate development of the private pension system, which has led to confusion and lack of interest among employers and employees in establishing EA schemes, as well as unnecessary competition in the market and even among ministerial agencies. Therefore, a better-designed tax regime for the purposes of pension arrangements would serve as a catalyst to promote further development of the system.

6. Conclusion

Statistics show that China has aged fast and that this demographic trend is likely to continue in the foreseeable future. The demographic evolution per se should not be a concern. However, as reviewed in the chapter, the current pension system in China suffers from various weaknesses and does not face up to the challenges, particularly in terms of the potentially huge fiscal burden and unfairness of the existing system. Given this background we proposed solutions to improve the pension arrangement in China. According to our proposal, the new pension structure should be as follows.

6.1. Proposed modified structure

A. **Pillar 0:** a universal old-age social assistance system. All urban citizens – regardless whether they have contributed to the system over their career life – are entitled to such benefits.

B. **Pillar 1:** mandatory urban pension system. The basic structure is the same as in the existing one; i.e. it consists of two components, and participation is mandatory. However, pillar 1B would be transformed into a notional defined-contribution scheme, while pillar 1A would still be run on a PAYG basis.

C. **Pillar 2:** EA. This pillar will be still the same as the current EA is, i.e. voluntary and fully funded.

D. **Pillar 3:** commercial life insurance products.

6.2. Main features of the modified pension system in China

The first main feature of our proposal (particularly related to the urban pension system) is that it largely fits in the basic structure of the current system, therefore avoiding significant changes related to it and so reducing reform resistance from various parties, which based on past Chinese experiences in many cases would make any reform almost impossible, regardless of how well it is designed.

Establishment of a national pension system: based on our proposals a notional pension system covering both urban and rural populations will be established. This objective is consistent with the recent decision by the Chinese government of establishing the basic pension system in both urban and rural areas by 2020.

Achievement of a national pooling: all China pension experts agree that national pooling is an ideal situation. However, ideas on how to achieve it vary between proposals. Under our proposal it would be easier to establish a national pooling scheme, not least because it encourages wider participation via a (much) lower contribution rate.

Mitigation of reform resistance: given that the current pillar 1B is empty and that "back-filling" it is extremely difficult, together with economic theory, it would make sense to have a legitimate notional defined-contribution scheme, which would greatly facilitate the reform process. Meanwhile, the notional defined-contribution model could help in tackling increasing longevity issues in China (Oksanen, 2010a).

Fairness of the system: the new system would be fair to all groups of the population if national coverage could be achieved. The current system is unfair partly because it mainly covers urban workers, thus disadvantaging the large number of uncovered people, given their insecurity after retirement.

Higher participation and lower evasion: as noted in the chapter, the current design of the system has not been able to encourage the public to join the system, even the mandatory part of the system. Therefore, largely because of the reduced contribution rate (approximately half of the existing rate) in the proposed system, it is expected that participation would increase, and thus the system could benefit from a large inflow of cash, further mitigating the fiscal burden.

Development of private (occupational) pensions: because of the lower contributions to public pensions, it is expected that firms and employees would be encouraged to join EA schemes, thus promoting development of the EA market. Further development of private pensions would of course reduce budgetary pressure son public pensions in the long run.

To tackle the key current topical issues, given the unification of the system, it is expected that the proposed system would greatly assist in solving many of the current reform proposals that mainly target a certain group of population. For example, the MOHRSS has recently released various guidelines in an attempt to reform different aspects of the system, notably "reform on pensions of the public service units (PSU) employees" in March 2008 and "tentative proposals on reforming the migrant workers pensions" in February 2009 (MOHRSS 2009). Meanwhile, it is believed that in order to effectively implement our recommended proposals as above, it is important to improve the current regulatory and supervisory framework related to old-age provision issues. The improvement is necessary in that any well-designed reform proposals would end up being in vain if the proper institutional structures do not exist, which is particularly relevant in China.

Furthermore, pension reform is nothing but complex, which might be particularly so in the case of China. Therefore, in this context, so as to successfully execute our reform proposals and maximize the benefits of the new system, it would be helpful to observe the evolution and reform of other parts of the economy and to view pension reform from a broader perspective.

Notes

1 Different estimates of the GDP arise from the different exchange rates used, given that the price for the same or similar goods and services might vary significantly across countries. The former, i.e. USD 2,206, was calculated by using nominal US dollar to Chinese RMB exchange rates, while the larger value, i.e. USD 6,200, was calculated by using assumed real exchange rates, based on PPP. The nominal exchange rate was much higher than the real rate.

2 Increasing income inequity in China has been argued to be a key factor contributing to social unrest across the country.

3 www.fhb.gov.hk/statistics/en/statistics/dependency_ratio.htm

4 The Public Service Unit (PSU) (or *shiye danwei* in Chinese) refers to those entities that mainly provide public services to society, e.g. hospitals and research institutions.

References

Asher, M. G., and Newman, D. D. (2002). *The challenge of social security reform in transition economics: The case of China* (Research Report No. 3-2002). Mexico: International Centre for Pension Research.

Blundell-Wignall, A., Hu, Y., and Yermo, J. (2008). *Sovereign wealth and pension fund issues* (OECD Working Papers on Insurance and Private Pensions No. 14). Paris: Organisation for Economic Co-operation and Development. doi:10.1787/243287223503.

Caijing Magazine. (2008). China is expected to launch the new rural pension schemes by the end of 2009. Retrieved from www.caijing.com.cn/2008-09-11/110011860.html.

Davis, E. P., and Hu, Y. (2006). Saving, funding and economic growth. In Clark, G. L., Munnell, A., and Orszag, M. (Eds.), *The Oxford handbook of pensions and retirement income.* Oxford, UK: Oxford University Press.

Development and Reform Center of the State Council. (2005). *Social security reform in China: Issues and options.* http://economics.mit.edu/files/691

Herd, R., Hu, Y., and Koen, V. (2010). *Providing greater old-age security in China.* (OECD Economics Department Working Papers 750). Paris: Organisation for Economic Co-operation and Development.

Holzmann, R., and Palmer, E. (Eds.). (2006). *Pension reform: Issues and prospects for non-financial defined contribution (NDC) schemes.* Washington, D.C.: World Bank.

Hu, Y. (2010a). Management of China's foreign exchange reserves: A case study on the state administration of foreign *exchange (SAFE)* (European Economy – Economic Papers 421). Brussels: Directorate General Economic and Monetary Affairs, European Commission.

Hu, Y. (2010b). Reforms to public sector unit pensions and civil service pensions in China, *A Vision for Pension Policy Reform in China*, Washington, DC: World Bank.

Hu, Y., and Davis, E. P. (2009). *China's pension reform: A simulation study and some policy recommendations.* Bandar Seri Bagawan: Economics and Finance Section, School of Social Sciences, Universiti Brunei Darussalam.

Hu, Y., and Stewart, F. (2009a). *Licensing regulation and the supervisory structure of private pensions: International experience and implications for China* (OECD Working Papers on Insurance and Private Pensions No. 33). Paris: Organisation for Economic Co-operation and Development.

Hu, Y., and Stewart, F. (2009b). *Pension coverage and informal sector workers* (OECD Working Papers on Insurance and Private Pensions No. 31). Paris: Organisation for Economic Co-operation and Development.

Impavido, G., Hu, Y., and Li, X. (2009). *Governance and fund management in the Chinese pension system* (IMF Working Papers 09/246). Washington, D.C.: International Monetary Fund.

Leisering, L., Sen, G., and Hussain, A. (2002). *Old-age pensions for the rural areas: From land reform to globalization* (ADB Report). Manila: Asian Development Bank.

Ministry of Human Resources and Social Security (MOHRSS). (2009). Retrieved from http://w1.mohrss.gov.cn/gb/zwxx/ghytj.htm on 28 March 2010.

National Bureau of Statistics. (2010). *China statistical yearbook (2010)*. Beijing: China Statistics Press.

Oksanen, H. (2010a). *The Chinese pension system – first results on assessing the reform options* (European Economy – Economic Papers 412). Brussels, Directorate General Economic and Monetary Affairs, European Commission.

Oksanen, H. (2010b). *Pegging the renminbi to a basket – facts, prospects and consequences* (CES info Working Paper No. 3254). Paris: Organisation for Economic Co-operation and Development.

Organisation for Economic Co-operation and Development. (2010). *Economic survey of China*. Paris: Organisation for Economic Co-operation and Development.

United Nations Development Program. (2008). *Access for all: Basic public services for 1.3 billion people* (China Human Development Report, 2007/8). New York: Author.

UN Population Database. (2008). Retrieved from http://esa.un.org/unpp/ on 28 March 2011.

Whitehouse, E., and Stewart, F. (2007). *Closing the pensions gap: The role of private pensions* (OECD Policy Brief). Washington, D.C.: World Bank.

World Bank. (1997). *Old age security: China 2020*. Washington DC: World Bank.

World Development Indicators. (2010). Retrieved from http://data.worldbank.org/data-catalog/world-development-indicatorson on 29 March 2011.

8 Extending the coverage of social protection among informal workers in India

Santanu Gupta

1. Introduction

It has been widely accepted that a large part of the Indian economy forms the informal sector, and there is now a consensus on the definition of the informal sector and informal employment. According to a note prepared by the 15th and 17th International Conferences of Labor Statisticians, there is a distinction between the informal sector and informal employment.[1] Unorganized/informal sector enterprises are those owned by enterprises or households that are not constituted as separate legal entities, for which separate accounting is not available, and at least some of whose goods and services must be available for sale or barter. Self-employed street vendors, taxi drivers, scissors and knife grinders, and home based workers are all considered informal enterprises. Even those with higher skill sets such as self-employed people including doctors, lawyers, accountants, architects, and engineers would be counted as informal own-account enterprises or as enterprises of informal employers. The key criterion is that they should be below a certain size with respect to employment, that there is no registration of its enterprises or its employees, and that there is no earnings ceiling. Employees will be considered to have informal employment if their employment is not subject to national legislation, income taxation, social protection, or entitlement to benefits such as paid leave or sick leave, amongst others.

An estimation of the magnitude of informal employment in India has been done by Raveendran, Murthy, and Naik (2006) based on the 55th round labor force survey done between July 2004 and June 2005. They estimated that the total informal employment is 362.08 million out of a total employment of 396.77 million, which means 91.26 percent of the total labor force was in informal employment. They reported that 98.84 percent of the employment in agriculture was informal, while in the non-agricultural sector, the highest number of informal employees was in retail trade, construction, land transport, and textiles. To give more updated figures, the projected labor force for 2009–2010 was 520 million (Government of India, Ministry of Labor, 2010, p. 11); assuming that even 10 percent of the labor force is in the formal sector would imply that the size of the informal sector will be around 468 million.

The Annual Report of the Government of India, Ministry of Labor (2010), for 2009–2010 mentions that the unorganized sector suffers from cycles of seasonal employment, lack of a formal employer–employee relationship, and absence of social protections. Given that labor in the informal sector is quite heterogeneous, providing social security to all types of workers will require a number of schemes. Keeping in mind that people below the poverty line will be the most hurt by the fluctuations in the informal sector, the government has initiated some employment oriented schemes, such as the Mahatma Gandhi National Rural Employment Guarantee Act, and also group insurance schemes, such as the Janasree Bima Yojana and Aam Aadmi Bima Yojana for the landless rural households. Since construction workers form one of the largest categories of workers in the unorganized sector, the government has enacted legislations for their welfare. A large section of the informal sector workforce also happen to be migrant workers or inter-state migrant workers, and therefore the Inter State Migrant Workmen (Regulation of Employment Conditions of Service) Act, 1979, was enacted to safeguard the rights of migrant workers. The Unorganized Sector Worker's Social Security Act of 2008 aims, amongst other things, to register such workers, provide them with identity cards, and initiate schemes for such workers namely a provident fund, an employment injury benefit, housing, educational schemes for children, skill upgrades for workers, funeral assistance, and old age homes.

Given that almost all workers happen to be part of the informal sector, we look into the social security schemes that are currently available, whether they address the needs of all income classes and can be expanded to cover a larger population. We will also be reviewing the health and old age benefits available to individuals working in the registered formal sector, and in that respect we find that their coverage, and the efficiency of service, leaves a lot to be desired. In recent years, given that many private agencies have come up with similar services, public agencies offering the same services can be compared and benchmarked.

The next section of this chapter looks into the functioning of the programs targeted for the poor: the National Social Assistance Program, which aims at providing old age pensions to people below the poverty line, as well as the health insurance program for the poor, namely the Rastriya Swasthya Bima Yojana. Section 3 looks into the functioning of the social security schemes for the formal sector, namely the Employees' State Insurance Corporation, which mainly provides health insurance coverage and unemployment benefits to people in the formal sector, and comments on the extent of coverage and the nature of the service. We also look into the role of the Employees' Provident Fund Organization, providing for social security assistance in old age, and comment on its coverage and operations. Section 4 discusses aspects of the New Pension System and its impact on coverage and scope to accommodate the informal sector. Section 5 discusses current options for old age security for the population. Section 6 concludes the chapter.

2. Social security programs for the poor

For the part of the labor force that earns a subsistence or below subsistence income, government intervention is necessary to provide them with direct social assistance. For this part of the workforce, programs such as the Mahatma Gandhi

National Rural Employment Guarantee Act, Swarnajayanti Gram Swarozgar Yojana, and Swarna Jayanti Shahari Rozgar Yojana resort to policies with direct intervention in the labor market. The Mahatma Gandhi National Rural Employment Guarantee Act aims at providing financial security by guaranteeing 100 days of employment in a financial year to adult members of rural households who volunteer to do unskilled manual work. Swarnajayanti Gram Swarozgar Yojana is a self-generating employment program that provides for credit and government subsidies to the rural poor for providing them with income generating assets. Swarna Jayanti Shahari Rozgar Yojana provides for employment for the urban poor as well as encouraging them to set up ventures for self-employment. Apart from these, the Prime Minister's Employment Generation Program was launched in August 2008 to provide a credit linked subsidy for generation of employment opportunities through the establishment of micro-enterprises in both rural and urban areas.

There are also programs and policies to look into social security aspects, namely old age pensions and health insurance aspects in the unorganized sector. The National Social Security Fund for unorganized sector workers has been set up with an initial amount of INR 10 billion. The two most important social security schemes are the National Social Assistance Program (NSAP) and the Rashtriya Swasthya Bima Yojana (RSBY). The NSAP is a welfare program initiated in 1995 with the aim of providing comprehensive social security to the poorest sections of the population in old age. The RSBY provides for health insurance coverage for people below the poverty line. In this section we look in detail at the performance of the NSAP and the RSBY.

At present, the NSAP comprises the following schemes with the following benefits:

1. Indira Gandhi National Old Age Pension Scheme (IGNOAPS): Persons over the age of 65 who live below the poverty line are entitled to a monthly pension of INR 200. The 2011 budget relaxed the eligibility of beneficiaries from 65 to 60 years of age. Those above the age of 80 will get a pension of INR 500 instead of INR 200 at present. These pensions will be paid from the central government's budget; however, state governments were urged to contribute equally towards the pension amount.
2. Indira Gandhi National Widow Pension Scheme: Widows between the ages of 40 and 64 are entitled to a monthly pension of INR 200.
3. Indira Gandhi National Disability Pension Scheme: Persons below the poverty line and between the ages of 18 and 64 with severe and multiple disabilities are entitled to a monthly pension of INR 200.
4. National Family Benefit Scheme (NFBS): A household below the poverty line is entitled to a lump sum amount of INR 10,000 on the death of a primary bread winner aged between 18 and 24 years.
5. Annapurna: 10 kilograms of food grains are provided free of cost to senior citizens who although eligible for IGNOAPS have yet remained uncovered.

Table 8.1 Beneficiaries of and expenditure on the IGNOAPS, the NFBS, and Annapurna

Year	IGNOAPS	NFBS	Annapurna	Total beneficiaries	Total expenditure (USD million)
2008–2009	15,020,640	423,292	1,011,240	16,455,172	872
2007–2008	11,514,026	334,153	1,050,885	12,899,064	694
2006–2007	8,708,837	243,972	871,424	9,824,233	437
2005–2006	8,002,598	276,737	851,509	9,130,844	230
2004–2005	8,079,386	261,981	820,583	9,161,950	193
2003–2004	6,624,000	209,456	937,155	7,770,611	146
2002–2003	6,697,509	85,209	774,129	7,556,847	132

Source: Compiled by the author from www.nsap.nic.in, accessed on January 30, 2011.

Note: Exchange rate taken as USD 1 = INR 46. IGNOAPS was known as NOAPS till 2006.

IGNOAPS = Indira Gandhi National Old Age Pension Scheme; NFBS = National Family Benefit Scheme.

The scheme looks novel and with good intentions. Table 8.1 reports the number of beneficiaries of the IGNOAPS, the NFBS, and Annapurna and the total expenditure on each of these three schemes. Although the number of beneficiaries has risen substantially over the years, what remains of interest is the extent of coverage of these schemes in relation to the population that should actually be served. To get an idea of the extent of coverage, one needs to know the population figures for the relevant age groups, and the proportion of the population in the relevant age group who fall below the poverty line. The yearly population projections for India and the states are available from the Census of India 2001 (2006). Since the financial year in India runs from April to March, it is possible from these figures to get the population figures for the financial year by giving a weight of 0.75 to the population figures of the current year and a weight of 0.25 to the population figures for the next year. For example, the 2008–2009 population figures give a weight of 0.75 to the 2008 population figures and 0.25 to the 2009 population figures.

A report based on the 2001 Census, had projected that the population of those over 60 years will rise from 6.9% of the total in 2001, to 7.5 percent in 2006, and further to 8.3% in 2011 (Government of India, Office of the Registrar General & Census Commissioner, 2006).[2] Assuming that 7.5 percent of the population is over 60, we have computed the number of people who fall into the 60+age group. Again, a computation was done in 2004–2005 that 27.5 percent of the people were below the poverty line, so taking this figure we computed the number of people who were below the poverty line in the 60+ age group.[3] We then computed the number of beneficiaries as a proportion of the population in the 60+ age group below the poverty line from 2002–2003 to 2008–2009, and that number is reported in Table 8.2. We observe that the coverage of the IGNOAPS and Annapurna, both of which target the elderly destitute (65+ in

Table 8.2 Coverage of the IGNOAPS and Annapurna schemes

Year	Beneficiaries (IGNOAPS + Annapurna)	Number of persons over 60	Beneficiaries/ 60+ persons (%)	60+ persons below poverty line	Beneficiaries/ 60+ persons below poverty line (%)
2008–2009	16,031,880	86,156,531	18.61	23,693,046	67.66
2007–2008	12,564,911	84,943,069	14.79	23,359,344	53.79
2006–2007	9,580,261	83,720,231	11.44	23,023,064	41.61
2005–2006	8,854,107	82,487,850	10.73	22,684,159	39.03
2004–2005	8,899,969	81,245,119	10.95	22,342,408	39.83
2003–2004	7,561,155	79,992,769	9.45	21,998,011	34.37
2002–2003	7,471,638	78,731,794	9.49	21,651,243	34.51

Sources: www.nsap.nic.in for beneficiaries; Census of India 2001 (Government of India, Office of the Registrar General & Census Commissioner, 2006) for population projections; Mehta et. al. (2011) for poverty line figures; authors' own calculations.

Note: IGNOAPS = Indira Gandhi National Old Age Pension Scheme.

this case), has risen steadily over the years, from 34.51 percent in 2002–2003 to 67.66 percent in 2008–2009.

By the NSAP's own review of physical and financial progress during 2010–2011, the coverage of the IGNOAPS has reached to almost 17.44 million, while the approved number was 16.96 million. In contrast, for the Indira Gandhi National Widow Pension Scheme and Indira Gandhi National Disability Pension Scheme, the coverage is less than the estimated number. Coverage for the Indira Gandhi National Widow Pension Scheme has reached 3.8 million, against the estimated number of 4.5 million, and coverage under Indira Gandhi National Disability Pension Scheme has reached 766,000, against an estimated number of 1.5 million. For the NFBS only 205,000 cases have been covered, rather than the estimated 436,465 cases per annum. During the financial year 2010–2011 INR 39,233.8 million (approximately USD 852.91 million) was released, as compared to a budgetary provision of INR 57,620 million (approximately USD 1,252.6 million). Fourteen states and two union territories reported a utilization rate of over 50 percent, while 10 states and two union territories reported a utilization rate of less than 50 percent. The utilization rate was not reported for the states of Jammu and Kashmir, Kerala, Arunachal Pradesh, Manipur, and National Capital Territory (NCT) Delhi.

It is interesting to note that the performance review committee made no observations on the administrative cost of the program, except for stating that 3 percent of the funds are available for the administration of the program, and an annual verification and a social audit have been introduced, although no such audits have been received from any state. The annual progress reports of the NSAP give information on the allocation, total release, and expenditure reported by states and the number of beneficiaries for the schemes of the IGNOAPS, the NFBS, and Annapurna. Unfortunately, for many of the states the disaggregated expenditure for each of the schemes is not available. Our following analysis is based on the disaggregated expenditures for the IGNOAPS, the NFBS, and Annapurna, which are available for 19, 18, and 11 states respectively. Given that the per month allocation per person in the IGNOAPS is INR 200 from the central government, the annual allocation per person is INR 2,400, and therefore the expenditure per person should be at least INR 2,400, and that for the NFBS must be at least INR 10,000. For the year 2008–2009, only three states, namely Orissa, Haryana, and Manipur, have an expenditure to beneficiary ratio equal to INR 2,400 for the IGNOAPS. For Jharkhand, Assam, Uttar Pradesh, Tripura, and Meghalaya the expenditure per beneficiary is higher than INR 2,400, which could either result from state contribution or indicate wastage in the use of resources. It should be noted that the highest expenditure per beneficiary is for Meghalaya, at INR 2,816, indicating that state contribution to the IGNOAPS has been low. However, the *Annual Report to the People on Employment* of the Ministry of Labor reports for 2009–2010 that 18 states are disbursing a pension of INR 400 or above per month, 11 states are disbursing between INR 250 and 400 per month, and 6 states are disbursing central assistance of INR 200 per month only (Government of India, Ministry of Labor, 2010). It is also interesting to note that for eight states, namely Kerala, Jammu and Kashmir, Punjab, Bihar, Tamil Nadu, Uttarakhand, Rajasthan, and Madhya Pradesh, the expenditure per beneficiary is less than INR 2,400. This can have two implications: either the disbursement is lower than the stipulated amount, or there is an over-reporting of the number of beneficiaries. If one looks at the expenditure per beneficiary for the NFBS, most of the values are close to INR 10,000, except for in Tripura and Jharkhand, where the amount is substantially less than the benchmark, and in Manipur, which is over the benchmark. For Annapurna, being a scheme with transfer in kind, benchmarks are difficult to obtain, and the variation amongst states is huge, with the lowest expenditure to beneficiary ratio found in Tamil Nadu, at INR 509.34 per person, and the highest in Manipur, at INR 1071.01.

It will also be interesting to analyze how states have performed over time, that is, to examine whether increases in expenditure over two successive years have been commensurate with increases in the number of beneficiaries. We look into the change in expenditures incurred by states over all the three schemes (the IGNOAPS, the NFBS, and Annapurna) in 2008–2009, compared to in 2007–2008, and the change in the total number of beneficiaries over these three schemes during the corresponding period. It is interesting to note that Kerala, Orissa, Arunachal Pradesh, and Goa added beneficiaries yet had a decline in their expenditure from 2007–2008 to 2008–2009. This implies that the per capita allocation declined during this period for these states. Assam and Andhra Pradesh witnessed an increase in expenditure yet served a smaller number of beneficiaries. In the absence of any leakage, the per capita allocation for these states would have increased during this period. How efficiently funds are being used depends not only on how low administrative expenditures are as a proportion of total expenditures but on the magnitude of exclusion and inclusion errors present in the system. In the context of India's public distribution system, Jha and Ramaswami (2010) estimate that for food grains in India, which are delivered at a subsidized rate to the families living below the poverty line, the exclusion error – the proportion of deserving population that is not served – is of the magnitude of 70 percent; the inclusion error –the proportion of recipients who are not deserving of the subsidy – was also as high as 70 percent in 2004–2005. A high exclusion and inclusion error of similar magnitude would imply that a very small proportion of the target population is being served, yet the allocation is enough to service all if both types of errors are avoided.

The RSBY program was initiated in April 2008, with the aim of providing health insurance coverage to families below the poverty line (BPL). It has been recognized that the poor may avoid treatment owing to a lack of resources, fearing wage loss; getting desired treatment may lead families to cut down on other expenses like children's education. Beneficiaries under the RSBY are entitled to hospitalization coverage up to INR 30,000. Transportation benefits of INR 100 per hospitalization, up to a maximum of INR 1,000 per annum, are also available. For a large number of interventions, the government has fixed package rates, pre-existing conditions are covered from the first day, and there are no age limits. Coverage extends to five members in a family, namely the head of the family, the spouse, and three dependents. Beneficiaries need to pay INR 30 as a registration fee, the insurer is selected by the state government on the basis of a competitive bidding process, and the premium is shared by the central and state governments at the ratio of 75:25.[4] Although similar schemes have been launched by the government in the past, the RSBY scheme has a lot of advantages for all stakeholders. Beneficiaries have the freedom to go to the hospital of their choice, be it public or private; hospitals for their part would like to provide service to such beneficiaries as remuneration will come directly from the insurer. Insurers for their part would like to monitor hospitals to prevent unnecessary procedures or fraud resulting in excessive claims. Since the insurer is paid a premium for every BPL family enrolled, it is in the interest of the insurer to enroll as many households as possible from the BPL list, resulting in better coverage of targeted beneficiaries. Since the government will pay a maximum of INR 750 per family, the government is able to control the cost of providing healthcare to BPL families. A healthy competition between public and private providers is also expected, which should improve the services of the public providers. Finally, intermediaries such as non-governmental organizations are involved in assisting BPL households, and they will be paid for their services.

A key feature of the RSBY is that every BPL family is issued a biometric enabled smart card containing the fingerprints and photographs of family members. All hospitals under the RSBY are information technology enabled and connected to the server at the district level. Issuance of smart cards has ensured that the grants under the RSBY are not misused; patients have the option of using the card in any of the hospitals empanelled by the RSBY. The card can be split for migrant workers, who carry a share of their coverage with them separately. Beneficiaries of the RSBY get cashless benefits after providing verification through their fingerprints. Health providers need not send any paper documents to the insurer, and payment is electronic.

As for coverage, till March 2011, enrollment has been completed in about 225 districts, which are a third more of the total districts in the country than covered by the RSBY; 43.9 million BPL families have been identified in the selected states, and 23.2 million BPL families have been enrolled. It is too early to make a state-wise comparison, since not all districts have been covered in the states. Evaluation of the scheme's performance is already under way. Swarup and Jain (2011) state that, according to survey reports, beneficiary response to the arrangement has been excellent for 29 percent, good for 51 percent, and average for 15 percent. With respect to hospitalization, beneficiary response has been excellent for 26 percent, good for 54 percent, and average for 19 percent. The total number of empanelled hospitals, both public and private, is 7,840 as of March 2011.

Apart from the NSAP and the RSBY, the government has also initiated the Aam Admi Bima Yojana to provide death and disability coverage to landless rural households between 18 and 59 years of age. Under this scheme the head of the family or one earning member of the family is insured. The central and state governments share the premium burden of INR 200 per year per person at a ratio of 50:50. The benefits under the scheme include a benefit of INR 30,000 in the case of natural death and of INR 75,000 in case of death from an accident or permanent disability. The insurance coverage for partial disability is INR 37,500. The scheme also envisages an add-on benefit for providing scholarship for up to two children of the beneficiary, studying in the 9th to 12th standard, at the rate of INR 300 per quarter per child. The scheme is intended to cover 15 million rural landless households, and a separate fund of INR 5 billion is being created to provide scholarships to the children of beneficiaries.

Apart from central government sponsored schemes, states like Rajasthan have also come up with a micro-pension scheme, namely the Rajasthan Vishwakarma Unorganized Sector Workers (Motivational) Contributory Pension Scheme 2007.[5] The minimum contribution is INR 100, and the maximum contribution is INR 1,000 per annum, with a matching contribution of the same amount by the Rajasthan government. There is an administered government interest rate of 8 percent per annum, and on reaching the age of 60, individuals will receive a pension based on their own contributions plus the matching contributions of the government. This is similar to the Swavalamban scheme of the New Pension System, which we will discuss later.

3. Social security in the formal sector

Social security for the poor in the informal sector is mainly being provided by the central and state governments. For the formal organized sector social security is provided by the Employees' State Insurance Corporation (ESIC) and the Employees' Provident Fund Organization (EPFO). The ESIC[6] provides health and unemployment benefits, while EPFO covers the provision of social security in old age.

ESIC activities are funded from the contributions of both employees and employers in factories and establishments. The employees' contribution is 1.75 percent of the wages, and the employer's contribution is 4.75 percent of the wages during the wage period. The ESIC budget runs a surplus, which has steadily increased, from USD 175.03 million in 2003–2004 to $518.18 million in 2008–2009.

As for the coverage of the ESIC, as of March 31, 2010, only 406,499 employers were part of the ESIC, along with 13.9 million employees, for a total of 55.48 million beneficiaries. The ESI Act of 1948[7] applies to all non-seasonal factories employing 10 or more persons on any day in the preceding 12 months. Most of the state governments have extended the provision of the act to include shops, hotels, restaurants, movie theaters, road and motor transport agencies, newspaper establishments, and private medical and educational institutions employing 20 or more people. For employees, there is a wage ceiling in effect from May 1, 2010, at INR 15,000 (approximately USD 326.10) a month. Only employees with a wage lower than the ceiling limit are part of the ESIC. Subrahmanya (1998) has made a critical review of the benefits that are available under the ESIC. With the increase in workers' wages over time, some workers' wages went over the ceiling, but they were brought back into the ESIC when the ceiling was increased. Many of the factories have their own health insurance schemes and feel that membership in the ESIC should be optional. There has been reported misuse of the sickness benefits by some workers, who ask for such benefits by submitting forged medical certificates.

A major concern is the concentration of ESIC hospitals in major cities or towns; even though there may be quite a few ESIC hospitals, they are concentrated in only about four or five cities in most states. Questions have also been raised on the functioning of the ESIC, as there is a lot of variation in the number of positions for medical officers that are vacant and the occupancy rates of beds in ESIC hospitals across states. In Bihar and Himachal Pradesh, all positions for medical officers are filled, while in Andhra Pradesh, Maharashtra, Punjab, Jharkhand, and Orissa more than 30 percent of the medical positions are unfilled. In Assam and Delhi, the occupancy rate for beds in ESIC hospitals is close to 90 percent, while the rate is less than 30 percent in Goa, Rajasthan, and Jharkhand. So the problem seems to go both ways: in Jharkhand there is a shortage of staff and low use of hospital services, whereas in Rajasthan, despite no apparent shortage of staff, the occupancy rates of hospital beds are low. As of March 2010, there were 787 ESIC centers, just 4 more than in the previous year. In contrast, private insurance companies offering health insurance, like Star Insurance, have connections with over 4,500 hospitals and offer tailor-made packages to suit different population profiles; these may in some sense work out to be cheaper and more relevant than the health services provided by the ESIC.

With regard to the unemployment benefits, amounting to half of wages, that are available as part of the ESIC, it is surprising that there were only 870 such claims in 2009 and 642 in 2008. The reason for such low numbers claiming unemployment insurance is that such benefits are usually given when a factory has shut down, which is not so common. Normally a factory gets shut or is in "lock up" for a period of time because of some problems, in which case people are not eligible to claim such benefits. Unemployment benefits are normally not given if an employee has lost a job at a factory. Therefore, it is not surprising that the ESIC has been having surplus budgets in all these years.

Just as the ESIC is trying to look into the social security aspects for people in the formal sector, the EPFO considers the social security of workers in the formal sector in old age. By the Employees' Provident Fund and Miscellaneous Provision Act, 1952, all establishments employing 20 or more people and engaged in any of the 181 industries and some classes of businesses specified, as well as cooperative societies employing 50 or more people working without power become members of EPFO. For most classes of industries the employer's contribution is 12 percent of the emoluments, while the contribution rate is 10 percent for certain other categories like brick and jute production. Employees also have to give a matching contribution. Firms may, however, with the consent of their employees, opt out of the EPFO if their own provident fund scheme is substantially better than the one provided by the EPFO. Since 1995, of the employer's share of the contribution, 8.33 percent is remitted towards the Employees' Pension Fund Scheme.

Table 8.3 gives the coverage of the EPFO in terms of the number of establishments covered, as well as the number of members enrolled. In 2008–2009, 573,063 establishments were covered, and 47.072 million members were enrolled. The National Sample Survey Organisation (NSSO) surveys of 1993–1994 to 1999–2000 and 1999–2000 to 2004–2005, the labor force for 2009–2010 had projected to be 520 million, and the coverage of the EPFO was less than 10 percent of the labor force. Although the definitions, in terms of the kinds of establishments, are fairly wide, one reason for such low coverage is the fact that only permanent employees are usually part of the EPFO. Although the act requires contractual workers to also be part of the EPFO, this is not usually the case, as in most situations contractual workers receive a fixed monthly salary with no social security coverage; in many situations even for better paying jobs, they are designated as "consultants," in which case they need not be part of that organization.

Asher (2010b) criticized the functioning of the EPFO on account of the large number of people in its governance structure and limited access to outside expertise. The service was quite poor in comparison to the cost imposed on the economy, which to a large extent was due to failure of modernization of the information technology systems. Shah (2006), apart from emphasizing the

Table 8.3 The coverage of the Employees' Provident Fund Organization

	2006–2007	2007–2008	2008–2009
Establishments covered	471,678	532,702	573,063
Members enrolled (million)	44.404	44.919	47.072

Source: Annual–09.

administrative inefficiency of the EPFO, has also highlighted the fiscal subsidies received by the EPFO, namely the special deposit that is maintained by the government at an above market rate of return, the subsidy associated with preferential tax treatment, and potential payments from the exchequer in future owning to funding gaps in either Employees Provident Fund (EPF) or Employees' Pension Scheme (EPS). According to Shah, the goals for pension reform should be to ensure good coverage, sustainability, and scalability; it should be able to reach out to financially unsophisticated participants and should ensure fair play and low costs; and the system should give a choice between competing pension fund managers, alternative investment styles, and multiple annuity vendors. All of these points have been taken care of to a large extent by the New Pension System.

4. The New Pension Scheme (NPS)

The New Pension System (NPS), operational from May 1, 2009, has gone a long way towards addressing the shortcomings of the earlier system. Although it is mandatory for people employed in the public sector, it is voluntary for others; it is based on the defined contribution pension system and is therefore sustainable in the long run. It is open to all citizens of India, and it also gives citizens the flexibility to choose an investment plan and a fund manager. It is simple to open such an account at any of the Points of Presence (POP) and get a Permanent Retirement Account Number. It is portable in the sense that it is operational even if an individual changes cities or jobs. The NPS is regulated by the Pension Funds Regulation and Development Authority (PFRDA) and therefore has transparent investment norms, regular monitoring, and performance reviews of fund managers by the NPS Trust.

Since the NPS was trying to reach to a wide section of the informal sector, two types of accounts, Tier I and Tier II, were established. Tier I and Tier II are two sub-accounts in which the subscribers can invest their money. While Tier I is a non-withdrawal account, Tier II offers a voluntary savings facility where subscribers can withdraw their savings from this account anytime they wish to. The minimum contribution at the time of account opening is INR 500 for Tier I and INR 1,000 for Tier II. The minimum amount per contribution is INR 500 for Tier I and INR 250 for Tier II. The minimum total contribution in a year is INR 6,000 for Tier I and INR 2,000 for Tier II. Such stipulations were intended to ensure that a minimum amount builds up for an individual, and dealing with very small sum of money also entails a huge administrative cost. However, it is widely understood by policy makers that even this minimal contribution would not be affordable to a vast section of the population, which is why the government introduced the scheme of NPS-Lite, under which investors can deposit any amount at any point in time. Interaction between the subscriber and the NPS architecture occurs via aggregators, who have the responsibility of pooling the small sums of money received and undertaking the investment between asset classes.

To further encourage people from the under-privileged sections of society, Swavalamban was established in 2010. Under this scheme, the government was initially to contribute INR 1,000 (approximately USD 21.74) to each NPS account opened in the year 2010–2011 and for the next three years. However, the 2011 budget announced that exit norms for members from the Swavalamban Scheme would be relaxed and the benefit of government contributions would be extended from three years to five years for all subscribers who enrolled during 2010–2011 and 2011–2012. This scheme will be available only to people who join the NPS with a minimum contribution of INR 1,000 and a maximum contribution of INR 12,000 per annum. To take advantage of this scheme a person must be from the unorganized sector, which is defined as a person who is not in service in any public sector and is not covered by any of the known social security schemes as listed by the NPS.

According to the NPS, aggregators will be intermediaries who are identified and approved by the PFRDA. Aggregators will be organizations having a continuous functional relationship with a known customer base for delivery of some socio-economic goods/services. It is interesting to note that microfinance institutions and non-governmental organizations have been identified as potential aggregators along with nodal offices running certain schemes for identified beneficiary groups under central and state governments, as well as entities running common service centers under the national e-governance plan and non-banking finance companies (NBFCs). Most microfinance institutions and non-governmental organizations at the moment offer loans for capacity building or health and related insurance services but rarely banking services. One of the biggest microfinance institutions in India, SKS Microfinance is a profit making enterprise offering group loans to people in amounts between INR 2,000 (approximately USD 43.46) and INR 12,000 (approximately USD 260.87). It will be interesting to see if such institutions do join as aggregators for the NPS, which depends on the profit margins from this line of business compared to the profit margins of their already established businesses. Other very well-known non-governmental organizations like the Self Employed Women's Association (SEWA) offer amongst other services healthcare, childcare, legal assistance, and capacity building as well as banking services. It has 93,000 savings accounts, giving 33,778 loans and generating a surplus of USD 6.65 million. So it looks as though organizations like the SEWA might actually contribute to the NPS by joining as aggregators.

As for the withdrawal norms, at any point before 60 years of age, subscribers would be required to invest at least 80 percent of the pension wealth in a life annuity purchased from any life insurance company regulated by the Insurance Development Regulatory Authority. The remaining 20 percent of the pension wealth may be withdrawn as a lump sum. Between the ages of 60 and 70 years, a subscriber on exit would be required to invest a minimum of 40 percent of the accumulated savings (pension wealth) in a life annuity. These withdrawal norms would ensure that there is no impulse withdrawal of accumulated savings.

Amongst the NPS intermediaries, the NPS Trust takes care of the assets and funds under the NPS in the best interest of the subscribers. A central record keeping agency has been set up by National Securities Depository Limited and the PFRDA to provide for record keeping, the issuing of a Permanent Retirement

Account Number to each subscriber, and other administrative aspects. The Points of Presence are an interface between the NPS and the subscriber, mainly for processing subscriber requests. The trustee banks are appointed for the collection of funds from the Points of Presence, the pooling of funds, the remittance of funds to the pension fund managers, and fund reconciliation with the central record keeping agency. The Pension Fund Managers are responsible for investment management in accordance with guidelines issued by the PFRDA/NPF Trust and provide daily net asset value under the NPS. The PFRDA has appointed the Stock Holding Corporation of India as custodian of the NPS, responsible for settlement processing of assets, safe keeping of securities, and corporate actions. Annuity service providers will be appointed by the PFRDA to provide annuities to the NPS subscribers in accordance with the annuity scheme chosen by the subscriber.

NPS also offers subscribers the ability to choose their portfolio mix amongst three different asset classes, namely equity market instruments, government securities, and credit risk bearing fixed income assets. Subscribers have two choices: Auto choice – Lifecycle Fund and Active choice – Individual Funds. Auto choice is for subscribers who do not have the required knowledge to manage funds or are unwilling to exercise their choice; the composition of their portfolio will change every year according to their age, with a greater proportion of their assets invested in government securities as their age advances. For those who opt for Active choice, there is a cap of 50 percent on investment in equity market instruments. Before the NPS, only private companies selling pension products offered such choices to subscribers to manage their own funds. Another interesting feature of the NPS is the low charges compared to those of the pension products available from private companies. Under the NPS, the investment management fee is 0.0009 percent per annum, and the asset servicing charges are 0.0075 percent per annum for the electronic segment and 0.05 percent for the physical segment. For private insurance companies, the fund management charges may be as high as 1.25 percent per annum. The NPS currently also allows private players to act as pension fund managers.[8] There thus remains a possibility that current subscribers of private insurance companies for pension products will move to the NPS on account of its low administrative charges. The participation of private insurance companies as pension fund managers in the NPS will work only if high volumes more than make up for the low administrative charges in the NPS. A reason why people may still wish to stick to the pension products of private companies is that they give the flexibility of withdrawal at any point, while for the NPS one has to wait until 60 years of age.

Asher (2010a) has three broad suggestions to improve the NPS. The current design requires that a member can withdraw 60 percent of the accumulation, but a mandatory 40 percent must be annuitized. Options must be made such that he/she maintains 40 percent of the assets in his/her own name, such that these can be inherited by designated nominees when a person dies. Options for the phased withdrawal program also need to be looked into. He also advocates a flexible age of exit from the NPS, given that many people continue with paid economic activities even after formal retirement, and better marketing and communication strategies are required given that fewer than 10,000 members had joined the scheme by May 2010.

5. Options for social security in old age

In India, for a vast section of the aged middle class, a popular way of receiving a steady income stream is to invest in the schemes of India Post, which give good and assured rates of return. The monthly income scheme from India Post offers an interest rate of 8 percent, with a maturity period of six years, with a 5 percent bonus on maturity and with auto credit facility to a savings bank account. The minimum deposit is INR 1,500 (approximately USD 32.61), and the maximum deposit is INR 450,000 (approximately USD 9,782.61) for a single account, while the maximum deposit can go up to INR 900,000 (approximately USD 19,565) for a joint account. At the current interest rates, the maximum deposit of INR 900,000 will yield a monthly income of INR 6,000 (approximately USD 130.43). At current prices, this amount may be just adequate to cover the expenses for two people, provided one does not need to pay for rent or electricity. As of March 2009, there were about 24.9 million Monthly Income Scheme (MIS) accounts. India Post also offers a Senior Citizens Savings Scheme. In this scheme, a person between 55 and 60 years of age who has taken retirement (conditions imposed) is eligible to open an account. An individual may open an account in multiples of INR 1,000 subject to a maximum of INR 1.5 million. No withdrawal is permitted before the maturity period of five years from the date of opening of the account; the depositor may extend the account for a further period of three years. An interest rate of 9 percent per annum is available in this scheme; the interest rate is deposited on a quarterly basis to the savings account of the individual in the same post office. At the current interest rate, deposits of INR 1.5 million will yield a quarterly interest of INR 33,750. An advantage of the Senior Citizens Savings Scheme over the monthly income scheme is that the ceiling limit is much higher; however, the interest is available on a quarterly basis. As of March 2009, there were slightly more than a million Senior Citizens Savings Scheme subscribers, for about 10 percent of the elderly population. India Post also has a 15-year Public Provident Fund, where the minimum and maximum deposits per annum are INR 500 and INR 70,000, respectively, at 8 percent per annum. Withdrawal is permitted from the seventh financial year but is limited to one year, and there is an option to take a loan starting in the third year. As of March 2009, there were about 2.2 million Public Provident Fund accounts.

The Life Insurance Corporation of India also offers five different pension plans. The fund management charges are between 0.7 percent and 0.8 percent per annum, which is lower than that charged by private insurance companies but higher than that for the NPS. The premium amounts are also higher; thus, most of the pension products of private insurance companies target the higher income segments of the population. In 2009–2010 there were 19,000 subscribers to pension policies and 23,000 subscribers to annuity policies of the Life Insurance Corporation of India. However, there have been attempts by private companies like ICICI Prudential has come up with the ICICI Pru Rural Business Initiative. ICICI -Pru Jana Sarv Suraksha is an insurance cum pension plan with a policy term of five years, with the minimum annual premium being as low as INR 50.

In ICICI –Pru Anmol Nivesh, the premium range is between INR 1,200 and INR 6,000, and the policy term is from 7 to 15 years. It is expected that with growth in the Indian economy, more private companies will tap the rural market.

6. Conclusion

We looked at the magnitude of informal employment in the Indian economy, the kind of schemes needed, and those that are currently available to meet the social security needs of all income classes. For those below the poverty line, the government has initiated old age pension schemes, the coverage of which has steadily improved over the years. However, there is a need to improve on the inclusion and exclusion errors, and on delivery. On the health front, the RSBY scheme gives poor individuals the flexibility to choose among hospitals and get cashless service through the use of smart cards. In contrast, the existing social security schemes available for the organized formal sector have low coverage, and there is limited scope for the expansion and scaling up of their operations. The initiation of the NPS to extend social security to the labor force in the informal sector is a step in the right direction. In India only a miniscule section of the population – those working for central and state governments and for a few private sector organizations – had the benefit of an old age pension, and even that was unsustainable; this is why the government moved from a defined benefit to a defined contribution scheme. Many other schemes of the government to provide social security in areas like healthcare have also failed owing to extremely poor coverage, very inefficient functioning of such schemes, and lack of proper targeting. Measures taken to ensure proper targeting, such as distribution of benefits to individuals through their bank accounts, also had the adverse impact of leaving out many deserving individuals owing to lack of financial inclusion. Recent efforts by the government to open a no frills bank account for individuals, and to assign every individual a unique identification number, should go a long way to directing public resources to efficient usage.

Notes

1 This part draws heavily from Bhalla (2009).
2 The actual figures have been somewhat lower. Thus UN population projections (2012) revised their medium-variant estimate for 2010 for India's 60+ population share at 7.7 percent. http://esa.un.org/unpd/wpp/unpp/p2k0data.asp
3 The poverty level in India is defined in terms of the cost required to achieve a certain minimum level of nutrition, which was estimated at 2,400 calories per capita per day in rural areas and 2,100 calories per day in urban areas by a task force constituted by the government in 1977. The poverty line was estimated to be approximately INR 49.63 per person per month in rural areas and INR 56.76 per person per month in urban areas for the year 1973–1974 based on the National Sample Survey Organisation surveys. Since then these prices have been adjusted for inflation. In 2004–2005 the poverty line was INR 356.3 per person per month in rural areas and INR 538.6 per person per month in urban areas. Generally the poverty is estimated for individuals only. See Mehta et al. (2011) for poverty line estimation and definitions.

4 In the northeastern states and Jammu and Kashmir the premium is shared by the central and the state governments at a ratio of 90:10.
5 See Shankar and Asher (2011) for details.
6 See www.esic.nic.in for details of the benefits provided by the ESIC.
7 www.esic.nic.in/Tender/ESIAct1948Amendedupto010610.pdf
8 It is to be noted that the NPS allows the following six entities as pension fund managers: ICICI Prudential Pension Funds Management Company Limited, Infrastructure Development Finance Company (IDFC) Pension Fund Management Company Limited, Kotak Mahindra Pension Fund Limited, Reliance Capital Pension Fund Limited, State Bank of India (SBI) Pension Funds Private Limited, and Unit Trust of India (UTI) Retirement Solutions Limited.

References

Asher M. (2010a). NPS: Some suggested refinements, *CFO Connect*. Gurgaon, India: International Market Assessment India Pvt. Ltd.

Asher M. (2010b). Pension plans, provident fund schemes and retirement policies: India's social security reform imperative. *ASCI Journal of Management*, 39(1), 1–18.

Bhalla S. (2009). *Definitional and statistical issues relating to workers in informal employment*, Working Paper No. 3. New Delhi: National Commission for Enterprises in the Unorganized Sector. http://nceus.gov.in/Working%20Paper%20-3.pdf, last accessed March 20, 2011.

Employees Provident Fund Organization (2009), Annual Report of EPFO 2008–09. New Delhi. www.epfindia.com/annual_reports.html, last accessed February 1, 2011.

Government of India, Ministry of Labor. (2010). *Annual Report to the People on Employment*. July. New Delhi: Author.

Government of India, Office of the Registrar General & Census Commissioner. (2006). Population Projections for India and States 2001–2026. www.education forallinindia.com/Population_Projection_Report_2006.pdf

Jha S. and Ramaswami B. (2010). *How can food subsidies work better? Answers from India and the Philippines*, Working paper No. 221. Manila: Asian Development Bank.

Mehta A. K. et al. (2011). *India chronic poverty report: Towards solutions and new compacts in a dynamic context*. New Delhi: Indian Institute of Public Administration.

Raveendran G., Murthy S.V.R., and Naik A. K. (2006). *Estimation of informal employment in India*, Working Paper No. 3. New Delhi: Expert Group on Informal Sector Statistics (Delhi Group).

Shah A. (2006). *A sustainable and scalable approach in Indian Pension Reform*, The Pension Institute Discussion Paper No. PI-0615. London: Cass Business School.

Shankar S. and Asher M. (2011). Micro-pensions in India: Issues and challenges. *International Social Security Review*, 64(2), 1–21.

Subrahmanya R. K. A. (1998). Extension of social insurance schemes in the formal sector. In Van Ginneken, W. (Ed.). *Social security for all Indians*. New York: Oxford University Press.

Swarup A. and Jain N. (2011). Rashtriya Swasthya Bima Yojana—a case study from India. Downloaded from www.rsby.gov.in/Documents.aspx?ID=14#sub79, last accessed March 20, 2011.

9 Extending social protection for informal sector workers in Indonesia

Budi Kuncoro, Friska Parulian and Mukul G. Asher

1. Introduction

The International Labour Organization (ILO) defined social security in the 1952 Convention No. 102 on Social Security (Minimum Standards) with a comprehensive definition including nine core contingencies leading to cessation, or substantial reduction, of earnings. These included benefits in cases of sickness, maternity, employment injury, unemployment, invalidity, old age and death, as well as the provision of medical care and subsidies for families with children.

This ILO definition actually covers two types of social security, social insurance and social assistance. Social assistance covers people with various types of disability such as old age, illness, physical or psychiatric infirmities, etc. It is more likely to be non-contributory. Social insurance covers workers of different categories and refers to a system through which they contribute to their future security, e.g., in case of injury at the workplace. The word *social* implies that the market alone cannot take care of these contingencies (Unni and Rani, 2002). *Social protection* is a new term and is used to encompass all these concepts as an umbrella term to depict social security. It is related to poverty reduction or alleviation, unlike social insurance and social assistance (Lund and Srinivas, 2000).

In developing countries, where large proportions of the population are engaged in self-employment and informal activities, it is difficult to cover individuals under formal schemes of insurance and benefits. The approach used in the developed world therefore may not be suitable, or effective, in developing countries. Rampant poverty in geographically dispersed populations also makes such schemes difficult to administer. Given the dimension of the informal economy and massive poverty, the concept of social protection should include the idea of productive employment and poverty reduction.

One of the essential features of the decent work approach (Hirose, 1999) is that everybody is entitled to basic social protection. However, it has been pointed out that the problem with broadening the scope of social protection is that the concentration remains on schemes of employment, income and poverty alleviation (Jhabvala and Subramanya, 2000), rather than on social security schemes.

It is also confirmed that social protection is an important means to prevent poverty and strengthen the capacity to move out of poverty. The absence of social protection is believed to lead to greater chances of falling into and remaining in a poverty trap. Some social protection measures consisting of direct transfer of funds to the poor (e.g., social assistance benefits that are means tested) have a direct and at least temporary effect on the level of poverty.

The lack of provision of social protection for most workers is one of the greatest challenges faced by Indonesia, as the majority of the workers do not have protection, such as employment security, pensions or coverage against risks such as illness, accidents and death. In practice, the most basic protection, such as a minimum wage, is also not ensured, as the majority of workers engaged in the informal sector usually have low incomes, such that it would be very difficult for them to make any contribution to a social security scheme. In addition, the *Workers Social Security (Jamsostek) Act No. 3* of 1992 also limits the mandatory coverage to firms with more than 10 employees, with a monthly payroll of more than IDR 1 million, which practically excludes informal sector workers from the mandatory social security scheme, Jamsostek.

A milestone in the development of the social security system in Indonesia is the enactment of the 2004 Act No. 40 on National Social Security System Law (Sistem Jaminan Sosial Nasional [SJSN]), which came into effect in October 2004. The law stipulates that every citizen has the right to social security and that it is the state's role to provide universal social security coverage. The law also mandates the enforcement of universal coverage (in a staged manner), and its implementation (to extend the coverage) for informal sector workers, who make up two-thirds of the workforce in Indonesia, should become a major public policy issue.

In line with the spirit to implement the act and achieve universal coverage of social security in Indonesia, this chapter attempts to explore the possibility of extending coverage to the informal sector by mapping out the current initiatives that have been undertaken by the government and other stakeholders, in particular for the informal sector workers. What are the challenges and the possible options in extending the coverage to informal sector workers in Indonesia?

This chapter is organized as follows. Section 2 presents an overview of the current social security in Indonesia, Section 3 presents the demographic and employment trends, Section 4 attempts to identify possible options for extending coverage to informal sector workers, and the last section offers concluding remarks and suggestions for further study.

2. Overview of the current social security system in Indonesia

2.1. The existing social security scheme

In Indonesia the government currently manages several social security schemes for different purposes and groups of participants, namely Jamsostek, Taspen, Asabri and Askes. PT Jamsostek manages the pension scheme, work-related insurance and health benefits intended for private sector workers, particularly in the formal sector. Taspen manages a pension scheme for current and retired civil servants and their families, and Asabri manages a pension program and health benefits for armed forces members. Health insurance is provided by PT Askes, mainly for civil servants and government employees.

2.1.1. *Jamsostek*

Jamsostek provides the following compulsory schemes for all "legal entity" workplaces with at least 10 employees or a monthly payroll of at least IDR 1 million.

OLD-AGE BENEFIT SCHEME (JAMINAN HARI TUA)

This scheme provides an old-age retirement benefit for compulsory early retirement as a result of invalidity or unemployment. The contribution rate is 3.7 percent of gross wages for employers and 2 percent of gross wages for employees. The benefits of participating in this scheme are that the scheme provides lump-sum payments plus interest, or regular periodical payments, for the following life events of a member: age 55, total permanent disability, benefits to the surviving spouse or children in the event of the member's death before age 55, or cessation of membership resulting from unemployment after at least five years of membership.

WORK ACCIDENT BENEFIT SCHEME (JAMINAN KECELAKAAN KERJA)

This scheme covers work-related accidents, which includes accidents while traveling to or from work. The employer contribution rate is 0.24 percent to 1.74 percent of gross wages, depending on the economic sector. The benefits include transportation costs, costs of medical examinations, medical treatment and nursing, rehabilitation expenses, monetary allowances for invalidity or loss of functions and a death allowance.

HEALTH CARE BENEFIT SCHEME (JAMINAN PEMELIHARAAN KESEHATAN)

This scheme provides for hospital and medical treatment for members and their spouse and children. Employers providing similar or better health care services for their employees are exempted from participation. The employer contribution is 3 percent of gross wages for a single worker and 6 percent for a family. The benefits provide primary outpatient care; subsequent outpatient care; inpatient hospital care; prenatal, delivery and postnatal care; diagnostic support; special care; and immediate lifesaving emergency services up to a maximum of IDR 6,500,000.

DEATH BENEFIT SCHEME (JAMINAN KEMATIAN)

This scheme covers loss of life during work and at the workplace or caused by illness or natural causes. The employer's contribution is 0.3 percent of gross wages. Benefits provided are payments for funeral expenses of IDR 1,000,000 and a death allowance of IDR 5,000,000.

The Jamsostek scheme had not been successful in preventing those who were badly affected by the economic crisis from falling below the poverty line (Arifianto, 2004), partly because Jamsostek coverage is limited, excluding informal sector workers and formal sector workers in small enterprises (with 10 employees or fewer), meaning that the majority of Indonesian workers are not covered by the scheme.

Meanwhile, the participation rate of employers in the Jamsostek scheme is relatively low: it is estimated that only half employers required to participate by the Social Security Act 3/ 1992 actually do so, which means that the number of workers that are actually covered would be even lower. A main reason for this is that employers and workers have little faith in Jamsostek, as the fund management has not been open and transparent (ILO, 2003). For instance, Leechor (1996) points out that PT Jamsostek as the sole provider of publicly funded retirement benefits in Indonesia has failed to provide financial statements and regular progress reports that could be accessed by workers participating in the scheme and by the general public.

2.1.2. Taspen (social insurance scheme for government employees)

Taspen is a state-owned enterprise that manages the social insurance scheme (and retirement savings) for civil servants. The Taspen scheme was created in 1963 to provide retirement benefits, death benefits and retirement savings by providing both a lump-sum payment and a monthly pension for government officials or their beneficiaries. This benefit is expected to be used as an economic resource for members after their retirement, as membership is compulsory for civil servants. This scheme was expanded to cover special pension schemes for elderly members, their successors and members who are disabled based on the Government Regulation No. 25/1981,"Social Insurance for Civil Servants."

Taspen consists of an old-age savings scheme and a pension scheme. Employees should contribute 8 percent of their monthly basic salary, of which 3.25 percent is used to finance the lump-sum benefit and 4.75 percent for the pension fund. The amount of monthly pension benefits for members is 2.5 percent of their basic salary times the number of years they served in the civil service. This scheme is funded mostly through the central government budget (Anggaran Pendapatan dan Belanja Negara) and from members' contributions.

In 2003 it was estimated that the total number of government employees was four million. Their total contribution makes up about 8 percent of the overall cost of funding the Taspen's schemes. PT Taspen contributes about 22.5 percent of the overall funding costs, derived from its substantial assets and investment income from members' contributions. The rest of the costs (69.5 percent) are paid for by the government budget (ILO, 2003).

2.1.3. Askes (health scheme for government employees)

Askes (Asuransi Kesehatan untuk Pegawai Negeri Sipil dan Pensiuna) started providing a health scheme for civil servants, with compulsory membership for civil servants and their families, in 1968. The membership was expanded in 1993, to include employees of the state-owned companies and private companies, although participation was voluntary. In 2005 compulsory membership for civil servants and retirees reached 14 million, while the voluntary membership was 1.6 million. The employees' contribution is 2 percent of salary for the health schemes, which includes primary and secondary health care and inpatient care. The providers of this health care are mainly public health centers and hospitals.

Since 1995 PT Askes was appointed by the Minister of Health to manage health insurance for the poor. Contributions for the poor are financed by the government through the central government's annual budget (Anggaran Pendapatan dan Belanja Negara). Health care service is comprehensive and consists of primary care at health centers and sub-health centers, midwife services in villages and outpatient and inpatient care at hospitals. To avail themselves of these services, members would go to a health center first, and could then be referred to a hospital with a referral letter from the health center.

Health insurance provided by Askes and Jamsostek has more extensive coverage, including family members compared to Jamkesmas (Jaminan Kesehatan masyarakat) and Jamkesda (Jaminan Kesehatan Daerah). The number of persons covered by the Jamsostek health care program is 3.1 million (of whom 1.4 million are workers and 1.7 million are dependent family members). The coverage of Askes is 15.6 million (of whom 5.6 million are workers, 8.4 million dependent family members, plus 1.6 million "commercial", or those who pay their own premiums on a voluntary basis, members). Thus, about 18.7 million people in Indonesia are covered by the formal health insurance schemes (ILO, 2008). Nevertheless, coverage at the informal economy level remains very low.

2.1.4. Asabri (social insurance for armed forces members)

Asabri is a social insurance scheme, founded in 1971, that is designed to provide pension and endowment insurance to Indonesian armed forces members and the police corps. The contribution rate for this pension scheme is similar to that of Taspen, while benefits depend on rank. The retirement age for military personnel is lower than that of civil servants, at 50 years old. Generally, the monthly pension is 2.5 percent of the last basic monthly salary multiplied by years of service.

In addition to these establishments on social security system in Indonesia, there are other schemes that are facilitated by government:

HEALTH CARE INSURANCE (JAMINAN PEMELIHARAAN KESEHATAN)

The government introduced a health care insurance scheme known as Jaminan Pemeliharaan Kesehatan Masyarakat (JPKM) through the Health Act No. 23

of 1992. It became a national scheme in 1995 and is considered as a means to deliver health care services (Bitran and Yip, 1998). By the end of 2002, there were 24 licensed "Badan Pelaksana" JPKM or non-insurance companies promoting health insurance products as carriers, covering less than half a million people. Although the Ministry of Health was very supportive of this scheme and funded the pilot projects, JPKM was not considered successful as the scheme was highly under-funded owing to lack of actuarial calculation for premiums, while the benefits are considered poor. The expansion of the scheme was held up because of very low membership (Scheil-Adlung, 2004).

COMMUNITY HEALTH FUND (DANA SEHAT)

The community health fund or micro-health financing scheme (Dana Sehat) was introduced in the mid-1970s, starting from a small scale, in a few locations in Indonesia. It was then extended to the national scale by introducing local schemes, particularly in the poor areas. The scheme was based on contributions from the people, through consensus among the beneficiary households. Some studies indicate that a smaller proportion of the population (less than 2 percent) either had health cards or were members of a community health fund. Following the wide introduction of the Social Safety Net (SSN) scheme in the health sector in the late 1990s, many of community-based schemes have stopped functioning (Suryahadi and Widyanti, 2004).

THE SOCIAL SAFETY NET (SSN) SCHEME

The SSN scheme was launched as part of national efforts to alleviate the poverty resulting from the economic crisis in 1997–1998. Several financial assistance schemes were implemented to ensure that the poor were able to get access to basic health care. The first SSN scheme was aimed at high-risk pregnant women by channeling a block grant to village midwives to support their patients for further treatment. The second SSN scheme promoted the JPKM scheme of the Ministry of Health. The third SSN scheme targeted public health facilities by providing a block grant for essential medicines to complement medical supplies provided by the Ministry of Health. The fourth SSN scheme was a block grant provided to public hospitals to assist with their operational costs to support the poor. However, those who are marginally poor still face financial issues in meeting their medical needs and are unable to pay for expensive medical care (World Bank Institute, 2004).

2.2. Existing Indonesian legislation regarding social security

An important development regarding social security in Indonesia is the enactment of the National Social Security System Act No. 40 of 2004 (SJSN). The important feature of the new act was that it mandates the establishment of social security schemes for all Indonesians, to include old-age pension, old-age savings, national health insurance, work injury insurance and death benefits. The schemes would be financed by a payroll tax imposed on workers' wages, but no stipulations were made on minimum or maximum amounts of benefits or contributions or other parameters, as such details need to be followed up by government regulations.

On informal workers, the National Social Security System states:

- Chapter 1, Article 1 states envisages, ". . . Social Security as one form of social protection to secure all people to fulfill their decent basic living needs." Thus, the scheme is intended for all citizens, which validates the inclusion of workers in the informal sectors as well. Chapter 3, Article 3 states that the ". . . National Social Security System intends to provide decent living needs to its members and/or his/her family members." By legislation, the implementation of the National Social Security System aims at the realization of social welfare for all Indonesians.

- Chapter 3, Article 5 states that this act provides for the formation of the Implementing Board of Social Security System with four agencies currently to undertake the task of implementation and facilitate social security extension to workers as they are at present, namely the Private Sector Workers' Social Security (Jamsostek), Civil Servant Insurance and Saving Fund Company (Taspen), Social Insurance of the Armed Forces (Asabri) and Indonesian Health Insurance (Askes).

- Chapter 5, Article 14, Clauses 1 and 2 stipulate that the government, in a staged manner, will register recipients, the poor in particular, and those financially incapable for accessing government assistance to the Implementing Board of Social Security.

- Under the mentioned scheme, a self-employed person may participate as an individual by paying the nominal rate determined by the government or may participate in the system through a community group. Workers receiving low wages are also encouraged to participate in the insurance scheme. They should be given access to claim their rights to social security not only for themselves but also for their families.

- The type of social security benefits depends on one's financial ability to pay. Hence, one may choose any of the following schemes: health, work accident, pension, old-age security, and death benefits.

The explanation in the Act No. 40 of 2004 specifically affirmed that social security shall protect all Indonesians from illness, accident, job loss, old-age population or those needing pension resulting from total loss or reduce in income. Informal workers, particularly the self-employed, are therefore by law not excluded from the said privileges.

On social security for workers, another regulation is Act No. 3 of 1992 concerning Workers' Social Security (1992, No. 14, pp.1–15).[1] This act, known as manpower social security (Jaminan Sosial Tenaga Kerja, or Jamsostek), was introduced in 1992 to include work-injury, death, old-age, and health care benefits for workers, managed by a state-owned insurance company (PT Jamsostek) under the scrutiny of the Ministry of Manpower. The act comprises 11 chapters and 35 sections. Chapter I provides for definitions. Chapters II and III concern administration of the Workers' Social Security Scheme. Chapter IV regulates participation in the scheme. Chapter V deals with contributions, amount of benefits and payment procedures. Chapter VI regulates the administering body. Chapters VII and VIII provide for penal provisions and investigation. Chapters IX, X and XI provide for miscellaneous provisions such as excess payments of compensation, regulations relating to the Workers' Social Insurance Scheme and transitional provisions.

The Workers' Social Security Scheme includes compensation for employment-related accidents, death benefits, old-age benefits and health care benefits. The scheme provides every employee the right to Workers' Social Security and requires compulsory participation of each business in the Workers' Social Security on behalf of its employees who perform work in an employment relationship.

The Workers' Social Security Scheme for employees who perform work outside an employment relationship is to be determined by regulation. Payment of contributions is the responsibility of the employer. The Employment Accidents Act No. 33 of 1947 was repealed on entry into force of this act.

- Implementation of the Workers' Social Security Scheme (Government Regulation No. 14 of 1993). The Workers' Social Security Scheme consists of monetary payments for occupational accident benefits, death benefits, old-age benefits and benefits in the form of health maintenance services. An employer employing 10 workers or more is obliged to insure its workers under the Workers' Social Security Scheme.
- Minister Regulation No. PER-03/MEN/1994, "Implementation of the Manpower Social Security Scheme for Casual Daily Workers, Workers Doing Piece Jobs and Workers on a Contract Basis Regulation." This regulation stipulates that employers must include all their casual daily workers; workers not qualified for SSN assistance such as self-employed workers, part-time workers, seasonal workers and landless farmers doing piece jobs; and workers on a contract basis in the Manpower Social Security Scheme managed by the executing agency. The regulations provide for rules in respect of types of social security schemes, contributions, procedures for implementation and amounts of security and supervision.
- Instruction of the Minister of Manpower No. INS.02/MEN/1995 on the Implementation of the Workers' Social Security Scheme for Expatriates in Companies.
- Government Regulation No. 28 of 1996 concerning Management of Funds for the Scheme of Workers' Social Security.
- Decree of the Minister of Manpower No. Kep-132/MEN/1998 as Revocation of the Instruction of the Minister of Manpower No. INS-02/MEN/1995 on the Implementation of the Workers' Social Security Scheme for Expatriates in Companies.

- Minister of Manpower and Transmigration's Regulation No. PER-24/MEN/VI/2006 Guideline the implementation of the Workers' Social Security Scheme for workers undertaking jobs outside formal working relations. This regulation provides guidelines for social security regulations to apply to workers engaged outside industrial relations. The regulation is based on the Act No. 3 of 1992 on Workers' Social Security and the Act No. 13 of 2003 on Manpower.[2]

2.3. Recent developments in social protection

The 1945 Constitution of the Republic of Indonesia's Article 28H, point (3) states that every citizen has the right to social security and underlines the role of the state in providing universal social security coverage. Furthermore, Article 34, point (2) stipulates that the state shall develop a system of social security for all people and shall empower the inadequate and underprivileged in society in accordance with human dignity. Such a notion is the principle of the Act No. 40 of 2004 on the National Social Security System, which came into effect in October 2004.

After the stipulation of Act No. 40 in 2004 there has been some progress, as well as some drawbacks, in the current state of social security in Indonesia for both pension and health protection. The progress is that the number of people covered by health protection has increased, while the drawbacks are low coverage, program fragmentation, uncertain but potentially significant challenges of fiscal sustainability, (Wiener, 2007) and an uncovered informal sector.

The first issue is low coverage. In terms of the pension program, there has been improvement after the stipulation of the SJSN law (Act No. 40 of 2004). This means that only 20 million workers in Indonesia, out of a total of 110 million people in the labor force, are covered by the Taspen, Asabri and Jamsostek schemes. The ratio is still low, at about 18 percent of the total workforce. In terms of health protection, with 116.8 million people currently covered, this still leaves another 114 million people without health protection. The ratio of people out of the total population who have health protection is around 50 percent, which is a good start. However, there is still a great need to protect the health of the rest of the population.

The second issue is the fragmentation of the program. Currently, there are three public pension institutions with three fragmented programs; as well as three public health institutions with five programs. There are benefits of having a coherent system of social protection. The first is an efficient allocation of administrative resources, both personnel and funding. The second is the ability to enhance coordination among programs targeting the poor. The existing National Social Security Council (Dewan Jaminan Sosial Nasional) fails to do these necessary tasks.

The third issue is the protection of the informal sector. The existing Non-Contracted Workers Protection Program held by PT Jamsostek failed to get membership from the informal sector workers. Widjaja (2008) as well as Badan Perencanaan Pembangunan Nasional (Bappenas) and the Deutsche Gesellschaftfür

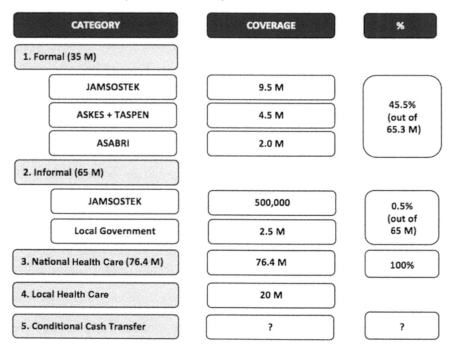

CATEGORY	COVERAGE	%
1. Formal (35 M)		
JAMSOSTEK	9.5 M	45.5% (out of 65.3 M)
ASKES + TASPEN	4.5 M	
ASABRI	2.0 M	
2. Informal (65 M)		
JAMSOSTEK	500,000	0.5% (out of 65 M)
Local Government	2.5 M	
3. National Health Care (76.4 M)	76.4 M	100%
4. Local Health Care	20 M	
5. Conditional Cash Transfer	?	?

Figure 9.1 The coverage of existing social protection programs
Source: Bappenas (2008).

Technische Zusammenarbeit (GTZ) (2008) has asserted that the number of workers in the informal production sectors is increasing relative to the total number of workers in Indonesia.

Approximately 70 percent of the labor force in the informal sector consists of unskilled workers. A large portion of this group, approximately 45 percent, works in the rural agricultural sector. The rest are distributed within the service production sectors. Therefore, a failure to protect the informal sector workers is actually a failure to protect the largest section of Indonesian workers. In short, the recent social protection system in Indonesia is highly fragmented in the formal sector, while informal workers and the poor do not have any protection system from social risks.

2.4. Current government and donor initiatives

As the Indonesian constitution mandates that every citizen has the right to social security, the government launched the National Social Security System in October 2004. Social security is imperative for workers outside a formal working relationship, who form the bulk of the labor force in Indonesia, and such workers have special characteristics, in that the provision of a social security scheme for those workers needs to be organized separately.

Since the government regulation for extending social security to workers outside of a working relationship is still in process, the government of Indonesia issued the Minister of Manpower and Transmigration's Regulation No. 24 of 2006 (Regulation No. PER-24/MEN/VI/2006) which became the guideline for extending social security to such workers. This is the current initiative of the government. This regulation in principle is based on Act No. 3 of 1992 on Jamsostek, which may accommodate provision of social security to all workers, both in formal and informal working relationships. The practice, however, makes it obligatory only for enterprises with at least 10 employees or a monthly payroll of IDR 1 million. This means that the act concerns only workers in the formal working relationship. It should also be noted, however, that the Minister of Manpower and Transmigration's Regulation No. 24 of 2006 is confined to the self-employed who work outside of a formal working relationship.

In addition, there are a number of studies on the possibility of providing social security coverage to informal sector workers in Indonesia that have been conducted by international agencies, including the ILO, the Asian Development Bank (ADB), the World Bank, the GTZ in collaboration with the Ministry of Manpower, Bappenas, the Ministry of Finance, the Ministry of Health and PT Jamsostek.

The ILO has supported Indonesia on the issue of social security and has been closely involved in assisting with the process of reform and improvement through the technical cooperation project *Restructuring of Social Security Systems in Indonesia* from 2001 to 2002. The ILO also carried out a comprehensive review of poverty and economic security in Indonesia. The review resulted in policy recommendations and institutional reform for the government on socio-economic security. The ILO has initiated a discussion on the new Country Scheme Framework of the ILO in Indonesia for 2001–2005, under the umbrella of the Decent Work Approach. Increased social protection for excluded vulnerable groups, in particular informal sector workers and migrant workers, is one of the main priorities of the Tripartite Decent Work Country Scheme for the period 2004–2005.

The ILO conducted two surveys regarding urban and rural informal sector workers, which aimed at collecting primary indicators of social security needs and information on the workers in the informal economy. The urban survey was conducted in 2001 in three areas that had large concentrations in the urban informal economy, and a total of 1,999 people were surveyed in East Jakarta, Bandung and Yogyakarta. The rural survey was carried out in November 2003 with a total of 2,169 respondents in the rural areas surrounding Bandung, Sukabumi and Pangandaran in West Java; around Cirebon in northeast of Jakarta; and around Semarang in Central Java.

The ADB has been working on projects that cover social security and pension reform. The following are the brief of such projects with a social protection component:

- *Financial Governance and Social Security Reform Scheme (2002)*

  The technical assistance contained two components, namely insurance sector restructuring and development of the social security system. The second component aimed (i) to raise awareness among the stakeholders, (ii) to consider possibilities for reform and extension of the scheme and (iii) to assist in preparing for a new legislation and agency for national social security. This loan aimed to strengthen the financial sector and improve the management and supervision of the funds of the mandatory schemes and the regulation and oversight of the voluntary plans. The last of the nine components initiates work for the development of a unified social security system.

- *Financial Governance and Social Security Reform Scheme II (2004)*

  This project builds on the Financial Governance and Social Security Reform Scheme I (Loan 33399-01), which supports a broad framework for overall strengthening of the financial sector and promotes the development of sound financial institutions necessary to promote good governance and growth.

- *Financial Governance and Social Security Reform III (2005) and Social Security Unification and Development (2005)*

  This project will focus on a unified social security system.

The GTZ attempts to help Indonesia provide its population with social health services, in the project *Development of a Social Health Insurance System in Indonesia*, with the objective that all Indonesian citizens are able to utilize social health insurance services. This is based on the notion that the issuance of the Act No. 40 of 2004 on National Social Security System, which stipulates a comprehensive insurance system for the entire population, may have a positive influence on Indonesia's economic development. The lead executing agency for the project is the Ministry of Health.

To undertake the project, the GTZ uses the following approaches:

- At the policy-making level, the project advises ministries, House of Representatives committees and national organizations on developing strategies and concepts for the implementation of efficient social health insurance. Partner institutions are given support in conducting relevant studies and research.
- At the institutional level, in order to strengthen the existing social insurance carriers and support the organizational development, the setting up of new institutions will be considered. The principles and procedures of social health insurance are explained in the comprehensive training schemes.
- The project also contributes substantially to the development of curricula for technical training seminars. Information and education campaigns inform people about the improvements in health insurance coverage. Since the enactment of the social security law, the project has promptly set up decentralized steering committees including representatives from the area of politics, the insurance carriers and health service providers. A demand for

advisory services was articulated at the national level and within the regions. The existing state health insurance carriers, PT Askes and PT Jamsostek, are currently discussing their new roles within a social health insurance system, including new business models and management systems in line with the principles of social health.

3. Overview of the demographic and labor market trends in Indonesia

3.1. Indonesia's population

Indonesia's population is projected to reach 300 million in the next 50 years (by 2060), from about 230 million in 2010. Although the rate of growth will decline steadily in the future, the age composition will change dramatically, resulting from lower birth rates and higher life expectancy. In 2010 the 55+ age group (currently used as the standard retirement age in Indonesia) was only 12 percent of the total population but is expected to more than double to 30 percent in the next 50 years.

As the life expectancy is expected to rise in the future, from age 71 at present to 79 by 50 years from now, age 60 or 65 could be a new standard for the retirement age in Indonesia. The population of those over 60 was around 20 million now (Statistical Office of Indonesia [BPS], 2010), or about 4.5 percent of the total population.

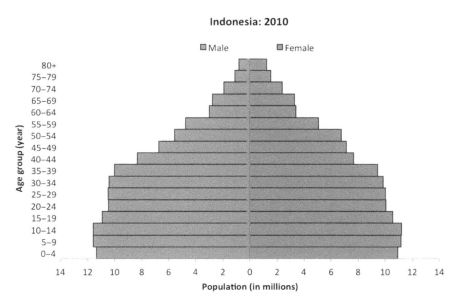

Figure 9.2 Indonesian population pyramid: age and sex distribution for 2010

Source: US Census Bureau. www.census.gov/population/international/data/idb/information Gateway.php

Indonesia: 2050

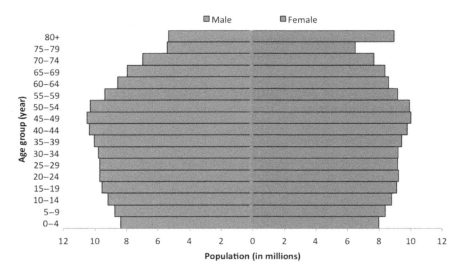

Figure 9.3 Indonesian population pyramid: predicted age and sex distribution in 2050

Source: US Census Bureau. www.census.gov/population/international/data/idb/information Gateway.php

The 65+ age group is expected to increase rapidly from 6 percent (2010) to about 20 percent in 50 years, while the working age group (15–64) will decline slightly, from 67 percent in 2010 to around 64 percent in the same period. The increasing size of the retirement age group will make the dependency ratio (ratio of pensioners to the working age group) increase from 9 percent to 30 percent, or 1.7 workers will be supporting one pensioner in the future compared to 5 workers in 2010. As the pension costs are directly related to the number of elderly, the dependency ratio is important.

3.2. The workforce in Indonesia

The size of the workforce in Indonesia has increased rapidly, from 90 million in 2001 to reach more than 120 million in 2012 (BPS, Sakernas 2012). About three-fourths of this workforce is in the informal economy, while the rest is employed in the formal sector. The Asian financial crisis resulted in a substantial increase in the share of the informal economy in the early 2000s, as the formal sector was badly hit by the crisis. The recent technological developments have led to lessening of the formal employer-employee relationships, giving impetus to informality in the labour market (ILO 2009b).

Table 9.1 Participation and unemployment rates (%), 2007

2007	Women	Men
Labor force participation rate	50.0	>80.0
Unemployment rate	11.8	8.5
Underemployment rate	41.3	25.1

Source: ILO/Jamsostek (2008).

Table 9.2 Labor force and employment

Year	2010	2030	2050	2070
Labor force (millions)	115.4	144.3	155.1	150.4
Labor force (as % of population)	50.7	52.7	52.4	51.4
Employed (millions)	104.2	132.3	143.4	139.4
Unemployment rate (%)	9.7	8.4	7.6	7.3

Source: ADB 2007.

The Indonesia's labour force participation rate in 2007 was around 80 percent for men and around 50 percent for women (see Table 9.1). The under-employment however remains high.

In the next 50 years, the workforce in Indonesia is projected to be about 150 million workers, or half of the population, while unemployment is expected to decline to around 7 to 8 percent (ADB, 2007).

3.4. Informal sector workers in Indonesia

The informal economy has been defined in a large variety of ways (GTZ, Menko Kesra, Departemen Kesehatan, 2007), while the BPS has developed an elaborate definition of informal employment based on a combination of main occupation and main employment status (Table 9.3). In general, the informal sector workers can be categorized as laborers, the self-employed and employers, with the first two representing 90–95 percent of total employment (ILO, 2009b).

In early 2010, 107 million of the 116 million labor force were absorbed by the labor market (with about an 8 percent unemployment rate). While the formal sector employed less than one-third (31.4 percent, or 33.7 million) of workers, the informal sector absorbed two-thirds of the pool, 65.6 percent, or about 74 million.

The majority of the informal workers work in the rural sector (about two-thirds work in agriculture), but increasingly it has become an urban phenomenon

Table 9.3 Definition of the informal sector

Main Employment Status	Main Occupation									
	Professional Technical and Related Workers	Administrative and Managerial Workers	Clerical and Related Workers	Sales Workers	Services Workers	Agricultural Workers	Production Workers	Operators	Laborers	Others
Self-employed	F	F	F	INF	INF	INF	INF	INF	INF	INF
Self-employed assisted by family or temporary worker	F	F	F	F	F	INF	F	F	F	INF
Employer	F	F	F	F	F	F	F	F	F	F
Employee	F	F	F	F	F	F	F	F	F	F
Agricultural freelance worker	F	F	F	INF	INF	INF	INF	INF	INF	INF
Non-agricultural freelance worker	F	F	F	INF	INF	INF	INF	INF	INF	INF
Unpaid worker	INF	INF	INF	INF	INF	INF	INF	INF	INF	INF

Source: BPS (2010).

Note: F = formal sector; INF = informal sector.

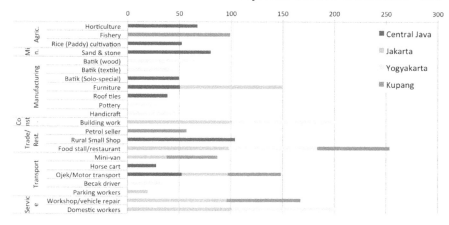

Figure 9.4 Examples of informal economic sectors
Source: ILO (2009a).

in Indonesia (ADB, 2007), as they have entered into other economic sectors such as manufacturing, construction, trade, transportation and services. In agriculture and fishery, most of them are daily laborers who do not own the productive assets (fields or boats) and work for landlords or boat owners. In the manufacturing sector, informal workers work for home industries or small plants making handicrafts, pottery, batik, wooden products, etc. Some of them are seasonal workers (carpenters, helpers) who work for construction projects in urban areas.

In many cities in Indonesia, small traders are easily found in busy locations as well as on street corners selling foods, cigarettes, beverages, newspapers, clothes, toys, etc. Many of them also work in service sectors as shopkeepers or domestic helpers (housemaids, gardeners, drivers, baby sitters); almost every household in Indonesia has domestic helpers. Informal workers also operate various transportation modes, including rickshaws, motorcycles, minivans (8–10 passengers), minibuses, buses and trucks.

3.5. The income level and ability to pay

In Indonesia the local government regulates the minimum wage for workers in its respective region. However, in practice, the minimum wage applies only for employment in the formal sector, while in the informal sector laborers normally receive less. The workers who work in Jakarta earn 20–30 percent more than those who work in other cities/regions; however, they also spend more for daily needs: food, clothes, rent and transportation costs.

On the income level, the majority are poor laborers earning less than IDR 800,000 (USD 85) per month, with an average wage of IDR 603,000 (USD 65), and the lowest level is less than IDR 400,000, or USD 45 (ILO's 2009b Survey on Social Security for Informal Economy Workers, Table 9.4). With the poverty level defined at between USD 1–2 per day (USD 30–60 a month), the informal workers live only marginally above the poverty line. In fact, their income was basically only enough for daily basic necessities such as food, clothing, shelter and the cost of transportation to the workplace.

Table 9.4 Minimum wage in some regions, 2009 (in IDR)

Wage Range (IDR thousands)	Male	Female	Total
<200	900,566	1,479,650	2,380,216
200–400	2,418,074	984,015	3,402,089
400–600	1,660,459	229,228	1,889,687
600–800	1,349,835	77,596	1,427,431
800–1,000	625,086	29,533	644,619
1,000–1,500	452,935	39,729	492,664
1,500–2,000	84,142	36,056	120,198
>2,000	50,772	55,439	106,211
Total	7,531,869	2,931,246	10,463,115

Source: BPS, Jakarta, Keadaan Pekerja di Indonesia Pebruari (2007). http://bali.bps.go.id/index_eng.php?reg=pub_det&id=Keadaan%20Pekerja%20di%20Indonesia%20Pebruari%202007

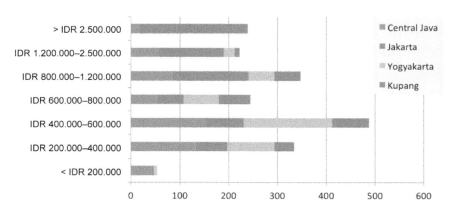

Figure 9.5 Income levels of informal workers in some regions
Source: ILO (2009b)

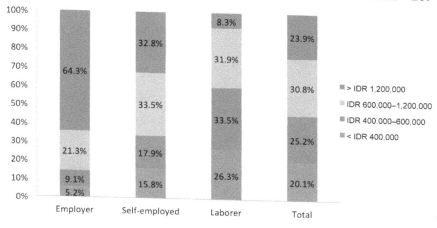

Figure 9.6 Income level of informal workers by type of employment

Source: ILO (2009b). This result is consistent with the BPS's statistic (at 2007 constant prices) that informal workers (self-employed) earn IDR 630,000 (USD 70) per month, while casual non-agricultural workers earn IDR 590,000 (USD 65) and casual agricultural laborers earn IDR 374,000 (USD 40) per month. Meanwhile, the average wage for informal sector labor is IDR 493,000, or about USD 55, per month.

4. Options for extending coverage for informal sector workers

4.1. The need of social protection for informal sector workers

Based on the access to and stability of the place, employment and resources, workers in the urban informal economy are classified as (a) highly mobile workers, (b) mobile or home based, (c) semi-fixed or recognized operating zones, (d) fixed location and (e) professional self-employed, fixed or home (Angelini and Hirose, 2004).

From a survey conducted by ILO in 2009 (2009b), both urban and rural informal sector workers need some form of social protection. Health insurance and old-age benefits were mentioned as the highest priorities by both urban and rural workers. Work-injury protection was also identified as a priority for urban informal workers, whereas education is considered a priority for rural informal workers.

The social security needs of those in the informal economy differ according to their demographic status, degree of hazard in the particular occupation (e.g., garbage scavengers, drivers of motorcycle taxis), location and work setting (at home, on the street, in a sweatshop), milieu (communities more than establishments) and ability to make regular contributions to the insurance fund.

It is important to understand the range and types of risks that are present and how they may be prioritized in order to develop appropriate mechanisms to cover the risks borne by workers in the informal sector. This would allow benefit packages and delivery systems to be designed that are responsive to their needs. It can be concluded from the ILO survey that it seems difficult for rural and urban informal sector workers to contribute without any form of cost sharing (from employers) or subsidy (from government).

4.2. Challenges in extending social protection to informal workers

There are a number of hindering factors for extending contributory social security coverage to the informal sector workers:

- The ability to pay (affordability) is a major issue, not only because of the low incomes of most of the workers in the informal sectors, but also because of the absence of employer participation in making contributions.
- Informal workers have an irregular income stream, as they will get paid only when they work, and no formal contractual arrangement has been made.
- Benefits are not related with their priority needs, as the flexibility of the current scheme may not be adequate to address their essential needs.
- Most of the informal sector workers lack awareness of the social security concept because of their educational background.
- There is distrust towards government institutions and the social security provider owing to a lack of openness and transparency in their operations, policies and administration.
- Willingness to participate (and to pay) also depends on the level of trust in the social protection provider and the complexity of participation (registration, collection of contribution, record keeping, compliance) and the coverage extension of the social protection provider (administrative capacity) owing to very broad geographical coverage.

4.3. Possible options for asocial protection scheme for informal sector workers

With this understanding of the situation, it can be concluded that in general three options can be pursued to provide social protection schemes for informal sector workers.

1. Extending the existing social security schemes (Jamsostek) to informal sector workers, with the government playing the role of the employer.
2. Creating a special social protection scheme uniquely designed for informal sector workers.
3. Designing a universal scheme under the SJSN law.

These are addressed in greater detail below.

4.3.1. Extending the Jamsostek scheme for informal sector workers

Jamsostek is currently the legislated social security system for workers and is widely perceived as the workers' social protection scheme. Despite its administrative capacity, it is the largest provider (compared to Taspen and Asabri) in delivering social protection for formal workers in almost all provinces in Indonesia. It may be more feasible for Jamsostek to jointly develop a policy together with private insurance companies and deliver a more flexible and suitable scheme for informal sector workers.

If the legislation on Jamsostek is not changed (a minimum of 10 workers and a payroll of IDR 1 million), the informal sector may still be included in the scheme as long as they participate (together) in a group. Consideration should be given to the administrative capacity of Jamsostek; e.g., to what extent Jamsostek can deliver its service and how efficient the administration would be. Such improvements are crucially dependent on procedures, administration and the use of information technology.

Alternatively, the ILO recommended that the government change the criteria for the enterprises that are obliged to participate in Jamsostek to:

1. progressively reduce the minimum number of employed workers;
2. examine the current criterion of the minimum payroll amount and develop adjustment rules to allow for regular indexation in line with increases in general wages;
3. link regular adjustment of the minimum payroll amount with the adjustment of the ceilings of the contributory earnings.

4.3.2. Creating a special scheme for informal sector workers

The current legislation and fund structure in the existing social security scheme has difficulty incorporating more variable programs that could cover all workers in the informal sectors. It is probably more effective to create a new contribution model for informal sector workers. In the case of Jamsostek, this could be achieved through the development of the government regulations as mentioned in Article 4 (2) of Act No.3 of 1992.

A viable social security scheme for informal sector workers would be necessary to develop a model that provides meaningful benefits with affordable contributions. The schemes should offer flexible options with a range of contribution rates and benefits to satisfy the needs and capacities of different groups and include at least injury, health, death, old-age and other voluntary savings schemes.

The administrative procedure and service delivery models for the scheme should focus on group schemes but still provide options for individual and self-employed contributors. Implementation of such schemes needs to be progressive and take into account the wide variety of occupations, organizations and geographical distribution of the workers.

4.3.3. Designing a universal scheme under SJSN law

Act No. 40 of 2004 (SJSN) requires the establishment of a universal scheme consisting of five separate mandatory social protection programs to cover all Indonesians.

1. Pension scheme: This scheme will pay a lifetime monthly annuity to workers who have retired, workers who become disabled and survivors of deceased workers or pensioners.
2. Old-age savings: Workers will make contributions to individual accounts throughout their working career. These contributions will be invested, and the account balance will be paid out as a lump sum at retirement.
3. Health benefits: This program will provide primary medical benefits based on medical need.
4. Work-related accident benefit: This program pays lump-sum compensations for those who are injured or die resulting from work-related accidents or sickness.
5. Death benefits: This program pays a modest lump-sum death benefit to the beneficiaries of a deceased worker that covers funeral expenses and may provide additional compensation to the family as well.

Under the SJSN law, the government is required to contribute to all five of those schemes for those who are considered poor. Currently the government had defined *poor* as people who consume less than 2,000 calories of food per day, or about USD 1 per day or USD 30 per month; meanwhile, USD 2 per day is considered near-poor. The government estimated that there are about 30 million poor citizens, while the near-poor number around 50–60 million.

PENSION SCHEME

The pension scheme provides workers with a guaranteed monthly income for the remainder of their lives following their retirement or disability, and it provides an annuity to survivors of deceased workers or old-age pensioners. Benefits can be based on average pay and years of contributions, or they can be a flat amount for each year of contribution and should be indexed to inflation following retirement. Given the current longer life expectancy in Indonesia, the retirement age for the SJSN pension program should be 60 and should be adjusted upward as life expectancy increases.

The SJSN law requires 15 years of contributions before workers are eligible for a pension benefit. Should this be implemented straight away, it will leave the current elderly and many older workers with no retirement income. To avoid this, government can provide a 'social pension' for the pensioners when the pension scheme is implemented. Starting in 2010, the Ministry of Social Welfare was piloting a social pension of IDR 300,000 (USD 30) per month, targeted to 10,000 poor elderly in a few years. In addition, the government may provide workers with some credit for years worked before the start of the SJSN pension system.

OLD-AGE SAVINGS

The old-age savings scheme provides a modest lump-sum payment to workers when they start retirement. This will provide workers with some cash to help them in financing their transition from employment to retirement. The contribution rate to the old-age savings program should be kept low in the beginning but could increase over time. As old-age savings are paid only as a lump sum at the time of retirement, it shouldn't be too difficult to develop, given a proper investment policy and asset management. It is more complex to provide pensions since these provide a lifetime annuity and become a major income for the pensioners.

The important task in this scheme is having a prudent investment policy, optimal asset allocation strategy, securities selection and good asset management governance in terms of accountability and transparency. These all ensure a proper annual rate of return, as small differences in the return will have a major impact on benefits received by the workers when they retire. In addition, good governance will prevent political intervention in the fund and its investment strategy.

HEALTH BENEFITS

The health benefits program will provide health services similar to those under the current Askes program for civil servants and the Jamkesmas program for the poor. Benefits are equal to all necessary basic medical care, which includes visits to primary and secondary care specialists, hospitalization, surgery, medicines, laboratory tests and other necessary care to assure good health. The system will be based on the managed care model, in which patients need to see a general medical doctor who serves as the access point for further medical services (seeing specialists or being admitted to hospitals), except for emergencies. The facilities are primarily public clinics and hospitals; however, some private health care providers can also be accessed.

The health scheme for the poor (Jamkesmas) has already started and currently provides more than 100 million people (half of the population) with access to public health facilities. As the program is intended for the poor, the government bears all the cost out of the state budget channeled through the Ministry of Health, without contributions from the poor. In the future, the cost will tend to increase owing to increases in coverage as well as increases in the utilization of services, costs of providing needed medical care, the number of facilities and providers, changes in medical procedures and technology, changes in the pattern of morbidity rates and changes in life expectancy.

WORK-RELATED ACCIDENT

The work-related accident scheme is a lump-sum compensation paid to the workers in case of accidents occurring in the workplace or accidents related to their work (basically similar to the current Jamsostek and Taspen programs). The compensation is provided, as the workers may not be able to continue working, or the accident may impact their capability to work. Under Jamsostek's scheme (in the formal sector), the employers pay the premium, and rates vary depending on the industry and job classification. For most of the informal sector workers, government should pay the premium, as these workers don't have employers, or it will create a burden for micro-scale employers if they have to pay the premium.

DEATH BENEFITS

The death benefit program is like life insurance, which provides a modest lump-sum pay-out (usually a flat amount) to the beneficiaries on the death of the worker. Normally, like a Jamsostek scheme, family members of the worker are not insured under this scheme, so benefits are not payable in case of the death of family members. This scheme is a complementary benefit, intended to provide cash assistance to cover funeral expenses and modest compensation for the family of the deceased worker. In addition, the beneficiaries of deceased workers will also receive a monthly annuity benefit from the pension program of SJSN.

5. Concluding remarks and ways forward

The current social security scheme in Indonesia is facing three challenges, namely fragmentation (based on market segments), low coverage and non-existence of protection for informal sector workers. Recently, only civil servants and less than half of formal sector workers were insured, while the informal sector workers were not covered by any kind of social protection.

The new act on the social security system (SJSN law, 2004) is a good start that provides a framework for a universal social security system for all Indonesians, including informal sector workers (70 percent of the labor force); however, the implementation is somewhat slow.

Recently, some line ministries started piloting some branches of social security schemes: e.g. the Ministry of Health for health benefits, the Ministry of Manpower for work-related benefits (accident, compensation benefits), the Ministry of Social Welfare for social pensions for the poor, as well as a social assistance program (conditional cash transfer) coordinated by the Ministry of National Planning. However, there is lack of coordination between the ministries in terms of programs provided.

In relation to the effort to provide universal social security schemes under SJSN, the informal sector workers, who are the majority of the labor force, are the first priority for some forms of social protection, namely health insurance and old-age benefits. The ILO survey (2009b) reported that, in general, informal workers in both urban and rural sectors have an interest in social security and are willing to contribute to a scheme that suits their needs and priorities. However, the findings confirm the limited contributory capacity of these workers; hence, without some form of cost sharing or government subsidies, they won't be able to participate in the schemes.

Understanding the issue of affordability for the informal sector workers, the government should step up and pay their contribution, as required by the SJSN law. This will also be seen as a 'fair' treatment, since employers pay most of the contributions for formal workers' scheme (Jamsostek).

With good progress in health benefits coverage, the government should start to implement the rest of the social protection schemes as mandated by SJSN law: pension, old-age, work accident and life insurance benefits. While the Ministry of Finance, with the help of international financial institutions, is trying to analyze and develop a universal (and affordable) scheme, the experiences of line ministries in piloting branches of social security schemes in their respective areas will bring important considerations in designing the overall scheme.

To avoid a fragmented scheme for informal sector workers, the Ministry of Finance should speed up the design and implementation of the universal scheme (for informal workers), since line ministries can roll out their specific schemes faster. In addition, the analysis of the fiscal impact (costs) of government contributions to informal sector schemes should be done in a comprehensive manner.

As currently there is no coverage for the informal sector workers, the universal scheme of SJSN should be implemented first for these types of workers. The harmonization between both schemes, formal and informal, could be implemented later, as the civil servants, military personnel, and formal sector workers already have schemes available. The Jamsostek scheme for formal workers can be used as the basis and reference in designing schemes for the informal sector workers.

Another important concern is the fiscal impact resulting from the contingent liabilities of extending the social protection scheme to the informal sector. A closer collaboration and coordination among various stakeholders – the Ministry of Manpower, the Minister of Finance, the SJSN team, Jamsostek, employers and trade unions, along with all participating donors who are conducting studies in this field (the ILO, ADB and World Bank) – is necessary.

To support the implementation of the program designed, capacity building for government officials from related agencies that handle social security issues would be very important, as line ministries need to have a comprehensive picture of the social security scheme. In the case that micro-insurance could be a means for extending social security to informal economy workers, it is important to evaluate the on-going pilot projects on this in some regions in Indonesia, and also to see how this scheme will fit in the big picture of a universal scheme of SJSN.

Notes

1 The proper name of the act is The Law of the Republic of Indonesia, Number 3, of 1992 Concerning Man Power Social Security. http://sjsn.menkokesra.go.id/dokumen/peruu/1992/uu3_1992_eng.pdf
2 www.ilo.org/dyn/natlex/docs/SERIAL/64764/56412/F861503702/idn64764.PDF

References

Angelini, J. and Hirose, K. (2004). *Extension of social security coverage for the informal economy in Indonesia: Surveys in the urban and rural informal economy.* Geneva: International Labour Organization.

Arifianto, A. (2004). *Social security reform in Indonesia: An analysis of the national social security bill* (RUU Jamsosnas). Jakarta: SMERU.

Cuevas, S., Mina, C., Barcenas, M., and Rosario, A. (2007). *Informal employment in Indonesia.* Jakarta: Asian Development Bank (ADB).

Bappenas (2008). *Options for social protection reform in Indonesia.* Jakarta: Author.

Bitran, R. and Winnie, C. Yip. (1998). *A review of health care provider payment reform in selected countries in Asia and Latin America.* Bethesda, MD: Partners for Health Reform plus.

GTZ, Menko Kesra, Departemen Kesehatan. (2007). *The informal sector in Indonesia and social security.* http://sjsn.menkokesra.go.id/dokumen/publikasi/informal_sector_in_indonesia.pdf

Health Act No.23 of 1992, Republic of Indonesia. http://rulebook-jica.ekon.go.id/english/6.23.1992.eng.qc.html

Hirose, K. (1999). Topics in quantitative analysis of social protection systems [Issues in Social Protection Series]. Geneva: Social Security Department, International Labour Organization.

ILO/Jamostek (2008). *Social security in Indonesia: Advancing the development agenda.* Jakarta: Author.

Implementation of Jamsostek Government Regulation No. 14 of 1993. Republic of Indonesia.

Implementation of the Manpower Social Security Scheme for Casual Daily Workers, Workers Doing Piece Jobs and Workers on a Contract Basis Regulation. Regulation No. PER-03/MEN/1994. Minister of Manpower.

Implementation of the Workers' Social Security Scheme for Expatriates in Companies Decree No. Kep-132/MEN/1998. As revocation of the Minister of Manpower Instruction No. INS-02/MEN/1995. Minister of Manpower.

Implementation of the Workers' Social Security Scheme for Expatriates in Companies Instruction No. INS.02/MEN/1995. Minister of Manpower.

International Labour Organization. (2003). *Indonesia: Extension of social insurance coverage to the informal economy.* Geneva: International Labour Organization.

International Labour Organization. (2008). *Indonesia: Providing health insurance for the poor.* Technical Paper. New Delhi: International Labour Organization.

International Labor Organization. (2009a). *Social security for informal economy workers in Indonesia: Looking for flexible and highly targeted programs.* Geneva: International Labour Organization.

International Labour Organization. (2009b). *Survey on social security for informal economy workers.* Geneva: International Labour Organization.

Jhabvala, R. and Subrahmanya, R. K. (2000). *The unorganised sector: Work security and social protection.* Thousand Oaks, CA: Sage.

Leechor, C. (1996). *Reforming Indonesia's pension system.* Policy Research Working Paper No. 1677. Washington, D.C.: World Bank. http://elibrary.worldbank.org/doi/pdf/10.1596/1813-9450-1677

Lund, F. J. and Srinivas, S. (2000). *Learning from experience: A gendered approach to social protection for workers in the informal economy.* Geneva: International Labour Organization.

National Social Security System Act No.40 of 2004. Republic of Indonesia.

Investment Fund Management and Labor Social Security Program Government Regulation No. 28 of 1996. Republic of Indonesia.

Scheil-Adlung, X. (2004). *Sharpening the focus on the poor: Policy options for advancing social health protection in Indonesia.* ESS Working Paper No. 19. Geneva: International Labour Organisation (ILO). http://europeanspallationsource.se/ilo-network

Social Insurance for Civil Servants Government Regulation No. 25 of 1981. Republic of Indonesia.

Social Security Program Implementation Guidelines for the Employment of Labor That Perform Work Outside Employment Regulation No. PER-24/MEN/VI/2006. Minister of Manpower and Transmigration.

Statistical Office of Indonesia (BPS). (2012). *National labor statistics* (Sakernas). Jakarta: Government of Indonesia.

Statistical Office of Indonesia (BPS). (2010). *Indonesia official census.* Jakarta: Government of Indonesia.

Suryahadi, S. S. A. and Widyanti, W. (2004). *Assessing the impact of Indonesian social safety net programs on household welfare and poverty dynamics.* SMERU Working Paper. Jakarta: SMERU. www.smeru.or.id/description.php?id=7

Unni, J. and Rani, U. (2002). *Social protection for informal workers: Insecurities, instruments and institutional mechanisms.* Geneva: International Labor Organization.

Widjaja, M. (2008). Designing pension programs to strengthen formal labor markets in developing countries: The case of Indonesia. *Pensions: An International Journal,* 15, 111–120.

Wiener, M. (2007). *White paper on old age saving program, pension program, and death benefit program, national social security system; prepared by the Ministry of Finance of the Republic of Indonesia assisted by Asian Development Bank (ADB).* Mandaluyong City, Philippines: Asian Development Bank.

Workers Social Security (Jamsostek) Act No.3 of 1992. Republic of Indonesia.

World Bank Institute. (2004). *Protecting the vulnerable: The design and implementation of effective safety nets, the case of a post-crisis country: Indonesia.* Washington, DC: World Bank Institute.

Index

Note: Page numbers in *italics* indicate figures and tables.

For Product Safety Concerns and Information please contact our EU
representative GPSR@taylorandfrancis.com
Taylor & Francis Verlag GmbH, Kaufingerstraße 24, 80331 München, Germany